JAMES JOYCE'S METAMORPHOSES

John Gordon

JAMES JOYCE'S METAMORPHOSES

GILL AND MACMILLAN
BARNES & NOBLE BOOKS

First Published 1981 by
Gill and Macmillan
Dublin
with associated companies in
London, New York, Delhi, Hong Kong,
Johannesburg, Lagos, Melbourne,
Singapore, Tokyo

SBN 7171 1024 9 (Gill and Macmillan)
ISBN 0-389-20167-7 (Barnes & Noble)

Printed in the USA 1981 by
Barnes & Noble Books * Totowa, N.J. 07512

A Joycean dedication to R.C.G., both of hem.

Contents

Acknowledgments

Any work on Joyce is indebted to an enormous number of scholars and critics. I have tried to acknowledge, in the course of this study, the works which have helped me most, and I would here like to single out a few whose influence the reader will find on almost every page. S. L. Goldberg's *The Classical Temper* has long guided my thinking on the larger issues of *Ulysses*. James H. Maddox Jr's *Joyce's Ulysses and the Assault Upon Character* seems to me simply the best close reading of *Ulysses* ever written. J. S. Atherton's essay 'The Gist of the Pantomime' seems to me the most illuminating few pages on *Finnegans Wake* ever written. Hugh Kenner, always provocative, brilliant, and uniquely willing to take chances, has been my model of what a Joyce critic should try to be, and has more than once, in these pages, stimulated a disagreement which has led to a discovery. Professor Kenner performs the indispensable service: he asks the right questions.

'Thou Leanest to the Shell of Night' from *Collected Poems* by James Joyce, copyright 1918 by B. W. Huebsch, renewed in 1946 by Nora Joyce, is reproduced by permission of Viking Penguin, Inc.

In the United States, I am indebted to Viking Penguin, Inc. for permission to quote from James Joyce: *Dubliners, A Portrait of the Artist as a Young Man, Exiles,* and *Finnegans Wake,* Stuart Gilbert and Richard Ellman, eds: *The Letters of James Joyce,* and Richard Ellman and Ellsworth Mason, eds: *The Critical Writings of James Joyce;* and to Random House, Inc. for permission to quote from *Ulysses* by James Joyce. In England, I am indebted to Faber and Faber Ltd. for permission to quote from *The Letters of James Joyce;* to the executors of the James Joyce Estate for permission to quote from *Stephen Hero, The Critical Writings of James Joyce, Exiles, Dubliners,* and *A Portrait of the Artist as a*

Young Man; and to the Society of Authors for permission to quote from *Finnegans Wake* and *Collected Poems.* Quotations from *Ulysses* are reprinted with permission of The Bodley Head.

This book began, several years ago, as a paper written for an independent study with Professor Harry Levin of Harvard University. Professors John V. Kelleher and Monroe Engel, both of Harvard University, supervised my dissertation on Joyce with extraordinary good sense: they are the ones without whom this book would still be a jungle of multicolored jottings in the margins of a few dogeared books. Professor Austin Briggs Jr of Hamilton College taught me to love Joyce in the first place and later gave me valuable advice on revising and civilising much of the manuscript. The advice and criticism of Professor William Dowling of the University of New Mexico at Albuquerque and his wife Linda Dowling were, simply, essential. Professor John Fyler of Tufts University and Professor Robert Bell of Williams College both offered very helpful advice which for the most part I have had the sense to take. Professors Ivan Marki, Dwight Lindley, and Edwin Barrett of Hamilton College have been kind enough to read over early drafts of the book in whole or part and help make it better. Professor Margaret Solomon of the University of Hawaii wrote a very helpful critique of what eventually became chapter 7.

I wish to also thank Professor Brendan O Hehir, of the University of California at Berkeley, Professor Riana O'Dwyer, of Tuam, Dr. John Garvin, of Dublin, and Dr. Roland McHugh, of Dublin. Hamilton College, through the offices of its former Dean of Faculty W. Lawrence Gulick, gave me generous financial support for much of my research. In the course of my travels in Ireland I received friendly and helpful communications from too many Joyces and Mulveys to mention. I hope that any of them who happen across this book will now be able to understand what I was about.

My greatest debt is expressed in the dedication.

1

Proteus and Narcissus

'Our object is to create a new fusion between the exterior world
and our contemporary selves . . . Sensation is our object,
heightened even to the point of hallucination.'—James Joyce,
speaking to Arthur Power.[1]

In the marketplace, 'hallucination' and 'sensation' are opposites;
in Joyce's work one is the flowering of the other. A woman in
Chamber Music listens to the sounds of the night and imagines
Shakespearian ghosts; a donkey in *Finnegans Wake* hears similar
sounds whispering the name of Shaun. In *A Portrait of the Artist
as a Young Man,* Stephen Dedalus looks at telegraph lines
punctuated by poles and sees staves on a sheet of music; later
the same image appears in *Finnegans Wake:* 'the song of sparrow-
notes on his stave of wires.'[2] Both Eveline and Earwicker, looking
from behind enclosures, see themselves as caged animals, and
become them; in 'The Sisters' a young boy's vision of life darkens
when he passes from a well-lighted room to a dim one and his
pupils are slow to dilate; in *Ulysses* the same thing happens
to the barmaid Miss Douce. A groggy Stephen Dedalus, coming to,
sees in stages that Leopold Bloom is dressed in black, crouched
like a panther, with skin that looks cadaverous in the lamplight,
and dubs him by degrees as 'black/panther/vampire'.[3] Similarly
Taff, his '*bulgeglarying stargapers razzledazzlingly full of eyes, full
of balls, full of holes, full of buttons, full of stains, full of medals,
full of blickblackblobs*' *(FW* 339.19-21) from the afterimages

1

stamped on his vision by Butt's lantern, sees the Russian general decked with buttons, medals, etc; similarly the myopic Gabriel Conroy, his glasses removed and his mind full of melancholy, looks out the window on a lamplit world all glowy, sad, and fuzzy, universals falling on universals.

It may be that Joyce's well-known eye troubles and eventual near-blindness, rather than sealing him off from the world of the senses, made him particularly studious of it: certainly he became, in the course of his ten eye operations, an authority on optics. Whatever the reason, up to the end of his career Joyce remained scrupulously attentive to the workings of sensation, even when evidently at his wildest and most visionary. When his characters and narrators hallucinate or in some way seem to lose touch with any established level of reality, they are not simply seeing crazy or symbolic things. Instead they are transforming real objects and people into visions recognisably derived from them, as when in the Busby Berkeley musical *Gold Diggers of 1935* a woman's head, viewed from beneath the chin and with a cigarette between the lips, melts into an image of the Manhattan skyline which then becomes the setting for the 'Lullaby of Broadway' number (*cf. U* 476-7), as when in the 1939 *Wizard of Oz* Dorothy's Kansas homestead turns into the pantheon of a new world transfigured by technicolour (cf *FW* 255.3-246.3). One of Joyce's sources for such effects was certainly the same as for his film-making contemporaries—the pantomime's traditional transformation scene, in which a gauze screen was illuminated from behind to reveal, as if magically, a gorgeous facsimile of the set and cast, 'streets [turned] into enchanted islands, shops into magicians' caves, and all the costumes of the actors . . . altered to match their new surroundings.'[4]

Joyce's transformation scenes differ from those of his contemporaries in the theatre and movies in that they are always in part the recognisable product of a particular observer. Perception, by itself and in its extreme manifestation of hallucination, is always in Joyce projection to some extent; to 'encounter the reality of experience' is always, to some extent, to encounter oneself. Joyce could have had this observation confirmed by, among others, Giambattista Vico, who observed the way that men named the landscape after themselves—as in foothill and cave mouth—and concluded that the story of Ulysses' encounter with Proteus, interpreted as 'first matter', was really the story of Narcissus, man's encounter with his own image.[5] It is not particularly Stephen's fault that, when he tries to encounter reality, he winds up being a Narcissus more than a Daedalus; that is just what happens. As an aspiring artist—and Joyce insisted on this (*CW* 31-7, 145; cf *SH* 171)—his perceptions differ from those of others in intensity but not in kind; he is simply doing what anyone does who opens his eyes and tries to say what he sees.

All of Joyce's work illustrates this with the exception of *Stephen Hero*, where the author has apparently not yet come to understand how much of ourselves is involved in what we encounter. (The growing realisation may have helped to prompt Joyce's decision to scrap *Stephen Hero* and start over.) *Stephen Hero* assumes that reality can be spoken of, just like that, without quotation marks, and that a sharp young man will encounter it as one encounters someone on the street. Stephen is forever 'realising' or becoming 'aware' of things that we know to be true, because the narrator tells us so. But in the later book, *A Portrait of the Artist as a Young Man,* reality has become 'reality', changing according to shifts in mood or setting, as in the change between Stephen's two perceptions of a decorated theatre: 'The light spread upwards from the glass roof making the theatre seem a festive ark, anchored among the hulks of houses, her frail cables of lanterns looping her to moorings' (*P* 74-5). 'On the lines which he had fancied the moorings of an ark a few lanterns swung in the night breeze, flickering cheerlessly' (*P* 85).

Changes like this are typical of *Portrait,* and so is the gloom accompanying it. For Stephen, to discover that an earlier vision came partly from his own fancy is to be, simply, disillusioned. But before writing *Portrait,* Joyce had produced a collection of poems in which such changes are allowed to occur lyrically, free of Stephen's dialectic of illusion and dis-illusion because free of the pressure for every vision to mean something profound and permanent. For instance, the first poem of *Chamber Music,* 'Strings in the earth and air', is a pictorial conceit of the same kind that Stephen makes of the theatre and lanterns. A musically inclined poet looks at willows drooping into a river and envisions a musician bending to his music, the willows' elongated leaves, drifting on the stream, metamorphosed to frail fingers 'straying/ Upon an instrument' (*CP* 9). The river's babbling becomes the music's melody. In a way, this is a case of projection—someone with music in his soul framing the landscape and making of it a snapshot from a concert. But the reverse is happening as well: the music is in the poet in the first place because, as Leopold Bloom will later put it, 'There's music everywhere,' strings in the earth and air. The poet of *Chamber Music* is an intermediary, neither determined nor determining, his soul the place where unheard melodies mate with sound and sight and gather rhythm and outline, his verse the enactment of that mating.

Here and throughout Joyce's work thereafter, the ideal is reciprocity—neither projection nor passive receptivity, but a working together of both. Long before *Finnegans Wake* calls itself a concave mirror,[6] reflecting, re-casting, and epitomising the world (like those other concave chambers, ear and eye), Poem XXVI will develop the comparison of art to a chamber wherein hearer and speaker are brought together:

> Thou leanest to the shell of night,
>   Dear lady, a divining ear.
> In that soft choiring of delight
>   What sound hath made thy heart to fear?
> Seemed it of rivers rushing forth
> From the grey deserts of the north?
>
>   That mood of thine, O timorous,
> Is his, if thou but scan it well,
>   Who a mad tale bequeaths to us
> At ghosting hour conjurable—
>   And all for some strange name he read
>   In Purchas or in Holinshed. (*CP* 34)

The night here is a shell because the ear listening to it is a shell, a 'soft choiring' (cf *U* 281), and so as usual Narcissus is looking at himself. But the lady of the poem, hearing the night reverberate back her imaginings as the shell's sea-roar gives back the pulsing in her ear, is listening to someone else as well—the storyteller whose 'mad tale' has tuned her ear to the air's ghostlier whispers. And that tale itself (it might be *Hamlet,* in the porches of her ear), was conjured when the teller chanced on an odd name in an old history that somehow harmonised, as does the night for the lady, with his own divinings. The poem itself—poet leaning to the lady—enacts the same process.

Much more than has the Stephen of *Portrait,* the twenty-one year old man writing this poem has already thought a good deal about the middle region where mind and world meet and inter-penetrate, especially about the ways in which each gives back the other, and has concluded already what, paraphrasing Vico, he will later tell Frank Budgen:[7] that imagination is memory, that its images are enabled by the shapes given to the mind's expectations from impressions received in the past—an old song or tale, for instance. The true artist can give us the right memories to encounter certain experiences, tuning our sensibilities as the tale-teller of 'Thou leanest to the shell of night' has tuned the ear of the lady to the night's more chilling resonances. He can do this because he has had the same encounters himself and has enacted faithfully, in his works, the sensations produced when a certain kind of sensibility reacts to a certain kind of setting—not simply river and trees, for instance, but river and trees as seen by someone musically preoccupied in a certain way.

The first requirement for the artist is, therefore, that he be open and supple, receptive to the world that others inhabit and able to reproduce his sensations from it with an unperturbed fidelity that will allow certain others to recognise them. At the outset of his career, Joyce told Yeats that he 'had thrown over metrical form . . . that he might get a form so fluent that it would respond to the motions of the spirit,'[8] and in the middle of writing *Finnegans Wake* he was to find a prophecy of his own work in the words of Father Marcel Jousse,[9] who taught that language originates in a sequence of gestures mimicking a universe which is itself a sequence of gestures.

For both Joyce and Jousse, that is the ideal: language before the fall, when Proteus and Narcissus worked together, when our bodies, voices, and verses were the places where the landscape found its form, and the imagination, a palimpsest of memories, took on flesh. Jousse associates our postlapsarian estrangement from the ideal with the introduction of writing, which petrified a supple and spontaneous mimetic language into a *'cadavre graphique'.*[10] To an extent, Joyce seems to concur. After *Chamber Music,* his work is full of horrible examples of literary 'dead language'—platitudes and parodies and journalese—which dem-onstrate what can happen when language is petrified in print, to it and the people who use it. But for him the problem is not so much with print as with the habit of mind which it reflects and engenders—a tendency to preserve old formulations and use them as weapons against new perceptions. Projection, as a result, overwhelms the balance between inner and outer worlds. The Narcissus side of the formula takes on exaggerated influence, imagination is not so much memory anymore as it is memorial, and the mind's encounters with reality call up a succession of once appropriate artifacts now cherished for their own sakes. The result is a kind of collective cultural self-love enacted individually—a kind of narcissism. The result, for instance, is the communicants of 'Grace', the hacks of 'Aeolus', the four old Annalists of *Finnegans Wake* and the middle episodes of *Ulysses,* symptoms of what happens when words stick in the mind, gum up its responses to the world's changes, and turn it into something closer to what it was once than what it is at the moment.

What the artist must avoid above all is what the young Joyce found wrong in an inferior novelist, the temptation to let his mind 'impress its own likeness upon that which it creates' (*CW* 130), allow his own codified set of memories to take over the landscape and turn it into a 'property'. When the Stephen of the 'Proteus' episode of *Ulysses* encounters something, for instance a dog on a beach, he illustrates how attempting to grasp the world with the senses can be retrograde, back into the self and its stored formulations:

> Their dog ambled about a bank of dwindling sand . . . Suddenly he made off like a bounding hare, ears flung back, chasing the shadow of a low-skimming gull. The man's shrieked whistle struck his limp ears. He turned, bounded back, came nearer, trotted on twinkling shanks. On a field tenney a buck, trippant, unattired . . .
>
> . . . The dog yelped running to them, reared up and pawed them, dropping on all fours, again reared up at them with mute bearish fawning. Unheeded he kept by them as they came towards the drier sand, a rag of wolf's tongue redpanting from his jaws. His speckled body ambled ahead of them and then loped off at a calf's gallop. (*U* 46)

Here, the determinants of the transformations from hare to buck to bear to wolf to calf are easy: one, some undistinguished mammalian protoplasm—a mutt, in fact—moving from one attitude to another; two, an observer equipped with a memory of rough equivalents for the attitudes struck—in this case, all of them from a handbook of heraldry. The dog takes on form and becomes named when his attitude comes for a moment to fit one of the heraldic silhouettes planted in Stephen's head. He becomes wolfish, for instance, when by hanging out his tongue he momentarily resembles a heraldic wolf, in heraldry distinguished from a dog by a large protruding tongue. He becomes a hare when 'bounding', his suddenly prominent ears 'flung back', because heraldic hares are generally 'courant', with ears bent back. And so on.

So the metamorphoses of this protean beach come not solely from shifts of primal matter nor Stephen's vagrant humour, but from momentary intersections of the two. As illustrated here, a perception is what a fairly recent study of the young Joyce's favourite philosopher, Giordano Bruno, calls the observation of 'the relationship of part to part'.[11] That Joyce shared this interpretation is indicated by his youthful review of J. Lewis McIntyre's *Giordano Bruno*, in which he agrees that Bruno's philosophy is 'a curious anticipation of Spinoza' (*CW* 132)—that is, a vision of the universe as a succession of shifting modes, temporary configurations of primal elements. In the passage selected from 'Proteus', it is as if the awareness of the observer's portion in giving these configurations their identity has caused Stephen to be overly conscious of himself as maker and so upset the equilibrium between projection and reception: the mind is too methodically 'impress[ing] its own likeness upon that which it creates'.

The significant difference from the fluid interactions of *Chamber Music* and *Finnegans Wake* is in how schematic and neat Stephen's formulations are, derived as they are from one more or less arbitrary frame of reference, as if the memory brought to bear were all in one plane. Like Bloom's Nymph, who enters in 'Circe' with the memorable words, 'Mortal! Nay, dost not weepest!', they resemble Hollywood histories, all stiff and 'antiqued'. Imagination here is still memory, but the kind that makes for family albums and cluttered attics—in this case, in fact, the source is probably one of the old heraldry books of Stephen's earlier reading, as recounted (*P* 180) in *Portrait*.

Everyone in Joyce's later work does this kind of thing at some time. Bloom does it, for instance, in 'Circe' when he has his own meeting with a protean dog (*U* 432-74). This time the metamorphoses recorded on the page are less likely to be heraldic—although the dog does become, like Stephen's mutt, a 'wolfdog' when he has 'his long black tongue lolling out (U 453)'—than materialised clichés, cued by one pose after another. It becomes a 'spaniel' when cringing, a 'mastiff' when growling, a 'bulldog' when showing something like 'bulldog courage', and so forth. Bloom is, however, an older, richer, more spontaneous and less predictable man than Stephen; his memory, and hence his imagination, is much less rigidly controlled, especially in 'Circe'. As a result the dog he encounters in Nighttown, though always liable to reappear as some stock figure from the conventional canine repertoire, can also take, in Bloom's eyes, any number of other peculiar shapes: it becomes, in succession, Mrs Breen (with a baggy, shaggy outfit and a little yelp of 'Yes, yes, yes . . .'), Molly's camel (he shakes hands with his mistress), Gerty MacDowell (she 'paws' Bloom and slobbers on him), Alf Bergan (he 'dogs' Dennis Breen), Richie Goulding (marching 'doggedly' ahead), and the pair of armless loiterers who 'flop' and 'frisk' around Bloom (two pairs of two legs plus no arms equals four legs; they are stuck together in 'playfight' like two men in a horse costume). For the last metamorphosis, 'dog' slant-rhymes into 'Dignam'.

The most substantial of the dog's transformations embodies one of Bloom's deepest preoccupations: 'The retriever approaches sniffling, nose to the ground . . . a stooped bearded figure appears garbed in the long caftan of an elder in Zion and a smoking cap with magenta tassels. Horned spectacles hang down at the wings of the nose. Yellow poison streaks are on the drawn face)' (U 437). This is Bloom's father metamorphosed from the dog: the shaggy coat has become a beard, caftan, coat, and tassels, the droopy flews a pair of glasses that 'hang down' 'at the wings of the nose', the nose-to-the-ground attitude a stoop, the liver-and-white markings (U 432) Rudolph's poison streaks, discoloured by the same Nighttown lights that have dyed his feathers magenta and, on the first page of 'Circe', changed the icecream of the children into copper snow.

The Rudolph apparition illustrates how, with a character like Bloom, sensation can reach back, past the levels of consciousness concerned simply with identifying, to hallucinations with their source in the deepest memories. Such moments are essential to *Ulysses* and *Finnegans Wake,* especially in their central, culminative sections; they are the main means by which the author gives depth to the characters and the books in which they appear. In the third chapter of Book III of *Finnegans Wake*, for instance, just such a moment reverberates backwards, revealing much about Shaun's deepest memories and their sources from his attempt to identify a simple shape. The inquisitors place an 'initial T square of burial jade' in different positions against three different parts of Shaun's supine body, and demand a report on the results:

> Now I, the lord of Tuttu, am placing that initial T square of burial jade upright to your temple a moment. Do you see anything, templar?
> —I see a blackfrinch pliestrycook . . . who is carrying on his brainpan . . . a cathedral of lovejelly for his . . . *Tiens,* how he is like somebodies!
> —Pious, a pious person. What sound of tistress isoles my ear? I horizont the same, this serpe with ramshead, and lay it lightly to your lip a little. What do you feel, liplove?
> —I feel a fine lady . . . floating on a stillstream of isisglass . . . with gold hair to the bed . . . and white arms to the twinklers . . . O la la!
> —Purely, in a pure manner. O, sey but swift and still a vain essaying! Trothed today, trenned tomorrow. I invert the initial of your tripartite and sign it sternly, and adze to girdle, on your breast. What do you hear, breastplate?
> —I ahear of a hopper behidin the door slappin his feet in a pool of bran.
> —Bellax, acting like a bellax. (*FW* 486.4-32)

The authors of *A Skeleton Key to Finnegans Wake* have shown that the inquisitors are rotating the T in order to suggest symbols of increasingly remote Irish history—first the Christian cross, then the Serpent with Ramshead of ancient Celtic religious ceremonies, finally 'a phallic monolith' dating from pre-Celtic times.[12] The sensations Shaun in fact experiences are, it turns out, more visceral in formation and ornate in form than they intend. In the first instance, he sees a vague T shape, feels a cold hard object against his forehead, and, with 'templar' ringing in his ears and food, as usual, on his mind, imagines (1) that the T is an upright man with some horizontal object across his head (from the shape);

(2) that the object is metal tray or pan (from the coldness, flatness, and harness of the jade, as well as the associational link head-brain-brainpan-pan); (3) that the pan contains pastry (from his perpetual appetite); (4) that the man is also a religious warrior (from the cross shape combined with 'templar'). Finally, the concepts of 'religious' and 'pastry' fuse in the figure of St Patrick, whose name is reminiscent of 'pastry', and who arrived from France, mother of pastry, bearing the T sign of the cross.

In the second position, the upper and lower prongs of the sideways T become the upreaching arms and downfalling hair of a lady levitating above her bed, borne on a mirror which is also a stream. In the third position, inverted, the T suggests a cartoon bunny, ears straight up and big feet sticking out horizontally. Its hopping originates from the sound of Shaun's heart, thumping under his breast (the T square is also a stethoscope), as the river of the second vision probably originated in the liquid sound from his lips, the characteristic noises of head, lips, and heart being, in *Finnegans Wake* (see *FW* 180.22, 477.28, 504.12), buzz, burble, and thump, respectively. As when Bloom meets the dog and evokes Rudolph, the immediate sensations work backwards through Shaun's memory to evoke certain images stored there. As with Bloom, the descent eventually reaches the level of some primal obsession, in this case what one critic, rightly I think, has called 'the primal scene' of *Finnegans Wake*, the intercourse of the parents, as overheard by the children.[13] (The first picture is of the arriving Tristram, the second of the waiting Iseult, the third is heard from behind a door, and the dialectic movement of the sequence requires that it be a union of the two, as 'pool of bran' unites solid and liquid, 'adze to girdle' connects male sign to female sign, and 'bellax' completes Vico's tag, 'pious and pure wars'.) Evidently, reaching out to the world with the senses can take Joyce's characters as far away from it, into themselves, as it is possible to get.

At the opposite extreme from Bloom's and Shaun's evocations of buried memories are moments when the memory is dormant, and consequently nothing at all, not even a name, is called up by encounters with the exterior world. Here are two such instances from the last chapters of *Ulysses*:

They thereupon stopped. Bloom looked at the head of a horse not worth anything like sixtyfive guineas, suddenly in the dark quite near, so that it seemed new, a different grouping of bones and even flesh, because palpably it was a fourwalker, a hipshaker, a blackbuttocker, a taildangler, a headhanger, putting his hind foot foremost the while the lord of his creation sat on the perch, busy with his thoughts. (*U* 662)

What discrete succession of images did Stephen meanwhile perceive?

Reclined against the area railings he perceived through the transparent kitchenpanes a man regulating a gasflame of 14 C P, a man lighting a candle, a man removing in turn each of his two boots, a man leaving the kitchen holding a candle of I C P. (*U* 669)

Both of these images are unfulfilled acts of apprehension according to the three-stage process outlined by Stephen in the fifth chapter of *Portrait*. There, Stephen demonstrates how to see a basket, for instance, by first drawing 'a bounding line about the object to be apprehended', then perceiving it as 'balanced part against part within its structure', and finally realising the *quidditas* by seeing that it 'is that thing which it is and no other thing' (*P* 212-13). Here the process is incomplete: the horse emerges 'suddenly in evidence' from the background of non-horse, the 'bounding line' of *integritas* separates its 'different grouping' from the background, and it is seen 'like new'—but its elements do not knit into any nameable set of relationships, any more than the generic man of the second passage becomes some iconic biped-with-light, Moses or Diogenes or the Statue of Liberty. Moments like these occur when the principals are exhausted, their memories asleep: Bloom is a virtual amnesiac when he meets the horse; Stephen, normally so erudite, cannot even remember Bloom's name.

Observing so wide a range, from the blankness of Bloom's encounter with the horse, to 'sensation', to the 'hallucination' of Bloom's encounter with the dog, Joyce had all the justification he may have needed for the stylistic experiments which especially characterise his later work. Beginning with *Dubliners* and *Portrait*, the shifting of a central character's apprehensions of a changing world are rendered in the shifting styles,[14] so that in effect the style is an extension of the character's encounter with reality, changing for instance from 'naturalist' to 'symbolist' as the nature of the encounters change from sensation to hallucination. In *Finnegans*

Wake especially, this is a very useful rule to keep in mind: the style is like the 'given' angle of a trigonometry exercise, and if we know it and can estimate the relative extent of each line running from it, we can derive each of the other two angles—first, the literal events transformed by the style, second, which of a particular mind's tricks are at work on them. In *Portrait,* for instance, the occasional irony reflects a mind abstracting itself like a ghostly double at a seance, hovering over and judging its own visions. It can do that because we do that, at least those who are as self-conscious as Stephen Dedalus. In *Ulysses* and *Finnegans Wake,* the mind gets muddled or stuck in different ways in different settings, and we have a kaleidoscope of voices, each resulting from the misperceptions of the moment. As for *Dubliners,* as we shall see, it is among other things, a series of early experiments in epitomising, through its styles, the apprehensions and misapprehensions of different minds at work bringing their senses and memories to bear on the city they inhabit in common.

2

The Dialogue of Dubliners

The style of each of the stories of *Dubliners* originates in the central character's reflection on the events narrated. The central characters (1) experience things, (2) formulate an immediate account of their experiences, and (3) reach a late, reflective judgement. Each of the stories is a kind of dialogue between two versions of one consciousness, one sensitive and one reflective. The style, always recognisably akin to the central character, but always to some extent beyond him or her, is the means by which the dialogue becomes possible. It takes us from the private gothic or sentimental, Marxist or 'realistic' myth of each character, to the vision which cancels it out, from illusion to disillusion.

The first three stories are first-person dialogues of a familiar literary type: an older man remembering his younger self. They set the pattern. At times, the family resemblance between character and narrator is a matter of fairly simple mimesis—'Clay' *sounds* like Maria. At other times it is subtler: one is not so much the other's twin as his or her descendant, sharing perceptions and assumptions.

The following pages will study the connection between narrator and character in the first and last stories of *Dubliners*, 'The Sisters' and 'The Dead', and will note their dialogue in each of the stories in between.

'The Sisters': 'Every night as I gazed up at the window I said softly to myself the word paralysis' (*D* 9). Early close readers of 'The Sisters' in effect took Father Flynn's paralysis to be a symbolic indicator of spiritual sickness, but there is no hard evidence for these readings. What, at first, seems to be Stanislaus Joyce's testimony about his brother's symbolic intentions turns out to be, when read in the original Italian, irrelevant to 'The Sisters',[1] and the only other piece of objective evidence, involving Joyce's choice of dates for Father Flynn's death, is tenuous at best.[2]

What are we then left with? We are left with two important facts: an old priest who for some reason has fallen apart, and a narrative which for some reason suggests that the event is significant. To begin with the first, James Flynn was born in 1830 in perhaps the worst of the Dublin slums. Somehow, he made it out. No doubt he was bright,[3] but as any ghetto-to-glamour biography will testify, it takes more than brains to make the escape. 'Making it', as Norman Podhoretz puts it, requires a special adaptive capacity. Podhoretz, writing *Making It* in his thirties, still remembered the grades he got in Professor Trilling's classes while in the process of working Brooklyn out of his system; Father Flynn, in his sixties, still dwells on the learning of his time at the Irish College in Rome.

The price of such an escape is usually one of enforced alienation from one's origins kept up by scrupulous attention to the rules of the new life. In Father Flynn's case, the separation was evidently tenuous. For fate has sent him back to Dublin to live with two sisters, well-meaning but pure Irishtown, who say things like 'rheumatic wheels'. It is not hard to imagine what his sisters must represent to him;[4] in fact, an earlier version of the story makes his feelings explicit:

He had an egoistic contempt for all women-folk and suffered all their services to him in polite silence. Of course neither of his sisters was very intelligent. Nannie, for instance, had been reading out the newspaper to him every day for years and could read tolerably well and yet she always spoke of it as the *Freeman's General*.[5]

If we want to know what the story's title means, we need only consult *Ulysses*: 'The aged sisters draw us into life; we wail, batten, sport, clip, clasp, sunder, dwindle, die: over us dead they bend' (*U* 394). They were there at the beginning of Jimmy Flynn's crossed quest and are there at the end, noting, in their puzzled way, the 'scrupulous' and 'nervous' way he attends to the various rituals, religious and social, that separate him from them. The most poignant part of Father Flynn's story is the suggestion that toward the end of his life, passing from stroke to stroke, he summoned up the early Irishtown days with them and regretted the loss of what he had spent his life fleeing:

—But still and all he kept on saying that before the summer was over he'd go out for a drive one fine day just to see the old house again where we were all born down in Irishtown and take me and Nannie with him. If we could only get one of them new-fangled carriages that makes no noise that Father O'Rourke told him about—them with the rheumatic wheels—for the day cheap, he said, at Johnny Rush's over the way there and drive out the three of us together of a Sunday evening. He had his mind set on that . . . Poor James! (*D* 17).

In the end he does come home, laid out by the sisters and fellow former Irishtown inhabitant ('no friends like the old friends') Father O'Rourke.

That seems to be about all that we can gather with reasonable assurance about the father's story. When we turn to the question of the narrator's interest in it, the most apparent reason for it is that he senses a similarity between Flynn and his younger self. The young boy of the story is a bookish, withdrawn child, taunted by his philistine uncle, imagining an escape like the one Flynn made—to an eastern land of ancient, exotic, and classy customs.

Above all, he shares with his older counterpart the quality of extreme sensitivity. The Flynn who wanted most to ride home in a noiseless carriage and who sought out the dark, quiet back room and the dark, quiet confessional is paralleled by a character acutely, often painfully affected by sights and sounds. He is especially sensitive to light, as the narrative records without comment when it says, 'I groped my way towards my usual chair in the corner' (*D* 14)—*groped* because he has just come from a brightly lit room (brightly enough to eclipse the candle flames) into the 'little dark room' (*D* 12), and his eyes have not yet adjusted.

That barely noticeable 'groped' tells us a good deal about the narrator—his relation to, and involvement with, his subject. It shows that the protagonist's sensitivity is re-enacted in the narrative—the highly reactive susceptibility matched by an older man who can recall, as if reliving, and pass on with effortless exactness what it is like for a weak-eyed child to go from light to shadow. (He also recalls how sight clears as the pupils dilate; after the boy is seated he begins to see things in greater detail.) This double sensitivity—protagonist attuned to details, narrator to his sensations—is presented as memory, but memory, as *Ulysses* demonstrates often, is seldom so lucid and immediate. Instead the narrative here presents a re-enactment of the original experience, selected with regard not to retrospective patterning, but to what made an impression. The man doing the writing shares the bewildered attentiveness of his younger self, and is generally willing to impart without comment his half-fledged conceptualisations of the things he sees. He resembles Cleanth Brooks and Robert Penn Warren's picture of 'Araby's' narrator, an older man reliving a childhood episode with great attention because 'he sees in the event, if he looks back on it, a kind of parable of a problem which has run through later experience',[6] if we add only that he does not know what that parable is. The major difference between the two is that the man is less certain of things, and so withholds his assent from the boy's suspicions without suggesting an alternative version. The boy may not know exactly what the events surrounding Father Flynn signify, but he is sure that they are full of portent in some way. Like most of the protagonists of *Dubliners*,[7] he has done some reading—evidently of Poe or some imitator—and becomes familiar with iconography of exotic menace. The first sentence, with its ominous fairy-tale 'third stroke', reflects a habit of looking for mystery in one's impressions which will eventually grow into the reflectiveness of the narrator, thus making the story's double focus possible.

The narrator recognises the affinity. In fact, his main business is recognition—the discovery or rediscovery of points of contact between one person and another. As Father Flynn's rediscovery of himself is at the centre of his story, so the narrator's recognition of his younger self is at the centre of his, worked out through the study of himself when young sensing affinities with Father Flynn. (If we follow this equation to its logical conclusion, Father Flynn must represent to the narrator what he may possibly become. Intimations of this possibility may lie behind his reasons for recalling the story.) There is no specifiable locus of meaning at which we can say, 'This is more or less what it all means.' At the heart of 'The Sisters' is not a point but a process, the process which Stephen, in *Ulysses,* says is enacted in *Hamlet*—the author, in the guise of father speaking with son, seeking communion with his younger self. It is a kind of telepathic dialogue: two persons of identical origin but separated by the passage of time, each bringing his own perspective to the other. In this, it sets the pattern for *Dubliners*.

'**An Encounter**': As in 'The Sisters', the young boy of 'An Encounter' is selectively attentive, in a word, 'sensitive'. He notices the sunlight slanting through the light green leaves, the squalor of Ringsend, above all signs of class. He sets himself apart from the wild Irish in preferring the romantic urbanity of American detective stories over Joe Dillon's wild west, naming himself and Mahoney 'Smith' and 'Murphy'.[8] In this he is influenced by Father Butler, who appeals to his sense of superiority to the 'National School Boys'. Counterpointed with the 'wild west' idiom of escape pointed out by Fritz Senn[9] is the Father Butler language of Latin history, rendered latinately. Grown up, looking back, writing this story, the narrator tends to use the latter: 'Hardly had the day dawned' (*D* 20), ran the boy's lesson, and so, years later, the good student grown up: 'Hardly had he sat down . . .' (*D* 26). His natural idiom comes across in phrases such as 'chronicles of disorder' and 'mimic warfare'. Consequently, he is conscious of a double separation—between himself now and his childhood, and between his childhood and the childhood of boyish innocence, represented by Mahoney, which any story about playing hooky has to entertain: '. . . *even I*, looking at the high masts, saw, or imagined, the geography . . . gradually taking substance under my eyes' (*D* 23—my italics). The temporary alliance between the young protagonist and the old man, begun, as Edward Brandabur has noted, with a hint that the latter may prophesy what will become of the former,[10] reflects on the older narrator's fears about himself: is he halfway to *that*? Like one of Wordsworth's returning travellers, he resurrects his childhood to invest it with a retrospective grace, to get things straight, to learn but also to teach. What he teaches his younger self, re-writing his personal history, is the limitation of his own values and the worth of Mahoney. At the end, it is the Mahoney story that prevails: he arrives 'as if to bring me aid', just in the nick of time, just like the cavalry of the wild west.

'**Araby**': As before, the moody child is recognisably father to the nostalgic man. More than anything else, the story is about a particular kind of poetic consciousness characterised by 'a romantic tendency to impose his own vision on the world',[11] turning things into visions, and this consciousness is also the narrator's. There is a modulation from the boy's apotheosis of Mangan's sister (*D* 32) to the man's description of houses gazing 'at one another with brown imperturbable faces' (p. 29)—the narrator, preparing to write about childhood, has read some Dickens—but the same cast of mind is in charge. To a large extent, 'Araby' is about the forging of its own style, and its dialogue is between a boy who looks for meaning everywhere and a man who looks for the meaning of such a boy, in order to find out which of his discoveries were true. In this light, its movement seems inevitable: it traverses numerous over-wrought 'epiphanies' to conclude with one on which both man and boy seem to be in agreement.

'Eveline': The narrator of 'Eveline' haunts its subject. It describes her gestures and everything she sees *a priori,* as part of some completed action: evening falling, invading the avenue as always, old playgrounds now covered with developments, the ever-circumambient dust. These reach us through Eveline's eyes, but the finality conveyed by their composition is the product of a mind that knows the outcome of her story ahead of time. The character does not yet see the extent to which she is a part of the picture; the narrator does. Aside from this, there is little difference between the two. The narrator is a grown-up, saddened version of her subject, occasionally echoing, sympathetically, her younger self. Her return to the emotions of the young Eveline is more than a case of imitative form: 'Amid the seas she sent a cry of anguish!' (*D* 41). That anguish is latent throughout. Eveline is no Gerty Mac-Dowell; as both girl and woman she seems to see things clearly. As a youth she knew what her life was and what it would become if she did not escape; as an older narrator she knows that she was right. Her cry of anguish, with its authorial exclamation mark, is in two voices.

'After The Race': A description of the narrator of 'After the Race': He admires 'solid instincts', and is capable of attributing them to Jimmy (*D* 44). He assumes the primacy of money. He likes to, as he would say, turn a phrase—'gratefully oppressed', 'reasonable recklessness'—and rather fancies himself as an essayist of some worldliness: 'The dinner was excellent, exquisite' (*D* 46). Nevertheless, his style is unsure, sometimes maladroit— the first page is a good example—sometimes precious, the writing of someone who has learned the poses but not the craft. He is half-educated in other ways, too. He hints at a conspiracy among Jimmy's companions, but (though he thinks himself sharp for his suspicions) doesn't really understand it, and the closest he comes to wisdom is a morning-after moral about youthful 'folly'.

This is a latter-day Jimmy writing. He has learned a little more about 'life', but not nearly as much as he thinks. Jimmy, for instance, plumes himself on his 'graceful' transformation of Segouin and Routh into a trite image (*D* 46), and the narrator is obviously proud of his own way with metaphor: 'The journey laid a magical finger on the genuine pulse of life and gallantly the machinery of human nerves strove to answer the bounding courses of the swift blue animal' (*D* 45). The younger Jimmy suspects he may be playing with fire; the older Jimmy knows now that he was, and his last sentence is so pat a summing-up that Joyceans are likely to thresh it for something else. The narrator is himself arrested, not nearly as advanced beyond the character as he thinks. All in all, the story is a horrible example of the benefits of a university education.

'Two Gallants': 'Two Gallants' belongs to Lenehan, a 'frustrated dreamer',[12] and its setting is accordingly a dreamy one of moon, harp, clouds, and plaintive notes. The story's symbolic intimations reveal his mind's mythopoeic bent. The harp turns into a betrayed woman because he is thinking of Corley and the slavey; the coin in the last scene recalls the moon in the way that Robert Boyle has demonstrated[13] because Lenehan sees one and then the other while thinking about betrayal and degradation. He is a perverted Platonist, mooning after noble ideals and lusting to see them defiled, a conflict reflected in his talk, which can always be taken two ways: when he calls Corley a 'Base betrayer', he half means it (*D* 53). (The narrator's mock-heroic title shows an identical double focus.) Like the boys of the first three stories, Lenehan feels himself out of place in dirty Dublin by virtue of his superior refinement, his 'air of gentility' (*D* 57), which he equates with class. (The environment of Kildare Street, one of Dublin's poshest, has a lot to do with triggering his romantic vision of the harp.) Although the narrator's deftness is beyond his scope, its wistful tone descends from his mood, and the parable of degraded innocence replicates his idea of moral order: he also divides things into above and below. 'Two Gallants' is the story Lenehan might have written if he had followed the career in sentimental lyricism that fate has denied him.

'The Boarding House': Mrs Mooney is a sharp-eyed, heartless woman, and the narrator is in her corner. He (it is a he, since Mrs Mooney is the man of the house) is disqualified from sympathy with his subject because Mrs Mooney is without sympathy; to be in tune with her is to see her coldly. As a modification of the sensitive, sign-reading consciousness of the previous stories, we have a narrator that senses and locks into its target, like the 'smart' weaponry of modern war, in the most functional language: 'butcher's daughter', 'short twelve', 'good screw'. The language works like her cleaver (*D* 63), going so far as to cut the story into three neat slices. The story can be told through three different characters and entitled 'The Boarding House' because Mrs Mooney knows all that matters about the others and holds complete dominion over the house; as sympathy with her leads us away from sympathy, so adopting her point of view takes us away from her to the borders of her establishment, her eyes being everywhere. Our closest approximation so far to an omniscient narrator is really an apotheosised busybody.

'A Little Cloud': The subject of 'A Little Cloud' is its own style, personified in Little Chandler; '*Mr. Chandler has the gift of easy and graceful verse . . . A wistful sadness pervades these poems . . .*' (*D* 74). The style is wistful and graceful and easy and sad, relying on the right pitch of elegance for the transient insight. The poetry Chandler would like to write would be a bijouterie of small metaphoric transubstantiations—a 'kindly golden dust' gilding old men and children and turning society women into 'alarmed Atalantas' (*D* 71, 72)—like the 'nocturnes' of Whistler that Joyce despised (*CW* 104). Chandler's judgement of his wife's picture, at the end of the story, is the style's commentary on itself: 'prim and pretty' (*D* 83). Again, the style represents a later, reflective version of the character, a man sitting at his desk. An older and even sadder Chandler is producing this act of refined self-loathing, in which every cherished *mot juste,* in showing us what he can do, serves more bitterly to show what he cannot do. Like the previous characters, excepting Mrs Mooney, Chandler sees himself poised between two worlds, one golden and one grubby, but he no longer believes in his capacity to reconcile the two, and can only recount gloomily his old strategies of mediation. As for the enigmatically allusive title, it also is Chandler's work: ''. . . besides that, he would put in allusions.''

'**Counterparts**': 'Eat pig, like pig', says Bloom in *Ulysses*. Farrington, with his red face 'the colour of dark wine or dark meat' (*D* 88) is a product of the food and drink he spends his days consuming and dreaming about, an embodied appetite. To see something through his bulging eyes is to track it as an object for the mouth, to be mauled or eaten. Characteristically, he has a zeroing-in consciousness, instinctively locking on moving objects, isolating what is of use and screening out everything else. With his sensitivity to what is exploitable, it comes as no surprise that he is a good mimic (*D* 92), able to catch the giveaway mannerism. As he keys in on exploitable distinctions, he backgrounds the useless, and the narrator's practice of pairing the story off in 'counterparts' is made possible by the selectively generalising fuzziness that accompanies his selective acuity—most dramatically when he makes his son into Mr Alleyne's counterpart (both being smaller creatures, one of whom he is constrained from thrashing). The narrative describing Farrington in the first and third sections is like his consciousness, murky but for a few insistent cues, Mr Alleyn's 'piercing North of Ireland accent' for instance. What is necessary is told us as it becomes necessary. Otherwise, people are presented as dehumanised objects, including Farrington himself, who is simply 'the man'.[14] He becomes 'Farrington' when he enters his first pub, and the narrative language gets much matier, because there he is in his element and can be 'himself'. So the pattern of the story follows and extends the movement of Farrington's vision—scanning, spotting, tracking in, bringing to a focus, with the story's second section the focal point, where we see Farrington close up. Before and after, we are in the mechanistic world of 'counterparts'. Though not written in his language (outside the pub he scarcely has any), the story shows the world as he sees it, a grind between stops at the snug. For all its jollity, the middle section cannot obscure the way it meshes with the gears of sections one and three—as we watch Farrington's coins, dependent on the world of watches and offices, dwindle to the twopence that will take him home. Through Farrington, 'Counterparts' tracks the effort to escape its own dreary understanding of the world; the title testifies to its failure.

'**Clay**': Critics of 'Clay' generally agree that it is notable for what it does not tell us. In fact the entire narrative represents a strategy of evasion, of leaving out what really matters, focusing on the politely peripheral. In this, the narrative functions as an extended wish fulfillment for Maria, who knows at some level that her situation is wretched and humiliating, who in the course of the story never gets looked at or listened to without some small calamity occurring, and who throughout escapes imaginatively into the future party until she gets there, when she immediately escapes into the past. She is comforted by the littleness of her body because she wants to disappear. The narrative suggestions picked up by critics that she is a witch or a saint[15] come from the speaker's response to her generalised wish to be not-Maria. As before, style extends (and conspires with) character: a character wishing her own disappearance portrayed in a story that wishes not to show things. Clearly a close copy of Maria's own idiom, the narrative preserves her doubleness and abets her in her desire that others not see what she has become.

'A Painful Case': By conventional Edwardian standards, Mr Duffy's story is the best-written of *Dubliners*, with the most refinement and tact. The self-deprecation of the 'Bile Beans' ad and rueful epigrammatic point revealed by his journal entries blend in the careful irony of the narrative: 'He lived in an old sombre house and from his windows he could look into the disused distillery and upwards along the shallow river on which Dublin is built. The lofty walls of his uncarpeted room were free from pictures' (*D* 107). No narrator in *Dubliners* chooses words more carefully. Duffy's habit of irony automatically short-circuits any metaphoric transformation, any urge to transcendence, and the resulting story is a one-dimensional narrative, its insistent flatness a version of Duffy's, which symbol hunting Joyceans have avoided in droves. The single exception occurs on the last page, when for a moment he can hear in the noise of the train engine Mrs Sinico's name and sense her presence in the air. It is a weak reminder of the imaginative transformations of earlier stories—musical harnesses, ravished harp-women, alarmed Atalantas. Such figures are, most elementarily, enactments of contiguity, one image or sensation made to touch another—harp fusing with woman; '*Puff*-puff-puff' with *Sin*-i-co'. But Duffy's style is to distinguish rather than join. When his habit of distance cancels out 'the reality of what memory had told him' (*D* 117) and he ceases to hear his lover's name on the air, the narrative leaves him in a withdrawal of contact that epitomises his own way with himself: 'He lived at a little distance from his body, regarding his own acts with doubtful side-glances' (*D* 108). The final silence (*D* 117) is as if he had stopped talking even to himself.

'**Ivy Day in the Committee Room**': There is no central character in 'Ivy Day in the Committee Room', its most important presences being, as M. J. C. Hodgart has noted, 'the absent and the dead'[16]—Tierney, the dozen bottles of stout, and, above all, Parnell. With no central character, there is, in effect, no narrator, so that 'Ivy Day' is the exception that proves the rule. The narrator is refined out of existence (in Stephen's words), in the interest of 'dramatic' writing—in effect, a play. Character is established through dialogue, costume, make-up, and gesture:

> A person resembling a poor clergyman or a poor actor appeared in the doorway. His black clothes were tightly buttoned on his short body and it was impossible to say whether he wore a clergyman's collar or a layman's because the collar of his shabby frock-coat, the uncovered buttons of which reflected the candlelight, was turned up about his neck. He wore a round hat of hard black felt. His face, shining with raindrops, had the appearance of damp yellow cheese save where two rosy spots indicated the cheekbones. He opened his very long mouth suddenly to express disappointment and at the same time opened wide his very bright blue eyes to express pleasure and surprise (*D* 125).

With no personified focal point to tell us where to look, the director relies on blocking and lighting: hence all the references to the fire illuminating characters or leaving them in shadow. There is only one scene, on which the perspective never changes (the unities are observed), and the performance concludes with an epilogue, a round of applause, and a critical review. Stephen called drama the highest form of literary art, but here its use is a negative comment on the action it represents: as Mr Duffy's narrative withdraws from him to match his militant agnosticism, so 'Ivy Day' renders the sold-out world of its principals by withdrawing from it. A collection of lives without centre (except perhaps drink) generates a play without dramatic centre (except perhaps the bottles of stout). Like 'A Painful Case', the story ends on a gesture of protest against the prevailing style—Hynes' impassioned return to the lyric mode—which is forthwith suppressed.

'**A Mother**': Mrs Kearney is distinguished by her sharp eyes for socially significant detail—the lines on an 'oldish' face (*D* 142), a house 'filled with paper' (*D* 140), and important distinctions of accent and breeding. When the narrator of her story sees things that she can't, it does so with her eyes: for instance Holohan's 'dirty pieces of paper' (*D* 136). The narrator is 'knowing' and frequently catty, and his handling of Mrs Kearney is another example of poetic justice: ' . . . she tried to console her romantic desires by eating a great deal of Turkish Delight in secret' (*D* 136-7). In her imagination a disappointed society priestess, Mrs Kearney judges according to the conventions, so that clichés cohabit with digs; the narrator is likewise alternately pitiless and platitudinous. Both have been around and know what's what, so that the events seen through their eyes are almost uniformly ritualistic: Mr Holohan always limping, the language movement a routine of trading post-cards and crossing hands. David Hayman[17] has distinguished the 'objective', 'omniscient', and subjective voices of the story, but the 'objective' passages seem to me simply to reflect Mrs Kearney when placid, safe 'amid the chilly circle of her accomplishments' (*D* 136), and the 'omniscience' is really a controlled shift of subjectivity: Mr O'Madden Burke taking over when Mrs Kearney loses control and her disembodied rectitude must look elsewhere for its avatar. (We can imagine what Mrs Kearney would think of someone who behaved as she does.) Mr Burke's last words are fully in keeping with the story's voice as established from the start: 'You did the proper thing, Holohan.'

'**Grace':** A seedy-genteel tea-taster whose first act on gaining consciousness is to twirl the ends of his moustache, Mr Kernan suffuses the first section of 'Grace'. A clot of blood is a 'medal'; everyone is a 'gentleman', including the two drinking buddies who have run out on him.[18] Toward the end of the first section the camera begins to pull back, and, as Richard M. Kain has written, the style of 'false elegance' becomes the subject.[19] Mr Kernan and his group, especially McCoy and Fogarty, jockey to establish their cultural credentials, and wind up, like the boy of 'The Sisters', turning to the church as the standard of all that is class. In inviting us to laugh at their ignorance and posturings, 'Grace' in effect invokes standards of genuine culture. If, as Stanislaus Joyce claimed, the second section of the story parallels the *Purgatorio,* the sin of which Kernan and company are purged is insufficient gentility: they lack 'grace' of the kind associated with Kernan's silk hat (*D* 154—later 'rehabilitated' at the end—173). What this means, we are to discover, is that they lack sufficient money. When in the last section this kind of grace is given voice by Father Purdon (*D* 174) and its conflict with the theological term becomes unblinkable, Joyce has achieved the most intricate act of narrative self-parody in *Dubliners*: a character absorbed into a narrative voice which is refracted in dramatic dialogue which in turn points to an embodied idea of order—Father Purdon, a Jesuit who knows the value of money and, in matters of doctrine, a Martin Cunningham *in excelsis*. From the first sentence, the Kernan narrative of 'Grace' points to Purdon and his speech, as all of *The Divine Comedy* points to Beatrice.

'The Dead': In 'The Dead', again, narrator and character notice the same kinds of things in the same ways. For instance: It is Gabriel who scrutinizes people's faces, looking for signs of youth or age, which he gauges according to the suffusion of blood through the complexion, and who accordingly thinks and speechifies about generations succeeding generations, 'on the rise' and 'on the wane'. But is it the narrator that, in his introductory Lily-voice, first sounds the generational 'thirty years' (*D* 176; later repeated on 194 and 211), and notes that 'a little colour struggled into Aunt Julia's face'; (*D* 193), or that Freddy eats celery as 'a capital thing for the blood' (*D* 200). The narrator is a ghostly extension of the central character, free to roam and see things that he doesn't and reach his own conclusions. This becomes clear, for instance, in a well-known line near the end: 'Generous tears filled Gabriel's eyes.' As John Wilson Foster has pointed out,[20] 'Generous' echoes Gretta's earlier words when learning of Gabriel's loan to Freddy Malins, 'You are a very generous person, Gabriel' (*D* 217). The narrator, that is, has picked up and made his own use of Gretta's word. He has learned something from her, and gone on to reach a fuller understanding of Gabriel than she (who is thinking mainly of the loan to Freddy) was capable of alone.

The narrator can reach his conclusions about the events of the story because, like Gabriel, he is able to reconstruct his provisional formulations as events change his outlook. Both have the capacity to reconsider things in the light of later understanding, remembering facts not included in the original narrative. For both, insignia from the party are combined and transmuted mythopoeically, as they are in the memory, in ways that make little conventional thematic or literary sense, according to private associative laws. Gabriel, for instance, recalls Freddy Malins' 'fork on high' (*D* 206) being held up by a young man with a hacking cough who, he knows, runs a Christmas card shop (*D* 217) and, he learns, has recently visited Mt Melleray, where the monks sleep in their coffins (*D* 200), and he unconsciously joins these elements into a half-knit pattern which he later connects with the image of a young man in the gasworks (Freddy's association with Browne, 'laid on here like the gas' (*D* 206), may help to close the synapse), whose last name suggests the avenging Eumenides to his literary consciousness[21] and whose first name suggests the church's avenging angel,[22] and who died, he presumes, of something like consumption—and the presence he conjures is of a dark avenger whose attendant image is the 'shaft of light' (*D* 216) which assimilates and transforms Freddy's fork and Michael's sword. For his part, the narrator is the one who closes the story with its complex vision of the snow, and with his last two words gives the story its portentous title. From the start, the narrative is so close a facsimile of Gabriel's own neurosensory and mental functions that it registers their effects without comment, as in 'The Sisters' it recorded without any explanation the boy's 'groping' to his chair: the way the sight of the largely old-ish faces around the table (the 'younger ones' having been served first (*D* 191), turns Gabriel's dinner speech into an elegy to the dead or dying, or the way the repeated disappearances into the darkened stairwell sharpen the chiaroscuro edges of his imagination and help implant therein the story of Orpheus and Eurydice,[23] or the Christian reverberations from Mr Browne's parting words: 'Make like a bird for Trinity College!' (*D* 209).

The danger of pointing out such presences as Orpheus or the Trinity is in assuming a structural consistency behind them which, in fact, is not present. Frank O'Connor has defined their nature precisely: they are like the 'dissociated metaphor of dreams' and when they combine, it is as a 'process of recollection' which is 'unconscious . . . built up out of odd scraps of metaphor'.[24] Like the metaphors of dreams they are personally oriented and conditioned. A case in point is the much-discussed ambivalence of the last page, an ambivalence which reflects Gabriel's notions of the profound. Reacting to a straitened upbringing[25] at the hands of a woman whose father, with classic Freudian displacement, he enjoys mocking as 'a very pompous old gentleman' (*D* 208), Gabriel has half-consciously formulated an idealised notion of 'escape' characterised, mainly, by inexactitude. He resists demarcations—between 'glue or starch' (*D* 207), the Three Graces and Paris' three goddesses (*D* 204), country and country—and feels his soul most at home in phrases like 'thought-tormented music', which glow vaguely in the mind. The critical disagreement over the exact meaning of the story's concluding images simply demonstrates the extent to which Gabriel's consciousness remains a presence, even when he may be asleep. Their vagueness may also owe something to the unrecorded removal of his glasses before going to bed.

*   *   *   *

'Fallacy or not', Clive Hart has written, 'imitative form was the one great literary theory which Joyce applied throughout his career.'[26] The statement holds true so long as 'imitative form' encompasses more than sound echoing sense. In Joyce's case it can mean a narrative attuned to the working of an individual mind as it makes its way through the world, guided by the senses— receiving impressions through ears and eyes, making words and sentences, formulating private mythologies, judging itself, talking to itself, remembering, and, at least once, achieving something like ek-stasis. His stories are governed more by the laws of the nervous system and elementary psychology than by literary codes, and their styles express more than anything else how the mind works.

3

The Dialogue of Ulysses

As 'The Dead' illustrates, Joyce's attention to the mind's workings
led him from the way it forms impressions to the way it stores and
sorts them, from sensation to memory. His longest short story
required a retrospective coda for the same reason that a long
journey requires a log. A good half of the vastly longer *Ulysses* is
retrospective, according to the same kind of logic: anyone who has
spent a day like Bloomsday and wants to understand it will have to
spend a good deal of time reviewing it. Behind the shifting styles of
Ulysses, there is one mind at work, clinically definable as a
sensorium connected to a highly developed but not photographic
memory, taking its voice in any given chapter according to its
position along a continuum which may be divided according to
three major points: (1) *Sensation:* the phenomenal world, moving
randomly, strikes an attitude which the memory fits to an earlier
similar attitude and the name that went with it. (2) *Hallucination:*
to paraphrase Hugh Kenner,[1] the word becomes a Trojan horse by
which the memory gets into the landscape and takes it over,
making it personify the deepest images of either the individual or
his inherited culture, or both. (3) *Pure Memory:* Lights out and
sound off, the mind passes back through words into a re-enactment
of the fundamental experiences of either the individual or his
inherited culture, or both.[2]

This last stage, relying as it does on the vaguely Jungian-
Yeatsian idea that at their deepest level one's private memories
may merge with something like the collective unconscious, so that

paradoxically the way out of oneself is inwards and backwards, gave Joyce the clue he needed to create characters not condemned to solipsism and a book which would be something besides a time capsule. Frank Budgen records Joyce's thoughts on the subject:

> Yeats held that the borders of our minds are always shifting, tending to become part of the universal mind, and that the borders of our memory also shift and form part of the universal memory. Joyce pointed this out to me, and added that in his own work he never used the recognized symbols, preferring instead to use trivial and quadrivial words and local geographical allusions. The intention of magical evocation, however, remained the same.[3]

When *Ulysses* stops to analyse itself in 'Scylla and Charybdis', the chapter which most critics agree is the clue to the book, Stephen's account of Shakespeare's struggle to escape himself by evoking his 'consubstantial' ancestry is clearly also about how the narcissistic Stephen can evoke his spiritual father, and about how a book set in 1904 Dublin can, by some kind of magical evocation, be called *Ulysses*. The answer in all cases is to turn 'elsewhere, backward' (*U* 197), in an extension of the act which for instance evokes Rudolph for Bloom and Tristram for Shaun. Stephen's Shakespeare, 'turned elsewhere, backward', is a version of Stephen, whose condition, we have seen, is general: Stephen in 'Proteus' sees in a mutt the heraldic emblem of himself as stag at bay; Stephen's Shakespeare finds in an old legend the picture of his traitorous brother Edmund, the result being *King Lear*.

In 'Scylla and Charybdis', Stephen's main task is to explain how this narcissistic licker of old wounds can also become the 'father of all his race'. First, however, he has to clear away some misconceptions—mainly the fashionable platitude, represented by his audience, that far from being concentrated on himself, Shakespeare is a 'myriadminded' mine of images 'in which everyone can find his own' (*U* 200). For the librarian Thomas Lyster, for instance, no version of Shakespeare may be allowed to exclude any other: 'All sides of life should be represented' (*U* 198). (William Schutte records that Lyster was the most 'ardent disciple' of Edward Dowden,[4] remembered as an 'urbane' keeper of

'intellectually open house',[5] given in his Shakespearian criticism
to urging that we 'fling away our . . . little rules' and surrender to
the 'larger harmony' of high art.)[6] Æ and Richard Best, who
envision this larger harmony as, respectively, 'formless spiritual
essences' and an endless recession of paradoxes, in effect agree.
The radically skeptical John Eglinton—'Esthetics and cosmetics
are for the boudoir,' he says in 'Circe' (*U* 510)—has reached the
same aversion to definition from the opposite direction. The
Shakespeare that they promote is like the nineteenth-century's
idea of Hamlet—brilliant and indecisive. (This version comes from
the grafting of two commonplaces, that Hamlet is too multifaceted
to act and that he is Shakespeare's self-portrait.) Stephen's theory
that the ghost rather than Prince Hamlet is a portrait of the artist is
a frontal attack on this image, there being nothing indecisive about
Hamlet Senior.

Stephen's biographical criticism depicts Shakespeare as a distinct individual, not less but more resistant than most to assimila-
tion, whether into 'formless spiritual essences' or into society.
Like Stephen, this Shakespeare is obsessive, suspicious,
'lonely'—one of the least clubable figures in literary history. Like
Stephen, who throughout 'Scylla and Charybdis' has a habit of
picking up someone else's innocuous comment and working it into
his performance,[7] he likes to turn others into 'grist' for his
productions. In his relations with the world he is a vortex more
than a mirror, a prodigy of self-absorption whose genius is mainly
the ability to draw an expanding range of material into his field of
gravity. Stephen's theory itself illustrates the nature of this Shakespeare's creativity by absorbing the remarks of others along with
various stray observations from the past and fusing them in the
intellect as, according to Stephen, *Hamlet* fused in Shakespeare's
imagination. For instance: 'By the way how did he [King Hamlet]
find that out? He died in his sleep. Or the other story, beast with
two backs?' (*U* 139). That was Stephen's question to himself, two
hours and several drinks ago, and here is what he has done with it:

> . . . those who are done to death in sleep cannot know the
> manner of their quell unless their Creator endow their souls with
> that knowledge in the life to come. The poisoning and the beast
> with two backs that urged it King Hamlet's ghost could not know

of were he not endowed with knowledge by his Creator. That is
why his speech (his lean unlovely English) is always turned
elsewhere, backward (*U* 196-7).

This is the (quite impressive) product of a centripetal intelligence
working hard to make everything fit.

The larger dimensions of the discussion, its applicability to the
major issues of *Ulysses,* are first intimated by Stephen's introduction of authors and ideas never thought to have any special bearing
on Shakespeare. Plato, Blavatskied into a misty pantheism
epitomised in Æ's Hindu-ish 'This verily is that' (*U* 185), can be
discerned doing battle with Stephen's 'Aristotelian' insistence that
something is what it is and not something else, that Shakespeare for
instance cannot be both this and that. Closer to the centre of things
is the parallel theological opposition between the heresies of
Arianism and Sabellianism, or 'modalism'—the doctrine that the
three persons of the Trinity are really three modes of one essential
being, 'The Father himself His own Son' (*U* 21). Stephen's
audience is Sabellian in his eyes because it believes that Father
Shakespeare, Son Hamlet, as well as Osric, Horatio, Ophelia, the
grave-diggers, etc. are as Eglinton puts it, 'all in all' (*U* 212),
modally incarnate in one another and all equally Shakespeare.
Opposite this Charybdean whirlpool, Stephen clings to the Scyllan
rock of another heretic, 'poor dear Arius' (*U* 38), 'warring', with
him, on the 'contransmagnificanjewbangtantiality', a boggler
which sums up and parodies the incarnational mysticism of Æ and
company.[8] Because something is what it is and not something else,
according to Stephen, Father and Son are of different substance
altogether, 'sundered' (*U* 207). Stephen's representation of the
first scene of *Hamlet* is an Arian parable: Hamlet Senior calling to
his son across the battlements, 'bidding him list' (*U* 188); father
Shakespeare calling to the dead Hamlet, both fathers sundered
from their sons by death.

Stephen promotes this Arian position for awhile in order to
generate an antithesis ('dialectic' is the 'technic' assigned this
episode on Joyce's schema) to the Sabellianism of his antagonists.
Eventually, he intends to bring things around to a synthesis in the
via media of orthodoxy.[9] This is shown, for instance, in his
interpretation of what happens when the two Hamlets commune
across the battlements: 'He is a ghost, a shadow now, the wind by

Elsinore's rocks or what you will, the sea's voice, a voice heard *only* in the heart of him who is the substance of his shadow, the son consubstantial with the father' (*U* 197) (my italics). There is a restricted communion here across the Arian void: King Hamlet is consubstantial *only* with his son, not with everyone in Elsinore, Shakespeare only with Hamlet and the ghost of his own past. Consubstantial fatherhood is a communion not of everything with everything else but of like with like, a connection both inclusive and exclusive.

This synthesis applies for all the chapter's oppositions. Shakespeare in relation to his own work, for instance, is neither refined out of existence nor 'all in all'. He is consubstantial with certain characters, such as King Hamlet, Prospero, Pericles, and Othello-Iago; others, like Richard III and Edmund, though they originate in his biography, are secondary figures, not variant self-portraits. The same goes for his relation to his audience. When Stephen describes him as becoming 'the father of his race' (*U* 208), he speaks not of the English or human race, but of a 'mystical estate' of rare consubstantial spirits, 'an apostolic succession, from *only* begetter to *only* begotten' (my italics). The identity of the resident apostolic successor is all too obvious: Stephen's theory virtually requires him to be as arrogant as he is.

This restricted consubstantiality, whether personal, paternal, or 'racial', is the province of memory which, as Joyce intimated to Budgen, can echo back beyond private recollections. King Hamlet's memory of his murder, an event which occurred in his sleep, is as Stephen points out supernatural, and God-given. Prince Hamlet learns something from his father which he could not know of from personal experience. And Stephen himself is occasionally able to remember past the borders of his own life to his spiritual father, the 'old artificer' of *A Portrait of the Artist as a Young Man*, the Shakespeare of *Ulysses,* to the timeless region where the past is the 'sister' (*U* 194) to the future. In Shakespeare's work, 'through the ghost of the unquiet father the image of the unliving son looks forth' (*U* 194), and so in Joyce's work: young Stephen's father sees him dressed for mass and remembers his own father; the speaker of 'Ecce Puer' sees his grandson and remembers his father; Bloom sees, through the ghost of Rudy, the ghost of Rudolph. In *Portrait,* Stephen studies his inherited name as a 'prophecy' and experiences, while reviewing his own memory, a reincarnation from his father's, evoked by the word *Foetus*: 'A vision of their life, which his father's words had been powerless to evoke, sprang up before him out of the word cut in the desk' (*P* 89). As Budgen suggests, such moments in Joyce's work recall ideas of racial memory, so long as the idea of 'race' is taken metaphorically to mean a few kindred spirits linked in an apostolic succession of the kind that Stephen imagines between himself and Shakespeare and that Joyce evidently envisioned between himself and Ibsen.

At bottom, then, Stephen's orthodox synthesis is quite simple. There has been some critical confusion about it because of the chapter's second half, where Stephen, as Frank Budgen puts it, 'blows his theory sky-high'.[10] The demolition begins when Mulligan appears. Mulligan is as Arian as the others are Sabellian. As a result he gives the impression—and encourages it, by 'antiphoning' and 'capping' Stephen's words—of being an ally.[11] In actuality Stephen is suddenly stuck between two extremes, with consequences familiar to any middle-of-the-roader who has ever found himself arguing with far-righter and far-lefter: extremes meet; the middle is excluded. Mulligan is invited to a party without Stephen because 'All sides of life should be represented' and Stephen is not a 'side'. His cue is Stephen's phrase 'the son consubstantial with the father', which he immediately reduces to Sabellian parody, as he had (*U* 18) at the beginning of the day: 'He Who Himself begot, middler the Holy Ghost, and Himself sent himself . . .' (*U* 197) and so on.[12] (The widespread belief that Mulligan's parody is a comical but accurate version of Stephen's theory is completely wrong.) Then the sharp-eyed Eglinton takes over, cornering Stephen by relentlessly reducing his theory to Sabellian pieties while appearing to agree with him. (This reaches a climax in the dialogue on pages 212-13.[13]) The result is that Stephen is forced off balance, and his Shakespeare becomes more and more a lonely neurotic, seeking not consubstantial fellowship but simply isolation. In the end, like Hamlet and Shakespeare, Stephen is self-haunted ('I am tired of my voice, the voice of Esau' (*U* 211)); in the end, like Hamlet making jokes about the voice in the cellarage and Shakespeare writing comedies about adultery and usurpation, he 'laughs to free his mind from his mind's bondage' (*U* 212).

Despite its defeat (or rather, given Joyce's usual approach, because of it), Stephen's theory is indeed a clue to *Ulysses*, a guide to the book in which it is set. The question of consubstantiality, of determining the nature and degree of affinity between first Stephen and Bloom and then Bloom and Odysseus, is certainly the central problem posed to the reader. Adopting Stephen's terms, we can conveniently talk of two antithetical extremes. The first, Arian, corresponds to ironic readings: Bloom is not Odysseus, Molly is no Penelope, Homer's presence, such as it is is, is a glum reflection on modern futility. This is the natural first response of any unguided reader, and it seems likely that Joyce commissioned Stuart Gilbert's catalogue of mythic parallels partly because he realised that such a reader would require a counterweight. Once Gilbert's notation became familiar and what everyone calls the Joyce industry got going, the opposite, Sabellian extreme took hold: that Bloom is indeed Odysseus because he is everybody, or at least an uncountable number of anybodies—all in all, like the Sabellian Shakespeare. At which point it becomes necessary to imitate Stephen: as the nature of Shakespeare's consubstantiality with others is highly exclusive, so there are in fact many figures, the great majority in fact, who have little or no affinity with this or that major character in *Ulysses*. Bloom may suggest parallels to Moses, Christ, Shakespeare, Odysseus and Charlie Chaplin, but for all practical purposes he has nothing in common with Nebuchadnezzar, St Paul, Titus Oates, Ajax or Mickey Mouse; if *Ulysses* in some ways re-enacts the *Odyssey, Hamlet* or *Don Giovanni,* its affinities with *Gilgamesh, The Duchess of Malfi* or *Lucia di Lammermoor* are slight.

As if to illustrate the lesson, ''Circe' gives two extreme examples of consubstantiality. First, 'Sabellian':

ELIJAH

. . . Are you a god or a doggone clod? . . . Florry Christ, Stephen Christ, Zoe Christ, Bloom Christ, Kitty Christ, Lynch Christ, it's up to you to sense that cosmic force . . . Be a prism . . . You can rub shoulders with a Jesus, a Gautama, an Ingersoll (*U* 507-8).

The gramophone in the background here turns 'Jerusalem' into 'Whorusalem', and no wonder. Jesus is 'all in all', incarnate everywhere—and so much for that.

The opposite, 'Arian' extreme is illustrated when Stephen and

Bloom, gazing together into Bella Cohen's mirror, produce 'the face of William Shakespeare, beardless . . . rigid in facial paralysis, crowned by the reflection of the reindeer antlered hatrack in the hall', to parrot some Bloomian versions of eloquence and then crow 'with a black capon's laugh' a garbled account of *Othello* and the name of its villain: 'Iagogo! How my Oldfellow chokit his Thursdaymomum. Iagogogo!' (*U* 567). Most of the determinants of this vision become clear when Stephen's theory from 'Scylla and Charybdis' is applied to *Ulysses*. Its cue has been Lynch's allusion to Hamlet's famous line—'The mirror up to nature' (*U* 567)—and so we get a Hamlet-Shakespeare whose thirty years put him just midway between the twenty-two year old Stephen and the thirty-eight year old Bloom, between the age at which Shakespeare is generally supposed to have spent his last full year in Stratford and the age at which, according to Joyce's notes,[14] he wrote *Hamlet* and became the father of his race, between Joyce's age on Bloomsday and his age when writing most of this chapter. He 'crows' because of Greene's famous blast, because Stephen has pictured him as a scavenger, and because Stephen and Bloom both wear black; he is 'crowned' with horns because 'Stephen' means 'crown', Bloom is a cuckold, and Stephen's Shakespeare is a type of Actaeon (*U* 193), with reindeer horns, probably, because of Bloom's associative chain Hamlet-Denmark-reindeer. He is Stephen's portrait of the upstart crow, the spurned scavenger, beautified with Bloom's rhetorical feathers, and the story he tries to tell is both the story of *Othello*—which according to Stephen is the story of *Hamlet*—and the story of *Ulysses*, something about an 'old fellow' (father) and a dead mother, occurring on a Thursday. And, of course, the name he keeps stammering is that of the hornmad hater to whom, according to Stephen in 'Scylla and Charybdis', all Shakespeare's work reduces, and the Spanish for the given name of our hornmad author, whose obsessive jealousy, even were it not documented, is present in overplus through the pages of *Ulysses*.

Like Stephen's reductively biographical criticism, this version of Shakespeare is a step in the right direction, away from the everything-goes alternative, but only a step: it obvious why this isolated, self-absorbed Shakespeare should be 'paralytic'. The dialectical synthesis, the embodiment of what Stephen was aiming at, appears not here but rather on the last page of the chapter:

standing over Stephen and staring at his own shadow against a wall, Bloom projects the after-image of the young man at his feet onto his own shadow, and begets a vision of his son as he might have been—bearing the name of Bloom's father, grown to the same age as Shakespeare's Hamnet, whose death at eleven, according to Stephen, begat *Hamlet*. In the process, not coincidentally, he has intimations of the two great consequences of the most significant day of Joyce's life: an alliance with 'Some girl' (*U* 609) and the birth of a male heir—of the reason for the significance of Bloomsday, in short.

This moment differs from the vision of hornmad Shakespeare-Iago because of the different act of memory that produces it. The earlier scene represents a case of obsessive fixation on one event, the memory of which consumes all later events and makes them into its image. The final scene is a blending of images, seen in three dimensions and held in equilibrium, so much so that it is impossible to pinpoint its center: is it Bloom's shadow, Bloom's memory of Rudy, the presence of Stephen or the never-never world, midway between Stephen and Rudy, where the apparitional changeling has grown to be eleven? This vision is neither Arian nor Sabellian, according to the meanings that the terms accrue in 'Scylla and Charybdis': it is not Sabellian because the determinants are neither infinite nor vague or unaccountable—in fact everything here can be accounted for;* it is not Arian because Bloom's recollection of Rudy contributes to it but does not seize and seal it off from the influence of other memories and impulses, does not paralyse or turn all utterance into a stammer. It exemplifies the *via media* that Stephen was trying to express.

The formation of this last scene exemplifies the act of memory that Joyce works to induce in the reader of *Ulysses,* who, to begin with, will obviously need to remember as much as he can in order to make sense of this very long, very dense book. The memory is of the sort described by Stephen, always on the verge of dissolving from the personal into the telepathic or 'racial', 'turned elsewhere, backward', 'endowed' by the 'creator', 'the sea's voice', 'the son consubstantial with the father' (*U* 197), echoing to the deepest reserves of the race (Homer, Shakespeare) and, inevitably, author.

It was just possible to induce something like that in the forty-

*See pp. 107-108, below.

page 'The Dead', but it obviously belongs mainly to the full-scale novel. Joyce, whose debt to Dickens is just beginning to be recognised, undoubtedly learned much from his Victorian predecessors in the art of constructing long narratives, especially about how to make the reader remember certain things in certain ways. From Thackeray in particular, an author with whom he is virtually never linked, he could have learned the extremely valuable (in fact, for his purposes, essential) technique of forcing the attentive reader to remember *through* the earlier episodes of a book. Here is one example from *Vanity Fair,* near the end:

> William [Dobbin] was too much hurt or ashamed to ask to fathom that disgraceful mystery, although once, and evidently with remorse on his mind, George had alluded to it. It was on the morning of Waterloo, as the young men stood together in front of their line, surveying the black masses of Frenchmen who crowned the opposite heights, and as the rain was coming down: 'I have been mixing in a foolish intrigue with a woman,' George said. 'I am glad we were marched away. If I drop, I hope Emmy will never know of that business.'

Although the reader of *Vanity Fair* will certainly recall the Waterloo chapters, Dobbin's memory of George 'surveying the black masses of Frenchmen' is different from his, because that picture is here given for the first time. It is a vivid sensation somehow missed by a narrator more intent on the world of Becky Sharp than the deeds of brave men in battle. With this reminder of something we haven't seen, two things happen. First, the authority of the narrator is diminished—his idea of the 'world' obviously leaves some things out. Second, William Dobbin is filled out somewhat, granted his own integrity, his own memories existing in some world apart from that of the narrator. With that, the reader is put on notice of a range of experience outside what he's been shown: there are other worlds beyond this one, some of them inhabited by characters without the narrator's knowledge.

A recollection similar to Dobbin's occurs fairly early in *A Portrait of the Artist as a Young Man*. Stephen, visiting his father's old haunts in Cork, feels suddenly unmoored from his past and tries to reorient himself by remembering the events of the first chapter:

The memory of his childhood suddenly grew dim. He tried to call forth some of its vivid moments but could not. He recalled only names. Dante, Parnell, Clane, Clongowes. A little boy had been taught geography by an old woman in her wardrobe. Then he had been sent away from home to a college, he had made his first communion and eaten slim jim out of his cricket cap and watched the firelight leaping and dancing on the wall of a little bedroom in the infirmary and dreamed of being dead, of mass being said for him by the rector in a black and gold cope, of being buried then in the little graveyard of the community off the main avenue of limes . . . He had not died but he had faded out like a film in the sun (*P* 92-3).

Every memory in this passage can be traced to some event or sensation in the first chapter, with one exception. There has been no previous mention of the 'slim jim in the cricket cap'. Nor is this recollection unique. Earlier in the chapter Stephen recalls sitting down at his table on the day after the disastrous Christmas dinner and writing down the names of his classmates, three of them— Roderick Kickham, John Lawton, and Simon Moonan—familiar names from the first chapter, one of them, Anthony MacSwiney, completely new (*P* 70). But Anthony MacSwiney, this recollection tells us, was *there* at Clongowes, like the slim jim in the cricket cap. Even if we did not know of the sprawling *Stephen Hero* from which this shorter book was quarried, such occurrences would point to a larger separate world beyond the narrative, from which it derives, to which it refers, and in comparison to which it is selective and incomplete.

It is incomplete both because it has left some things out and because those things which it includes can evidently be remembered differently. 'A little boy had been taught geography by an old woman' is strangely diminished when compared with the original: 'Dante knew a lot of things. She taught him where the Mozambique Channel was and what was the longest river in America and what was the name of the highest mountain in the moon' (*P* 10-11). Clongowes becomes 'a college'; the fire that was rising and falling 'like waves' (*P* 27) is now recalled as 'leaping and dancing'.

Stephen has discovered a truth on his visit to Cork that will later be part of his Shakespeare theory: 'So in the future, the sister of the past, I may see myself as I sit here now but by reflection from that which then I shall be' (*U* 194). Such 'reflections' of the substance of one's past are the equivalent of the proverbial Shakespearian mirror held up to life, turning it into art. In Joyce's work, the 'reflection' is always a projection backward of the subject's present state —and this is what Joyce may have learned from Thackeray—on the raw material from which his earlier perceptions were formed, rather than the perceptions themselves. So in Cork Stephen remembers Dante not as he thought of her but as he has come to think of her, as 'an old woman', as earlier he remembers in the midst of his new poverty some 'second moiety notices' of his father's from the time of the Christmas dinner fight (*P* 70) which in the first chapter had escaped a narrator attending to other issues. Although such involuntary revisions of his past naturally make him feel somewhat lost, fading 'out like a film in the sun', they reveal as much about the world's enduring substance as they do about its transience. That fire, for instance: the first time, feeling nauseous and hearing a vague muttering in the background, he saw waves at the seaside rising and falling; later as an adolescent, seething with the 'infuriated cries' inside him (*P* 96) and his world spinning out of control, he remembers demonic dervishes. But in both cases there really was something constant there, a fire casting shadows that went up and down, just as there is a real dog on the beach in 'Proteus', just as there was a real personal history of Shakespeare to reflect in his plays. And there really was a moiety notice, a cricket cap, an Anthony MacSwiney, whether recorded once or twice or not at all. These and many other details rest immanent in the virtual source of the first chapter's selections, waiting to be unlocked by some later 'reflection'. As a result, the details which do appear convey a sense of a larger reality within or behind them, whose immanence may or may not be divulged later. Like Stephen, the reader is made to feel conscious that 'he had failed to perceive some vital circumstance in them' (*P* 157).

The sense of immanence is increased by the very short distance, simply in reading time, between the Clongowes Stephen and the adolescent in Cork remembering him. That characters should grow or dwindle in the course of a novel is common enough, but the kind of radical change which Stephen goes through in a few pages is different, at least in degree, from the growing-up story of the usual *bildungsroman*. It resembles instead the primal changes of the chronicle or historical novel: cycles rather than stages, generations rather than years. In a chronicle like *The Forsythe Saga* or the Barchester novels, or in a historical novel like *Vanity Fair,* that long time span is to a degree embodied in, simply, the bulk of the work. When the Reverend Septimus Harding dies at the end of *The Last Chronicle of Barset,* the effect largely depends first on the memory of his drama in *The Warden,* second on the fact that it is a memory. That the reader's most substantial impression of him comes from a separate work is important; it suggests an elastic expanse between two related but distant worlds. Likewise, in the standard triple-decker Victorian novel, major changes in a character or setting are in a sense validated by the lengthy reading time required to get from one incarnation to another. (Dickens plays on the equivalence between reading time and represented time at the end of *Little Dorrit,* when a character compares the three stages of Amy Dorrit's life to three volumes.) The presence of time itself is palpable, as palpable as the thickness of several hundred pages between thumb and finger, and its nature becomes one of the subjects of the book.

In one way, all this is reversed in *A Portrait of the Artist as a Young Man.* Excepting perhaps the opening chapters of *The Rainbow,* nothing in literature that I know of equals the speed with which the cycles and generations of this book wax and wane. Uncle Charles, who was lively enough on p. 36 and at least hale on p. 60, is by p. 66 'witless' with age, and by p. 87 is long dead, 'an image fading out of memory.' The events of Clongowes, thirty or forty pages after they occur, seem terribly remote. *The Rainbow* essentially just speeds up the traditional movement of the chronicle, flipping through the calendar leaves at a great rate; Joyce, by contrast, never moves ahead more than a few years at a time. Still, his book, as much as Lawrence's, conveys the passage of vast tracts of time between the guide-posts—not by dealing in decades, but by creating a sense of all units of time as infinitely extensive, swollen with uncounted changes, attributes, and variations. As much as any Victorian novel of four times its length, *Portrait* can look back on things it has not witnessed in the first place because it is looking back on something much larger than its own earlier narrative—the succession of distending and ramifying moments on which it has drawn. Stephen's memory of his childhood can grow 'dim' in a few years because those years have contained enough to change an age. Joyce's incarnational perspective, always finding the universal in the particular, applies to units of time as much as to the atoms of the material world. In the words of Bruno, 'there is no difference between the hour and the day, between the day and the year, between the year and the century, between the century and the moment.'[15]

If this is true of *Portrait*, it is much truer of *Ulysses*, one of whose major premises is that one day will yield the material of an epic, that units of daily time are microcosms. The shifting styles of *Ulysses'* chapters change its world more dramatically from hour to hour than Stephen's changed from childhood to adolescence. Like the earlier book, it repeatedly leads the reader to remember *through* a vast but finite surface to an imagined source which is infinite. As *Portrait* revealed retrospectively with a reference to the slim jim that the earlier record had been fragmentary, so the later chapters of *Ulysses* are full of pieces of information from the time covered by the earlier chapters that the first or second-time reader will probably feel he somehow missed. The connections holding the book together turn out to be, not variations on unchanging themes, but apprehensions of an immanent reality behind the perceptions of character or narrator.

The reader who finds a character reminded on p. 500 of something else on p. 100 is therefore being directed to do more than put together two pieces of a puzzle. In fact, he is being informed in at least five different ways. First, the new detail tells him something more about what was seen or what really happened behind the recorded account on p. 100—the virtual source on which the narrative draws. Second, it gives him a new perspective on the state of mind of whoever first recorded the original event on p. 100. Third, it is almost certain to tell him something about the immediate events or conditions which are now, on p. 500, evoking the memory of four hundred pages ago: there must be a congruence of some kind between the two moments, and if he cannot see it right away, he should look around. Fourth, it tells him a good deal about the present state of mind of whoever is now registering that congruence. Fifth, and probably of most interest, it enables the reader to reach new conclusions about the typical principles of metamorphosis which define a given character by noting what has changed and what has stayed constant over 400 pages, as well as about the world which that character is interpreting. It gives him two co-ordinates and the information for plotting the curve of

personality which joins them and extends past them. It enables the
reader to experience Stephen's version of consubstantiality.
   An example:

> A scene disengages itself in the observer's memory, evoked, it
> would seem, by a word of so natural a homeliness as if those days
> were really present there (as some thought) with their immediate
> pleasures. A shaven space of lawn one soft May evening, the
> wellremembered grove of lilacs at Roundtown, purple and white
> . . . and yonder about that grey urn where the water moves at
> times in thoughtful irrigation you saw another as fragrant
> sisterhood, Floey, Atty, Tiny and their darker friend with I know
> now what of arresting in her pose then, Our Lady of the
> Cherries, a comely brace of them pendent from an ear, bringing
> out the foreign warmth of the skin so daintily against the cool
> ardent fruit (*U* 422).

To take the five kinds of information supplied by this passage, in
the order given above: first, this tells us a good deal more about the
events at Roundtown than was revealed by the fullest mention
previous, on p. 275. Second, it helps explain why Bloom has got
so misty-eyed over this scene when it has surfaced in his memory
before: for the first time we see him singling out Molly, the 'darker
friend', from her girl friends. Third, with a little hunting, we can
figure out what in the present scene has elicited this vision from the
past: as it happens, it is Stephen's expression 'staggering bob' (*U*
420)—'bob' being the 'word of so natural a homeliness' that
reminds Bloom here of the bob of cherries on Molly's ear.
(Speculating backward from this discovery, it seems probable that
the young women circling the 'grey urn' have been bobbing for
cherries while the young men have been bowling, and that Molly
has won.) Fourth, the contrast between this vision and the earlier
fragmented reflections of the same scene tells us that Bloom is right
now experiencing a prolonged, vivid recollection beyond his usual
powers—that he is, as indeed turns out to be the case, in a trance.
Fifth, if we can see what has changed and what has stayed constant
in the man who, gazing at Molly with cherries, fixed in his mind the
image which has now become 'Our Lady of the Cherries', who
seventeen years ago saw her amid the violet lilacs and has just
recently tried to rekindle old feelings by buying her violet garters,

who has been resisting all day just this sort of sentimental abandon and now, knowing what he knows, finally yields to it anyway, many of whose thoughts and actions during the day are here illuminated by this instance of Paterian myth-making, then we have got Bloom in the way that, Stephen's Shakespeare theory suggests, Joyce wants us to—as a constant activity of self-definition and self-communion. As with 'The Sisters' and the rest of *Dubliners,* the centre of *Ulysses* is not a point but a process: a dialogue between consubstantial spirits.

We make meaning of *Ulysses* by following the way that the characters who compose it make meanings of their world. That explains a long-noticed feature of the book—that as it moves along and the chapters get longer, they become more 'mythic' and the reasons for the title become clearer.[16] As its material accumulates, the narrative enacts the same kind of mental accommodations shown, for instance, by Gabriel Conroy when dealing with a long, bewildering evening: first, recasting the details according to some personal or cultural stereotype (such as Gretta as 'Distant Music') drawn from the memory, second, dwelling for a time in a trance-like revery which, cut off from the world around, follows its own dynamic (e.g. Gabriel's sentimental memories, leading to his access of lust and then his revulsion from it), third, passing on 'elsewhere, backward' to a large and lucid retrospective that overflows narrative limits as it overcomes the central character's fixations (for example the snow, the dead): from sensation to hallucination to 'racial' memory. The abstracting, inward-turning movement becomes a movement outward, the looking-back a looking-through. Like Stephen's Shakespeare, what begins as 'an old dog licking an old sore . . . passes on toward eternity in undiminished personality' (*U* 197).

The recall of events from the first episodes works as a facsimile and a prompting for the recall of myths from outside the book. There is no essential difference between remembering Molly Bloom as 'Our Lady of the Cherries' and remembering her as Penelope. Of course such memories belong mainly in the second half of the book—which is why the Homeric parallels of the opening episodes are for the most part playful and perfunctory. Starting well before 'Circe', over half of *Ulysses* is to a large extent engaged in recalling what has earlier been experienced or imagined or recalled, drawing on a realm which begins largely within the frame of the earlier narrative and ends largely outside it.

The wish to create just such effects accounts for a much discussed feature of *Ulysses,* the narrative gaps between and within the episodes. They make a long story even longer, virtually unending, in fact, and see to it that reading *Ulysses* means reading beyond it, through the lines instead of between them. Like a psychoanalyst showing incomplete illustrations to a patient, Joyce wants the reader to rush in with his own conditioned readings, because that is the main action of the book: the middle episodes read the Rorschach pictures sketched out earlier, themselves the result of similar readings. (Events such as the metamorphoses of 'throw it away' into Throwaway and 'mackintosh' into 'M'Intosh' (*U* 86, 675-6; 112, 647) remind the reader that this sort of thing goes on all the time.) Joyce wants to make the reader think, in a certain way: mainly, to remember, and to keep getting the feeling that he hasn't remembered back far enough. So he starts his novel twice, establishing a yawning discontinuity before the main action begins, and send out all sorts of clues—Stephen's and Bloom's synchronous reactions to the cloud covering the sun (*U* 9, 61) is the most obvious example—that one beginning is to be understood by reference to the other. He sees to it that most of Bloom's memories are of events ten years or more in the past[17] and names his book after the story told by the West's most ancient story-teller. He wants the reader, finally, to feel like Stephen's Hamlet hearing and then recognising a ghost who may well have originated in his own prophetic soul but for all that is there, talking to him, telling him things he didn't know. Neither Sabellian identity nor Arian separation: rather a conversation between two related spirits, a dialogue of father and son taking place continuously between, for instance, chapter and chapter, Stephen and Bloom, Dublin and Ithaca, and finally—the unavoidable conclusion from Stephen's *Hamlet* theory[18]—between James Joyce and the reader who is all the while being taught to recognise Joyce's ghost, and recognise himself in it.

4

The Idea of Order in Dublin

In following the evolution of *Ulysses* from sensation, through hallucination, to the kind of resolution described in the previous chapter, we should concentrate on three things: the characteristic kind of thinking recorded in each episode, the connection between that thinking and the episode's style, and the psychological continuity or discontinuity between episodes—emotional rather than thematic or narrative development. Such an approach will in turn test three assumptions: that a given chapter's style is, as in *Dubliners,* an extension of the central character's way of seeing things, that *Ulysses* consistently reflects one recognisable intelligence, variously incarnate in Stephen, Bloom, and other characters, and—putting the first two together—that the book's stylistic changes reflect the development of one person's encounter with the world, that *Ulysses* is the journal of one figure's progress through reality.

A Portrait of the Artist as a Young Man, being a simpler record of such a progress, can give us an idea of what to expect if these assumptions hold true. There, Stephen begins by gathering senses and impressions, knits them into generalisations, formulates from these generalisations a comprehensive myth with which he identifies, and suffers disillusion as the myth succumbs to the pressures of new realities. That is the essential story of the first chapter and a half of *Portrait,* and indeed it is repeated in the first 255 pages of *Ulysses,* in the ten chapters from 'Telemachus' to 'Wandering Rocks'. In turn, Stephen and then Bloom waken to a

47

new world of sensations, scrutinise it, and draw preliminary conclusions which lead, with Bloom's philosophisings and Stephen's Shakespeare theory, to a comprehensive myth, no sooner formulated than it starts to disintegrate.

'**Telemachus**': At the outset, on the opening pages of 'Telemachus', we begin, appropriately, with the sun and the sea: not first principles, but first things. Principles will come later. The sequence is logical: data before hypothesis. The first sentence of 'Telemachus' conveys facts; the first sentence of 'Calypso', three episodes later, is a generalisation drawn from a knowledge of former facts. If, as Marilyn French suggests,[1] the reader is the real voyager of this book, then his journey from the Stephen chapters to the parallel Bloom chapters is like the one we all make from the infancy of sensations to the distinctions and generalisations of experience—as the Stephen of *Portrait* passes from the pure sensations of the opening section to formulations like this in the second: 'But soon the gas would be lit and in burning it made a light noise like a little song. Always the same' (*P* 12).

The order is Lockean.[2] The Stephen of *Ulysses* is no *tabula rasa,* of course, but he is under the weather—'We're always tired in the morning,' he says, meaning himself—and the style of his chapter is taken over, in the book's first usurpation, by the 'mercurial' Mulligan,[3] whose nature is to have none: 'I can't remember anything' (*U* 8). The result is 'mercurial' writing never hampered by the various hypotactic devices that enable a narrator to comment on the impact of his own narration, free of the 'varieties of embedded sentence so dear to the heart of the modern grammarian'.[4] Throughout 'Telemachus' there are plenty of metaphors, many adjectives and adverbs, and an unfailing sense for the *mot juste,* all directed to the immediacy of the thing itself, for that moment only. Comparisons, of Mulligan to Mercury (*U* 19), for instance, are calibrated extensions of vocabulary, and nothing else. The prose, like the setting it reflects, is all light and bright and sparkling, aglitter with volatile mirrorings and changings: 'warm sunshine mirroring over the sea', the sea itself a 'mirror' reflecting the mutant shapes and shadows of the morning sky, the nickel shaving bowl glinting on the parapet (*U* 9, 11)—brightly polished, maximally susceptible to one another's reflections and the mutability of the whole scene, the sea a setting of 'morning peace' one moment and a 'bowl of bitter waters' the next

(*U* 9). Often the language seems on the verge of some epiphanic significance that remains undelineated in the end.

Watching the embodiment of this style, Stephen thinks, 'Dressing, undressing' (*U* 23). He might also be thinking of the chapter's words, which outfit and re-outfit sensations as they shift around. Haines's hand becomes a 'shell'—when he cups it, for instance—just as Shaun's will in *Finnegans Wake* (*U* 20, *FW* 402.34); Mulligan's panama hat becomes a 'Mercury's hat' when its brim starts flapping, like wings (*U* 19). Perceptions are simply momentary, more or less adequate comparisons, as the chapter emphasises by showing them in the process of forming: Haines looming obscurely as a 'dark figure' (*U* 11) before accruing his Haines-ness; 'a limp black missile' puzzling for an instant before Mulligan names it as Stephen's 'Latin Quarter hat' (*U* 17)— Stephen will later rename it his Hamlet hat—and Mulligan's hands caught momentarily in mid-gesture as 'fins or wings' (*U* 19). Dressing, undressing: 'Isn't the sea what Algy calls it?' asks Mulligan (*U* 5), and then calls it something else.

'**Nestor**': 'Telemachus' establishes the typical narrative act of the first six chapters: attention to details. These chapters, whether dominated by Mulligan, by Stephen observing the fibers of tobacco adhering to Haines's underlip, or by the avid Bloom, typically zero in on selected stimuli. In the next chapter, 'Nestor', as the style passes from the control of bright-eyed Mulligan to that of the sharp-eyed Stephen,[5] the narrator becomes a brooder who more than anything wants what he sees to mean something. Impressionism changes to the kind of solemn, portentous descriptiveness still familiar in many serious novels, especially first ones. A novel by Stephen right now would sound like 'Nestor', sifting every sand for significance, finding 'symbols' and 'signatures' in a coin or a shell (*U* 30), incessantly modifying, looking at a page of numbers and evoking gloomy Moors (*U* 28). One problem with this approach is that it allows no sense of proportion, no hierarchy of values. The intimations have nowhere to point except into the general gloom. History, as taught in the history lesson, is a lie agreed upon; literature is a bored boy pretending to like 'Lycidas'; the search for sources engenders conspiracy theories, such as Mr Deasy's anti-semitism. Money, Stephen's symbol of symbols, is 'useless' (*U* 31). The dialogue is full of riddles with unsatisfactory answers.[6] I have never understood, for instance, what Stephen means by calling God a shout in the street (*U* 34), and I have come to think that he does not know either.

'**Proteus**': In the next episode, 'Proteus', Stephen takes the narrative from the symbols of the school to the 'signatures' of the sea shore, studying 'signatures of all things I am here to read' (*U* 37). The result is one prolonged riddle with no good answer. Nature, said Fenollosa, is without grammar; the 'philology' which Joyce assigned as the science of this episode in his schema refers to the study of diction only. (A 'signature' identifies someone without saying anything about him.) I count sixty-six questions in the episode's fourteen pages, almost five per page, none of them answered adequately. One of the last sums them all up: 'Why is that, I wonder, or does it mean something perhaps?' (*U* 50) The answer is, maybe yes, maybe no. The fundamental questions raised keep receding into yet more fundamental questions. A fair expository summation of what is established definitely would be that everything changes and so do we. The other questions, about form and substance, appearance and reality, Aristotle vs Berkeley, and so forth are left hanging.

'**Calypso**': The style of 'Proteus' is the style of 'Nestor' taken to its extreme—what happens when the young man who had earlier teased Mulligan's shaving bowl (*U* 11) or Deasey's shells (*U* 30) into ponderous epiphanies is allowed to have a chapter all to himself.[7] In the *Odyssey*, Menelaus finally pins Proteus but Stephen is Telemachus in Joyce's Linati schema, and he obviously has not a clue as to how to handle the old monster. The narrator of 'Proteus' simply cannot take one observation here, one observation there, and say for certain in what way they connect. The language of the next chapter, 'Calypso', almost all of it Bloom's, does that sort of thing all the time. The movement from the Stephen chapters to the Bloom chapters is one of puzzles to answers, 'signatures' to sentences, question marks to full points. 'Calypso' forecasts the Bloom whose fantasy in 'Circe' is to be an omniscient answer-man (*U* 487-9), whose most gratifying exchange with Stephen in 'Eumaeus' is a simple answer to a simple question (*U* 660), whose return home, in 'Ithaca', will find its expressive form in a catechism. In fact it would be possible to make a sort of miniature 'Ithaca' from the materials of 'Calypso':

Are cats stupid?
No (*U* 55).

Why are cats' tongues so rough?
To lap better (*U* 56).
Can one cross Dublin without passing a pub?
Save it they can't (*U* 58).
Why are oranges dearer than olives?
They need artificial irrigation (*U* 60).

The biggest question of the chapter is Molly's about metempsychosis, and Bloom's response is characteristic: 'An example would be better' (*U* 65). This new attitude, accompanying a vagueness of diction (expressions such as 'they', 'what-doyoucallhim' are frequent) unimagineable in Stephen's episodes, signals a change in focus away from words by themselves to the patterns they fall into and the more general areas of experience they encompass—from diction to grammar. If it is possible to talk about examples, it is possible to talk about the general statements which they illustrate. Because Bloom can think thoughts such as 'Fresh air helps memory', the narrator for the first time can say things such as 'He liked to read at stool.'

'Lotus-Eaters': The book can therefore start to form what can be called, after Wallace Stevens, certain ideas of order. Things connect and correspond, often in unexpected ways. For instance: '
. . . parlour windows plastered with bills. Plasters on a sore eye' (*U* 61). Occurring in 'Calypso', this is a fairly witty instance of the belief in occult correspondences underlying alchemy, near by a version of the words inscribed on the Emerald Tablet of Hermes Trismegistus, 'As above, so below', and an example of the related doctrine of sympathetic magic: 'Watering cart. To provoke the rain. On earth as it is in heaven' (*U* 61). In the next chapter, 'Lotus-Eaters', such notions become the main determinants of Bloom's ideas of how things are. The episode's assigned science on Joyce's schema is 'chemistry', traced back to its origins in alchemy. It is in 'Lotus-Eaters' that Bloom's thoughts most resemble those of the magus Giordano Bruno.[8] There are loads of pots all through the episode, as William York Tindall points out.[9] Tindall associates them with the ciborium, but 'pot' is an alchemical rather than a liturgical word, and the kinds of transformations taking place within the chapter's many enclosures are mainly chemical. One is even taking place in a chemist's shop: stopping off at Sweny the chemist's on an errand, Bloom remarks on how the

shop's drugs have affected the shop-keeper: 'Gradually changes your character. Living all day among herbs, ointments, disinfectants' (*U* 84).

An alchemical pot is a receptacle in which substances are brought together in order to influence one another. A corollary of the 'lotus-eaters' theme is the theme of influence, for instance, the 'influence of the climate' (*U* 71). Thinking of such things, Bloom becomes choosier about what he allows admittance into his own head. In 'Calypso', he felt 'relish' for the servant girl's 'moving hams' (*U* 59); the corresponding vision in 'Lotus-Eaters' is much more refined: 'Silk flash rich stockings white' (*U* 71). After the main course, dessert. Replete and bombarded by sensations, Bloom's mind pots itself, muting and transmuting the outside world, nesting among choice sweets and its own sugared reveries as if in a drawer full of sachets.

Bloom's developing idea of order, of an occult network of influences and correspondences, reflects what is happening to him. He considers himself scientific, but his idea of science is the old idea of magic—the play of mysterious forces affecting him in mysterious ways. 'It's a law something like that' (*U* 472). 'Weight', for instance, gets defined as the force that pulls bodies together (*U* 72) but why does it do that? (Love is a force too—Martha Clifford feels herself 'drawn' to Henry Flower (*U* 78). To be precise, it is a 'correspondence'.) Why do poisons cure one another, or why does 'moisture about' give long sight (*U* 84, 74)? Bloom's answer is that it just does—the world is a web of correspondences, of attractions and repulsions. He makes it a point to notice such correspondences, for instance between the mass and cannibalism, *hoc est corpus meum* and hocus-pocus (folk etymology is another kind of hunt for connections), Catholic confession and Salvation Army testimonial (*U* 81, 83)—and, admiring St Patrick for capitalising on the correspondence between the shamrock and the Trinity, wonders if some missionary in China could work a similar trick by making a cross out of two chopsticks (*U* 80). There are connections everywhere, many of them hidden by 'Clever' nature (*U* 84), and the kind of problem-solving intelligence that Bloom values in turn is Patrick's, the ability to see some of them that others don't.

Correspondingly, the narrative is suddenly full of unexpected contiguities—*double entendres,* serendipitous discoveries, puns: 'Who's getting it up?', Plumtree's potted meat (*U* 75), a man named Hornblower standing by the gates of a place named Trinity on a 'Heavenly' day (*U* 86), 'word' becoming 'world' (*U* 77), INRI becoming 'Iron nails ran in' (*U* 81), a misunderstanding becoming a prophecy (*U* 86). You can't throw a brick over a wall without hitting some new congruence. Like 'Nestor', 'Lotus-Eaters' is full of riddles, but these ones have answers. For instance—Question: Why is a missionary (Peter Claver) like a British informer (Dennis Carey)? (see p. 81.) Answer: Both undermine, both are appendages of authority, both pretend to be something else.

'Lotus-Eaters' is the first markedly 'thematic' chapter of *Ulysses*. A naive reader, seeing that it is full of flowers, lethargy, and public sights, might well recognise it as a kind of allegory, might even come up with its title, though he would probably get it from Tennyson instead of Homer. This new feature of the style is a formal expression of Bloom's mind, which assumes that the world is complicated but eventually 'all works out' (*U* 154). The professionally anthropological stance struck by the title—which suggests that Dublin is going to be studied as if it were the home of some strange tribe—reflects Bloom's pose as a cosmopolite among provincials. The idea of literary coherence emerging will take hold for the next four chapters, each one of which invites the reader to approach it the way Caroline Spurgeon taught a generation to approach Shakespeare: noting the dominant images, assembling them into themes, and abstracting thence an expository argument. (The movement culminates in 'Scylla and Charybdis', which is mainly exposition.) It is literature 'about' things.

'Hades': The next chapter, 'Hades', for instance, is 'about' death, and thematically the transition from the preceding chapter's concluding image of Bloom taking a bath 'in a womb of warmth' (*U* 86) couldn't be neater: from womb to tomb, from pots to the potting of the dead. The function of the pots of 'Hades' is mainly to seal things off. The action begins in a box on wheels and moves to a coffin, and throughout is full of enclosures and acts of enclosing, most of them simply part of the natural communal response to the chapter's main expository message, voiced repeatedly by Bloom and symbolically seconded in many ways. That message is that the 'stream of life' flows into Hades, and that quick and dead are both alive to the same qualified extent—the dead, disagreeably, in the maze of their underground metropolis, with worms for couriers, the living a parade of zombies. The natural response, epitomised by the mind of Leopold Bloom, is to establish borders between things. Bloom's growing habit of drawing conclusions allows him here to draw brackets around certain entities and divide them from other entities—most importantly, living from dead, and himself from 'them', the other Dubliners, whose antipathy first becomes clear in 'Hades'. Combine these two distinctions, and you have his definitive statement on the experience: 'They are not going to get me this innings' (*U* 115). In an episode of things swelling, simmering, threatening to burst (Simon Dedalus alone breaks out and breaks down), Bloom's response is always the same: 'Looks horrid open . . . Seal up all' (*U* 98). The resulting style is a sequence of self-contained vignettes, including the book's one certifiable 'epiphany'[10] and has reminded at least one critic of Flaubert.[11] Framed by the carriage windows, Dublin is witnessed as a sequence of snapshots, such as the seaside Mutoscope show that Stephen is simultaneously making of the dog on the beach or the 'silhouettes' that the young Joyce was going to write about the city:[12] 'Oot: a dullgarbed old man from the curbstone tendered his wares, his mouth open: oot' (*U* 93). Sound as well as sight is condensed, bracketed, epitomised: 'I'm sorry, sir, for your trouble' becomes 'Sorry, sir: trouble' (*U* 112), Bloom is interrupted (*U* 94) when his story-telling is too discursive (there are in fact a lot of interruptions and changing-of-subjects:[13] another way of drawing lines), narrative, monologue, and dialogue all congeal into epitaphs, clichés, jokes, epiphanies, and self-consciously punchy descriptions: 'A raindrop spat on his hat' (*U* 90). Even those raindrops fall 'Apart . . . like through a colander'.

'**Aeolus**': In the next episode, 'Aeolus', the bracketing turn of mind takes over completely. In 'Hades', Hynes had begun the business of turning Bloom into L. Boom (cf. *U* 111, 647) and the mystery man in the raincoat into McIntosh; in the newspaper office everyone is given that nutshell treatment:

A DAYFATHER

He walked through the caseroom, passing an old man, bowed, spectacled, aproned. Old Monks, the dayfather . . . Nearing the end of his tether now. Sober serious man with a bit in the savings-bank I'd say. Wife a good cook and washer. Daughter working the machine in the parlour. Plain Jane, no damn nonsense (122).

The style is a sequence of that sort of thing. It develops Bloom's ideas of order, but there's a touch of the artist about old Bloom (*U* 235) and his vision here coincides with that of the book's resident artist, Stephen Dedalus, the one who talked about epiphanies in *Stephen Hero* and something very like them in *A Portrait of the Artist as a Young Man,* and who, in 'Aeolus', seems to get the idea for a book called 'Dubliners' (*U* 145). Of course—it is one of the chapter's many tricks with time—we know what that book will be like. It will be written in a style of scrupulous meanness. Its three keynotes, given on the first page, will be 'paralysis', 'simony', and 'gnomon'. Not coincidentally, all are prominent in 'Aeolus'. (Simony—the profession of journalism which represents one way for Stephen to sell out. Gnomon—the theme of frustration and incompleteness.[14] Paralysis—paralysis both of trams—they become stalled on p. 149—and people.) 'Aeolus' is an elaborate *Dubliners* story,[15] resembling 'Counterparts' more than any other, which results from the convergence of two intelligences, Stephen and Bloom, sharing their first episode together, both given at the moment to epiphanies and parables. The idea of order revealed is classically formal, in fact geometrical: things are laid out as if in a formal garden, in circles and rectangles. Monks, for instance, is 'bowed, spectacled, aproned' (*U* 122)—that is, a curve, two circles, and a rectangle. The writing is 'Mainly All Pictures' (*U* 119) drawn with compass and straightedge: 'Shapely bathers in golden strand. World's biggest balloon. Double marriage of sisters celebrated. Two bridegrooms laughing heartily at each other.' Two figure eights, one large circle, two groups of two.

The first principle is symmetry. As Richard Ellmann remarks, 'Almost everything is coupled'[16] in both space and time. History is a hall of mirrors, and always was, so that its reflections recede infinitely. Rhetoric is mainly made up of tricks such as alliteration and antithesis. Wit, epitomised in Lenehan, is a facility for puns, parallels, palindromes and reversals: 'rows of cast steel', 'clamn dever'. Inspiration is 'vision', and that vision is double, like the 'double vision' which, according to Joyce's biographer Herbert Gorman, allowed Joyce his 'Pisgah sight of Dublin'.[17] (The only one in 'Aeolus' to understand Stephen's Pisgah sight, recorded in the concluding 'Parable of the Plums', is McHugh, who 'mostly sees double' (*U* 134).) Literature is double vision rendered in doubled sounds—at its most complex, as in Dante, it is quadruple vision rendered in triple rhyme. Stephen, lamenting his bondage to the leaden pairings of English poetry, has trouble remembering anything from one of Dante's stanzas but the rhymes (*U* 135) and in his confusion gives away the main reason for the chapter's parallels: that making order with words depends on memory, and memory has a natural affinity for symmetries. Bloom reveals this as well when he remembers Keyes's phone number because it is the same as Citron's house number (*U* 122); Crawford shows it in a different way when he misremembers the year of the Phoenix Park murders as 1881 (*U* 136), a numerical palindrome, similar to the 'perfect cretic' 'Ohio', which also sticks in his memory.

Memory is suddenly an issue in 'Aeolus' because the reader has just been reintroduced to Stephen, after sixty very dense pages, and has to remember a lot of things about him in order to form any idea of what he is doing back on the scene with Bloom. Almost certainly, the reader is drawing a lot of blanks. But there is also, of course, what Bloom would call a phenomenal explanation for what seems to be everyone's weakening of memory. Bloom supplies it in the next chapter, 'Lestrygonians', when he blames his forgetting of Penrose's name on the 'noise of the trams' (*U* 156) and then blames a similar lapse by Nannetti in 'Aeolus' on the sounds surrounding him. 'Aeolus' opens with clanging trams and bawling timekeepers, is punctuated with screaming headlines, and is fitfully clamorous throughout. Mental continuity becomes impossible, with the result that the mind naturally does what memory experts up to the present have prescribed: it visualises, and sticks one picture onto another. (The art of memory has long been central to the study of rhetoric, as Joyce would have found from his readings in Bruno if nowhere else, and 'rhetoric' is the assigned science of 'Aeolus' in Joyce's schema.) A map of Dublin is superimposed on an advertisement (*U* 136), the map of Irish history on Jewish history, and so on. The chapter is therefore full of double significations, one character or word rhyming with another. Almost all its headlines, for instance, have double meanings at least.

Stephen will have a good deal more to say about memory in 'Scylla and Charybdis'. In the meantime, 'Aeolus' functions as an introductory lesson, a radically simplified first step in the reading of *Ulysses,* now that things are getting complicated. Its elementary geometry suggests that the whole may be reducible to a map or picture, and in fact to an extent Dublin is reduced to both. It is introduced, in the first scene, as having a 'heart' from which trams and red mailcars circulate; 'circulation' is obviously double in meaning (*U* 118), as is the plumseed-spouting pillar of the one-handed adulterer (*U* 148), as are the inhaling and exhaling windbags of the paired newspapers (*U* 117). There even seems to be a lymph system, to go with the blood circulation: when the tram system has a heart attack, the 'aerated mineral water floats with rattling crates of bottles' (*U* 149) keep circulating. (Joyce learned something in medical school after all.)

So the author of 'Aeolus'—the 'arranger', as he has come to be called[18]—works like the Great Gallaher, by placing a picture over a map and drawing correspondences. The seed of Bloom's 'parlour windows plastered with bills. Plasters on a sore eye' in 'Calypso' has flourished in its natural habitat. The result is clamn dever and awfully silly. When we realise that we are probably supposed to take the 'vermilion mailcars' being loaded with sacks of letters as red corpuscles picking up oxygen and running it to the edges of the body, we may be reminded of educational cartoons, popular in elementary school, with titles like 'Our Friends the Antibodies'. The fact is that memory systems have a natural affinity for the stupid, since the loonier a picture is, the more likely it is to stick in the mind. We are always being advised to picture the Miss Cadbury we've just been introduced to as rubbing chocolate bars into her hair, or something of the sort. Here, Dublin is presented an-thropomorphically in a chapter where such tricks are the specialty of people like the public orator Dan Dawson, who likes to talk about the forest's 'pensive bosom' (*U* 123), and who is Dublin's most famous fathead.

Aside from its trivial complexity, such 'double vision' is reductive: something is always like something else. For instance, machines are 'Almost human' (*U* 121), and humans are almost machines: memory is mechanistic, coupling one impression with another and sometimes getting derailed in damaged minds like that of Crawford. Consequently the trams introduced in the opening lines can function as a separate, all-purpose symbol of the sort we would expect such a chapter to have: they are noisy, they circulate on parallel tracks, 'their rows of cast steel provide a parallel network to the linotype machines and the rows of printed mat-ter,'[19] and their termini, like those of everyone in the chapter possibly excepting Stephen and Bloom, are set from the start: 'Come on, Sandymount Green!' (Crawford to Stephen: 'You can do it. I see it in your face' (*U* 135). A tram's 'face' tells it where it is going.) As a result, the future becomes depressingly easy to see. 'Aeolus' is full of prophecies[20]—Nannetti's election to Lord Mayor, The First World War, *Dubliners, Ulysses,* the fates of most of the men present are all predicted—which seem to be nothing special; tomorrow's newspaper is after all usually a close double of yesterday's.

To an extent, everything in 'Aeolus' is just as easy to see. It begins and ends with pictorial epitomes, the emblem of the trams and the parable of the plums, the former drawn with parallel lines, the latter opening up a vista of circles, 'Rathmines' blue dome, Adam and Eves', saint Laurence O'Toole's (*U* 148). But the bird's-eye perspective comes heavily qualified, because it is simple-minded: it sees things whole by leaving a lot of things out. The result is a picture of 'gaps in human conceptions', of 'frustrated success' in the effort to communicate.[21] One of the chapter's most striking features is the way that the wind and noise gain a presence of their own and make palpable the spaces between person and person or age and age. In the next episode, 'Lestrygonians', Bloom continues to see Dublin in the round, but always makes clear how provisional his conclusions are.

'Lestrygonians': 'Lestrygonians' continues to expand the narrative scope while returning to the interior monologue. The result is a good deal of strain. Bloom's mind becomes baroque for the same reason that poetry did—the traditional anagogical correspondences are stretched to new limits in an effort to keep linked together the particles of an expanding field of apprehension. Trying to keep everything centred, Bloom is suddenly as fascinated with the idea of the microcosm and its problematical correspondences to the macrocosm as was John Donne. He is a little world made cunningly; Guinness's brewery is a 'Regular world in itself' (*U* 152), 'peace and war depend on some fellow's digestion' (*U* 172), and a little finger can blot out the sun.* The anthropomorphic conceits, considerably more extravagant than in the previous episode, suggest Donne at his most outrageous, if not Phineas Fletcher.[22] When Bloom is reminded of his love for Molly by the sight of two copulating flies, the source is obvious: 'Call her one, me another fly.' Above all, he is a metaphysical wit, full of puns and conceits.[23]

As always, the narrative and dialogue extend his mental habits: even when he is offstage, Nosy Flynn carries on about Tom

*Cf. Stephen's Shakespeare: 31-2, above.

Rochford's 'main drainage'. Robert M. Adams has played Dr Johnson by complaining about this passage that 'heartburn and acid indigestion are afflictions not dignified enough to "stand for" anything very portentous';[24] the episode is built out of such correspondences all the same. Others have noted, without reproof, that the syntax shows a great deal of tension.[25]

The intelligence in control is the same one that has been drawing conclusions since 'Calypso', but as the scope widens from the local to the universal, the answers become more obviously provisional. The new philosophy calls all in doubt. The previous episode has just upset established ideas of order by introducing the troublesome fact of doubleness, of there being at least two ways of looking at something. That is why Bloom here begins grappling with parallax (*U* 154) and why, as he senses both his world and himself coming apart,[26] he seems willing to consider almost any way, no matter how far out, of accounting for the curious connections and coincidences around him. Throughout 'Lestrygonians' his mind is full of superstitions—that fish food is brain food, for instance, or that oysters are aphrodisiacs—and in general he believes that what 'they' say, even the vegetarians and Methodists, has some truth in it. Some truth: no school has all of it. Although at his lowest point he feels that nothing is or means anything (*U* 164) the thought reaches him midway between two mysterious coincidences that make him suspect a designer: 'Wheels within wheels' (*U* 163). 'Now that's a coincidence' (*U* 165). (In fact the low point occurs because the sun is beclouded; the sun, like the moon influencing the local lunatics, has its correspondences below.) Something is behind it all. The feeling of conspiracy is evidently widespread: when Bloom leaves Davy Byrne's the talk is of racing tips and freemasonry. At times the indications seem to be pointing to Marxism, which would fit in many ways. 'Aeolus' has just pictured industrial labour doing to its people just what Marx said it did, and its representation of 'historical' attitudinising precisely illustrates the famous first page of *The Eighteenth Brumaire of Louis Bonaparte*. The capitalism of 'Lestrygonians' is dog-eat-dog, with 'a swindle in it somewhere' (*U* 164): religion is shown to be the opiate of the people; Bloom's 'metaphysical' dynamic, like the dialectic, works by contraries; things seem to go in circles; people are determined by class, environment, and job. But the mind which strained at 'the ineffability of the tetragrammaton'

(*U* 724) is not about the swallow the withering-away of the state. 'Ah, get along with your great times coming' (*U* 163). Instead Bloom follows Donne's advice to 'doubt wisely'. He thinks in maybes and admits when he cannot answer a big question: 'Where is the justice being born that way?' The world is mysterious and perilous, and the various saws and superstitions running through Bloom's mind—'no ar no oysters', 'Behind a bull, in front of a horse'—are watchwords for getting through it which may or may not have a larger application.

Energetically agnostic, 'Lestrygonians' seeks, if not final answers, at least more adequate ways of seeing things. Like Donne, it is seriously witty, much more serious than the rhymester writing 'Aeolus' (which is perhaps why Bloom, as if to admonish the Stephen of the previous episode, points out that there's more to poetry than rhyme. Compare pp. 138, 152). Where Donne uses paradox, Bloom uses parallax: he portions a given entity or concept into its extremes and then yokes them by violence together, thinking 'Look on this picture then on that' about a man starting to eat next to a man finishing his meal (*U* 169), passing rapidly from a vision of elegant women (*U* 168) to 'Men, men, men' (*U* 169). As usual, the narrative complies: the apples it shows us, for instance (*U* 156), come from Australia, the antipodes.

The main purpose of parallax in this episode is to try to resolve the incompatibility of subject and object. It is the problematic answer to the solipsism which goes with the metaphysical wit's collapsing of macrocosm into microcosm. At his most intellectual, Bloom balances between thinking that we project our visions onto the world—'If you imagine its there you can almost see it'—and thinking the reverse—'Coming events cast their shadows before' (*U* 166, 165). (In either case, he continues to sense correspondences.) In practice, he sees people (in one case a bird) from the vantage of his own concerns, then consciously tries to imagine them doing the same to him. Paradoxically, his most claustrophic chapter can generate, dialectically, a way out. The clue is the return to his thoughts of metempsychosis, which is to time what parallax is to space—two incarnations juxtaposed so as to reveal their paradoxical communion. 'Aeolus', doubling everything, rhymed Jesus with Mario (*U* 117), or Stephen with Simon; Bloom has a much subtler understanding of the affinities which connect the Parnells with one another, or Dilly Dedalus with her father (*U*

165, 151). He lacks the erudition to put this sense into formulae, but his subtle, tensile imagination has prepared things for Stephen's Trinitarian dialectic, and the next chapter takes up the implied gist of his thought like a relay runner grabbing a baton.

'Scylla and Charybdis': The beginning 'description of Shakespeare in 'Scylla and Charybdis' also describes the Bloom last glimpsed in 'Lestrygonians': 'A hesitating soul taking arms against a sea of troubles, torn by conflicting doubts, as one sees in real life' (*U* 184), and takes his concerns as its own. The first of these is to get away from 'real life' for a while. The library and adjoining museum, like Davy Byrne's earlier, fill the bill: they are places where you can think. So Lyster begins by quieting everything down with his librarian's purr, and the writing becomes euphoniously contemplative, thus confirming Bloom's idea in 'Lestrygonians', developed from 'Lotus-Eaters', that thought is the product of environment. So his ideas about metempsychosis, reincarnated in Stephen, are finally able to work themselves out. (However, at the end of the chapter a second metempsychosis will confound the first—one alliteratively named usurper Malachi Mulligan, bringing consternation to Stephen as another, Blazes Boylan, had to Bloom.) It is as if Bloom's mood swings of the previous episode had been personified and turned into the cast of a Platonic dialogue. For Bloom the dialect had been between Pyrrhonism[27] ('No one is anything') and 'symbolistic' credulity, (Everything is everything else), at one point epitomised, as for Stephen, in Æ. Like Stephen he has hugged the rock to escape the whirlpool (his Æ, like Stephen's, is also aqueous, talking about an octopus (*U* 165)), but concludes by doubting wisely. Now both his doubts and his intimations of metempsychosis are systematised and extended. Opposite Æ is now Eglinton, whose 'eclectic' habit of viewing all Shakespeare theories as frivolous curiosities parallels the side of Bloom that thinks all belief may be superstition. Stephen tries to sustain a plausible system of belief explaining the occult affinities sensed by Bloom earlier, preserving doubt without succumbing to it. The connection across the void is a 'mystery' like the mystery of Communion which connects God with matter. The debate is a re-enactment, on one level, of the Reformation's disputes over the Real Presence, with 'merry Puritan' Eglinton (*U* 208) on the side of the Protestants. Its highly mannered style, pointed out by many commentators, is an act of resistance paralleling Stephen's own to Eglinton's roundheaded idiom of 'plain facts' (*U* 510). It is as if in Stephen's imagination Shakespeare had lived until the Civil War and taken sides with the cavaliers.

'Wandering Rocks': That would put him, of course, on the losing side—which is where Stephen is after the final rout of his Shakespeare theory, as was Bloom after Boylan's appearance at the end of 'Lestrygonians' put an end to his strenuous meditations. In 'Wandering Rocks', the chapter in which the sister who reminds Bloom of Stephen reminds Stephen of Charles I (*U* 243), we behold a Georgian landscape whose evolution from the Shakespearian 'Scylla and Charybdis' is described, for instance, by J. Hillis Miller when discussing the intellectual world to evolve from the Protestant rejection of the Real Presence:

> In the High Renaissance, God is both transcendent and immanent, and in many writers there is an intuition of nature as everywhere inhabited by God. There is a turn toward panpsychism, even to pantheism, as in Giordano Bruno. But the God within nature and the God beyond nature gradually separate from one another, and by the eighteenth century we have the watchmaker God, maker of a universe which is a perfect machine, and no longer needs his presence.[28]

So from the immanence envisioned in 'Lestrygonians' and 'Scylla and Charybdis' to the clockwork of 'Wandering Rocks', which was planned with a stopwatch and, it seems, should be read with one too.[29] When in this chapter Stephen comments on a window full of watches (*U* 242), it is clear that he is also talking about the world.

God is not so much non-existent here as irrelevant, probably too much trouble. The minor character, Miss Dunne, reading a complicated story like *The Woman in White,* speaks for everybody in dismissing it: 'Too much mystery business in it' (*U* 229). (Likewise Bloom passes from three books providing dark mysteries to *Sweets of Sin,* and Stephen flips through the 'Eighth and ninth book of Moses', with its 'secret of all secrets', looking for a surefire way to get a girlfriend.) It is tea time, and everyone has apparently decided to give the big questions a rest for a while—especially the narrator. For those readers who cannot bring themselves to do the same, the chapter is full of traps,[30] dark intimations and clues which point nowhere very gratifying. The worst thing one could do would be to draw conclusions. An example is offered in the first person one meets, Father Conmee, toward whom one is invited to feel smug by Joyce's cattiest narrator since 'A Mother': '[a beggar] held out a peaked cap for alms towards the very reverend John Conmee S. J. Father Conmee blessed him in the sun for his purse held, he knew, one silver crown' (*U* 219). Now, it is not Conmee's fault that he has only one crown in his purse, which technically is not his, and which he needs to complete a charitable mission—he can hardly ask the beggar for change—just as it is not his fault that in the same chapter Bloom gives the Dignams a 'crown', or that Dilly Dedalus asks another father for a 'crown', or that the coin should have its suggestive name. Nor is there anything contemptible in his failure, in the continuation of this passage, to indulge in morose delectation about the *General Slocum* explosion in faraway America while looking after widows and orphans, Mrs Dignam and her children, at home. Like his fellow citizens—like most of us, for that matter—he is able to function in his useful way only by ignoring or simplifying large areas of experience. In inviting us to despise him, the narrator is inviting us to adopt his myopia without his charity. Such invitations are always traps in 'Wandering Rocks'.

The other characters, despite appearances, are also quite good—not great, but more than all right. They worry about clothes and money and status, of course, but also about one another. They are almost uniformly polite and kind, and Joyce considered neither virtue negligible. Representatives of church and state are both 'on errands of mercy bent';[31] so are Ben Dollard, Martin Cunningham, and their cronies. As for the rest, Molly throws the sailor a coin, Simon Dedalus gives his daughter what probably really is most of what he has, charitable nuns are feeding the other Dedalus children, Bloom is getting Molly a book, Tom Rochford has risked his life to save another, McCoy thoughtfully nudges a banana peel into the gutter, and Lenehan pays Bloom his highest compliment of the day. Even Mulligan helps the waitress in the DBC, and even Boylan is sending a gift.

Of course some of these kindnesses are dubious or qualified—Boylan's for instance. 'Wandering Rocks' impresses many readers as the picture of a wasteland partly because of the way it frustrates the wish for final answers, for acts either all good or all bad, whose repercussions will conclude within the range of our vision. The frustration is all the greater because of what has recently been promised: after the 'Pisgah sight' concluding 'Aeolus', *Ulysses* has given, in its 'Lestrygonians' and 'Scylla and Charybdis', its 'Eighth and ninth book of Moses' (*U* 242)—its closest approach to a statement on how things cohere in space and time. Much of *Finnegans Wake* could be deduced from these two chapters. From 'Wandering Rocks', 'still seen from the top of a tower',[32] nothing can be deduced, not Inferno, Purgatorio, or Paradiso. The grammar of meanings built up for 200 pages out of coincidences that are not coincidental is now dispersed in random coincidences that may or may not mean something. In a way, 'Wandering Rocks' confirms that 'Scylla and Charybdis' was *it*—as far as the book is going to go in the exposition of its premises. Taken together, the two chapters amount to a signal that a new kind of writing is coming up, because it is time to stop expounding its ideas of order and start enacting them.

5

The Romantic Temper

'The romantic temper,' says Stephen in *Stephen Hero,* 'is an insecure, unsatisfied, impatient temper which sees no fit abode here for its ideals and chooses therefore to behold them under insensible figures. As a result of this choice it comes to disregard certain limitations. Its figures are blown to wild adventures, lacking the gravity of solid bodies, and the mind that has conceived them ends by disowning them' (*SH* 78). In contrast, 'the classical temper' grows, with 'security and satisfaction and patience' out of a faith in the accessibility of the 'world of experience' to 'the world of . . . dreams'. Years later, Joyce said essentially the same thing about romanticism to Arthur Power—that by 'puffing . . . up' life, it became 'fundamentally false' to it.[1] At the same time he rejected the classical style as 'inadequate' to the 'mystery' of life, the 'subterranean complexities which dominate the average man and compose his life'.

The way out of this apparent contradiction is suggested in the early essay on James Clarence Mangan, in which Joyce calls romanticism and classicism both 'constant states of mind' whose conflict is 'the condition of all achievement' (*CW* 74). The 'classical' state of mind sees things as they are; the 'romantic', in trying to make sense of them, in effect tries to make them into something else, and eventually loses touch. One state leads naturally to the other. Joyce's eventual solution was to represent accurately— 'classically'—the processes by which the mind comes to create its 'romantic' phantasms. Thus 'Circe', a series of hallucinations, was according to Joyce the chapter in which he 'approached reality closer . . . than anywhere else in the book'.[2]

65

Midway between the two states is the mannerist temper, which bends and fashions its subject out of all proportion, but does not fly away from it. This is what happens in 'Lestrygonians' and 'Scylla and Charybdis' before the effort collapses into the anomie of 'Wandering Rocks', which gives a demonstration of why the classical temper by itself will not do. The next chapter, 'Sirens', begins the book's swing to the other extreme. Analogically, 'Scylla and Charybdis', 'Wandering Rocks' and 'Sirens' are the only three chapters to occur away from land, and the point seems clear: for these hundred plus pages, *Ulysses* is at sea, without its bearings. 'Sirens' begins to point it in the new direction. For the next four chapters, 'Cyclops' to 'Circe', *Ulysses* is 'romantic' in Stephen's and Joyce's sense, puffed up and given over to 'wild adventures'. In the final three chapters, 'Eumaeus', 'Ithaca' and 'Penelope', 'the mind that has conceived them ends by disowning them.'

Each of the five episodes from 'Sirens' to 'Circe' is, like the ten preceding episodes, an imitative extension of the mentality of its central characters. The styles are more extravagant, more 'romantic' than in the previous chapters because the characters, having had their attempts to make sense of the world collapse at the end of 'Lestrygonians' and 'Scylla and Charybdis', are in Stephen's words 'insecure, unsatisfied, impatient'. Bloom is obsessed with Molly and Boylan, and Stephen, when he returns in 'Oxen of the Sun', is drunk. The result is that all five episodes are 'romantic'—in Stephen's and Joyce's sense, in the colloquial sense, and, to an extent, in the more traditional literary sense as well. Their intellectual affinities are with Blake, Wagner, Wordsworth and Carlyle, with ideas of primal innocence, transcendent states behind the veil or transforming passions under the surface, nostalgic primitivism, and metempsychosis. The main thing is to break loose and follow the passions whither they lead, not worrying about decorum. The predictable result is that each episode contains at least one disgraceful occurrence. Stylistically, the result is the liberation of what Joyce called the two 'eternal qualities'—the imagination and the sexual instinct.[3] Each of these five chapters is heavily sexual in theme and technique, explicitly ('Sirens', 'Nausicaa', 'Circe') or symbolically ('Cyclops', 'Oxen of the Sun'). Typically, the writing gathers force, builds to crescendo, and subsides, as if controlled by some consuming endogenous power. In fact there is some indication that these chapters are to be taken together as one continuous instance of sexual creation: Stephen has defined conception as an 'instant of blind rut' (*U* 208); 'Cyclops' culminates as the Citizen is blinded by the sun; 'Nausicaa' climaxes when a skyrocket shoots 'blind'; 'Oxen of the Sun' is a tenebrous bringing forth; 'Circe' begins and ends with images of children.

As for the other of Joyce's two 'eternal qualities', imagination—imagination, remember, is memory, the recognition of things of the past in things of the present. The styles of these episodes are consistently imaginative in this sense. As the resident characters, they identify something and give it literary form by casting it in the language of the past. As the characters travel deeper into themselves, passing from reverie to trance to hallucination, the styles become more 'imaginative'—more antique, parodic, more revealing about the history of the character doing the talking or writing.

Both 'the imagination and the sexual instinct' are ways of imposing order on the world, displayed in 'Wandering Rocks', of half-tones, womanly men and moral neutrality. From 'Sirens' to 'Circe', it is as if these two supposedly primal forces were able to run away with the book because they are both functions of an even more fundamental rage to order, whose liberation constitutes Joycean 'romanticism'. 'Lust is more abstract than logic,' writes C. S. Lewis in *The Allegory of Love*. 'It seeks . . . for some purely sexual, hence purely imaginative conjunction of an impossible maleness with an impossible femaleness.' In *Ulysses,* that imaginative conjunction is always drawn from the past, either public or private. Like Gerty as she looks at Bloom, everyone is always 'thinking of someone else all the time'. Molly doesn't go to bed with Hugh E. Boylan so much as with Raoul, or 'the savage bruit', or a 'lion', or an imaginary collage of sloe gin, jingle, carnation, flashy clothes and nickname which stirs her music hall fantasies. Sexual passion suffuses these chapters because it is inseparable from fantasy, and the formation of fantasies, of abstract or lurid images derived from the memory and imposed on the landscape which has called them up, is what these chapters are mainly about.

In fact, what unifies them more than anything else is that all five are variations on the Frankenstein story of a creator's impulses taking on form and coming to life, interpreted by Joyce as a parable of what happens when the mind's image-making power is freed of

normal constraints. The earlier experiments with narrative extension of one central character are allowed to run wild. In 'Cyclops'
the analogue is Mary Shelley's *Frankenstein* itself; in 'Nausicaa'
it is the Pygmalion and Galatea story; in 'Oxen of the Sun' the
style is represented as a child conceived by a mating of the mind's
free-associative and puzzle-making faculties, personified in Bloom
and Stephen; 'Circe' is a series of embodied fantasies which
constantly brings to mind the Faustian original of the Frankenstein
story, especially as interpreted by Joyce's nineteenth century
predecessors.

   'Sirens': In the first episode of the five, 'Sirens', the resident
Frankenstein is Orpheus, the very type of the romantic artist,
whose music made the trees uproot themselves and dance. The
role is taken by Simon Dedalus. Joyce's Linati schema lists
Orpheus as one of the 'persons' of 'Sirens', and Simon is clearly
the one who fits: his wife is dead, he has recently visited her in
'Hades', he plays the piano which is Orpheus' lyre metamorphosed (his son will later be symbolised by a constellated lyre, and
his brother in law is, according to Bloom, a 'Wonderful liar' (*U*
277)), thinking of his wife he calls to her to come to him (*U* 275),
and at that moment the Ormond apparitions around him are rapt.
His song is 'symbolistic . . . high, ethereal', that is, Orphic. (See
the *Argonautica* of Apollonius for the story of Orpheus' charming
of the Sirens—Joyce's sanction for putting Orpheus in this stage of
his Dublin Odyssey.)

   That the maudlin and seedy Simon should take the part of this
musical chapter's supreme musician says a lot about Joyce's
divided feelings towards what he considered a seductive but
inferior art.[4] He had earlier said of Stephen that he was 'shut off
. . . from music by vigour of the mind',[5] and here Bloom agrees:
'Thinking strictly prohibited' (*U* 288). Certainly the music of
'Sirens', all of it sentimental and escapist, is as Bloom says 'a kind
of drunkenness', its sound a 'souse in the ear' (*U* 288, 281).[6]

   The music is sentimental and escapist because that's the way the
central character, Bloom, feels throughout 'Sirens' as he remembers good times with Molly and tries not to think about the adultery
going on at the present. The same imitative principle is at work as
in the other chapters, here carried farther than ever before: Bloom
is given in Simon Dedalus a double to serve as an instrument of his
dominant mood, a conductor between his feelings and the style.

Simon personifies the music which is Bloom's expressive form, and thus becomes the first of a series of flesh-and-blood characters conjured out of Bloom's mind. Both are non-bachelors who have lost their women (although Bloom's equation of his symbolic loss with Dedalus's real one is an index of his slide into sentiment); so, in a different way, is Richie Goulding, who lost his sister when Dedalus lost his wife. That is why all three can harmonise in one chord, each returning briefly in his imagination to the same Eurydice: 'When first they saw, lost Richie, Poldy, mercy of beauty, heard from a person wouldn't expect it in the least, her first merciful lovesoft oftloved word' (*U* 274). Using as justification the old romantic instance of sympathetic vibration, *Ulysses* here begins what over the next 300 plus pages will become an increasingly important part of the action, the embodiment of moods or thoughts in other human forms.

Reflecting Bloom's inner state, the music is more dissonant than harmonious. As the preceding 'Wandering Rocks', 'Sirens' is essentially post-transcendental and relativist: nothing means anything except by comparison and contrast. 'Everything is dear if you don't want it' (*U* 290). Typically, Dedalus the tenor thinks that the 'lower register' is preferable (*U* 289).When he was married he sang 'Fair one we had better part.' Now as a widower he implores his fair one to come back. The attractiveness of women is a matter of supply and demand, as Miss Douce discovers, for what can hardly be the first time, when she gives Boylan what he wants and immediately loses him (*U* 267). Separated, the people in the Ormond feel as meaningless as random notes struck on a keyboard, as lost as Bloom feels. Accordingly, they sing about meetings and sunderings, paradises lost and the wish to regain them, from the opening 'In the Shade of the Palm', about an abandoned 'valley of Eden',[7] to 'The Croppy Boy', about a saintly martyr's death. And accordingly, the Orphic musician of their moods, having inherited the fragmented world of the previous episode and the same 'simultanist manner'[8] of making it cohere, tries very hard ('Begin!') to fabricate a version of transcendent permanence with the tools of relativism: contrast (bronze by gold, bass and tenor, sloe gin and bitter, young and old, men and women), and fusion (harmony, coincidence).

Fusion, of the sort that occurs most spectacularly in the 'Siopold' chord, is music's facsimile of the ideal. The Ormond's sentiment points to a heaven envisioned as a place of polymorphous perversity, everybody fusing with everybody else. Bloom, no free-lover, is not sympathetic. For him the most important fusion of the chapter is after all an act of adultery which in the world of real people cannot help deepening one division insofar as it bridges another. When he accompanies 'M'Appari' and 'Love and War' by mashing his steak, kidney, liver, gravy and potato into one 'mashed mashed' mess (*U* 270, 272), Bloom makes his sharpest criticism of the Ormond's musical love-feast.

Still, Simon Dedalus did for a spell personify and voice Bloom's yearnings for a return to a sentimental Eden. And Simon has started something: each of the next three chapters will feature some kind of prelapsarian ideal, the nature of which will be determined by the controlling character's state of mind, and in each case some figure, created out of some part of him or her, will appear to give it voice.

'Cyclops': In the twelfth episode, 'Cyclops', Eden is the citizen's idea of Ireland before England, the Jews, or women had anything to do with it. James Maddox neatly sums up the transition between the two episodes: 'Were *Ulysses* about the American South, "Sirens" and "Cyclops" would link the Good Old Boys with the Ku Klux Klan.'[9] (And 'Nausicaa' would be *Gone With The Wind*.) Behind the transition is an evolution in Bloom's moods, from self-pity to repressed fury and self-torment. Like 'Sirens', 'Cyclops' is a refracted projection of his mental state. He arrives having just been humiliatingly cuckolded by 'the worst man in Dublin', passing on his way displays of gutted fish. Publicly mild, he is unquestionably fermenting underneath[10] with thoughts of either revenge or the internalised aggression that produces ulcers. In an early draft Joyce had him looking at old clothes in a shop window and, in a mood to be sacrificed, envisioning hanged martyrs (*B* 154). The interior monologue was removed in later drafts, but Bloom's cast of mind is the same, and the persecutions of the parodies are simply instances of the narrative's continuing accommodation to the character's impulses. 'Martyrs long for it' (*BM* 121), writes Joyce in one of his notebooks; 'Cyclops' obliges.

This time around, Bloom is projected into three voices, the Citizen, the narrator, and the parodies. (The increased complexity indicates that he feels torn between rage, embitterment, and pompous self-justification.) The Citizen is the part most deeply buried, the Bloom who would like to go home, break down the door, knock Boylan over the head, and slap some sense into Molly. The Citizen, Polyphemus, according to Joyce's etymology the spirit of 'exaggeration' (*BM* 82), magnifies the forces traditionally associated with his race. He is monstrous because Bloom sees himself as a cuckold, and a cuckold, as Iago says, 'is a monster and a beast'.

Joyce says as much in a note: 'Polyphemus is Ul's shadow' (*JJA* 3,81). If read by themselves, the Citizen's statements almost invariably sound like Bloom's *cri de cœur*: the Citizen, for instance, is the one who attacks Boylan (*U* 318) while Bloom is pretending not to care. Take the Citizen's speeches, replace 'Ireland' with 'Israel', and you have an enflamed Zionist whose idea of a homeland keeps getting mixed up with thoughts of Marion Tweedy Bloom, lamenting 'our lost tribes . . . our Foxford tweeds . . . the Gibraltar now grabbed by the foe of mankind', the English, who are also responsible for 'our ruined trade and our ruined hearths' (*U* 326). (The Citizen has already fingered Boylan as an English stooge.) Even the anti-semitism comes from Bloom's projected masochism and illustrates Joyce's trite observation that 'the Jew hates the jew in the jew' (*BM* 82).

Bloom can make a monster like the Cyclops because he is the Prometheus listed in Joyce's Linati schema. When he lights his cigar he brings fire to the dark pub (his apotheosis is in a chariot of fire), he is introduced as 'prudent', an English translation of 'Prometheus' through a Latin intermediary, and he suffers persecution by a hangman god. (The story about the eagle eating the liver is distributed elsewhere through the narrative: we hear of another Jew suffering at the hands of an anti-semite named Falconer; the hangman Rumbold comes from Liverpool and disembowels his victim.) The Citizen just misses getting Bloom right when he insinuates that Molly is a Pandora like a Devorgilla (*U* 324), since Pandora was not Prometheus' wife but his sister-in-law. In the *Metamorphoses*, Ovid records the legend that Prometheus at the Creation moulded clay 'into the form of the all-controlling gods', and Bloom is likewise the maker of his 'shadow', although his creation resembles not so much a god as the monster of Mary Shelley's 'Modern Prometheus', Frankenstein.

The second voice, that of the parodies, magnifies the Bloom whose idea of art is the nymph out of *Titbits*. We see a trace of the connection when the first parody wilts momentarily into expressions, such as 'first class foliage', 'built expressly for that purpose', and 'strawberries fit for princes', which forecast the Bloom of 'Eumaeus'. ('Fit for princes' is also a Bloomian echo from 'Sirens'.) Bloom is a newspaperman, unusually formal in bearing, with the on-the-one-hand-on-the-other-hand idea of fairness typical of editorials in the establishment press, and a journalistic notion of elegance in diction which does not require much exaggeration to produce the parodies of 'Cyclops'.[11] When overwrought he aspires to the mantle of Christ or Mendelsohn, just as a newspaper writer trying to sound impressive is likely to use words such as 'epic' and 'Herculean'.

The third voice, that of the narrator, represents the Bloom who, in deciding that revenge would be senseless, has decided that everything is senseless, nothing but sham and lechery. 'Would you mind, please, telling me the right time? I'll tell you the right time up a dark lane' (*U* 371). The narrator is the 'gigantic' expression of the Bloom revealed in that last sentence, the wilfully cynical seeker-out of nature's secret cruelties. Joyce's schema calls the narrator 'No one', which of course is the name assumed by Odysseus in the Cyclops' cave. In conversation he also called him 'Thersites',[12] paired with Ulysses from *Troilus and Cressida;* he is also a type of Iago, paired with the Citizen's Othello. Odysseus-Noman, Ulysses-Thersites, Othello-Iago: each of these sets of Cyclopean eyes are the polarised vision of one man, the cuckold Leopold Bloom, as summed up by Stephen's description of Shakespeare: 'His unremitting intellect is the hornmad Iago ceaselessly willing that the moor in him shall suffer' (*U* 212). (A bill-collector, the narrator is quite literally 'unremitting'.) It is as if Bloom had been liquefied and whirled in a centrifuge according to the episode's technic, given in the Linati schema, of 'Alternating asymmetry', moor-particles and Iago-particles spun out of the equilibrium previously suspended in one personality.

In fact, Bloom's loss of control following Molly's betrayal is just what triggers the exaggerations of the episode. The loss corresponds to what Joyce evidently considered Odysseus' single most significant act in Polyphemus' cave, the denial of his identity, the substitution of 'No one' for 'Odysseus'. That is doubtless what Joyce had in mind in calling the 'meaning' of the episode 'The Egocidal Terror' in the Linati schema. Padraic Colum records a conversation that shows what this 'meaning' has to do with Bloom: 'Ulysses, as Joyce recalled it to me, denied his name by suppressing the 'Zeus', the divine part of it. It may be, Joyce commented, that people deny the divine part of themselves in denying something belonging to themselves such as their name; it may be that whole peoples have denied the divine part in themselves; it may be that the Jews have done so.'[13] Like Shakespeare, whom Stephen has 'proven' to be a Jew, jarred into alternating asymmetry—first Othello then Iago—by Ann's betrayal, the cuckolded and shaken Bloom breaks down into his constituent extremes. He breaks down into, for instance, Prometheus and Cyclops: both giants, both fiery (in 'Circe' the Citizen is remembered (*U* 436) as 'that fireeater'), both enemies of Zeus, the repudiated 'divine part'.

So 'Cyclops' is a chapter of asymmetrical exaggerations of parts of one human figure, turned into monstrous personifications of distinct impulses. People become fragmented and the fragments selectively swollen into other people and things: Garryowen is a partial epitome of the Citizen, for instance. The analogue to this action which Joyce has the most fun with is male sexuality, also a matter of selective engorgement.[14] Aside from being funny, the analogy comments on what has happened to the book's language, which at this point can be expressive in only one way, by getting bigger—elevated diction, multiplying lists—and has taken on a stiffness both erectile and morbid. Language is the instrument of a passion out of control, cut loose from its original purpose. The impulse to make words is seen as one part of the desire to make images. As the inhabitants have no use for women, for all the locker-room talk, so the writer, for all his words, has no use for reality, for anything like the evolutions of neologism and metaphor with which poets have kept their changing perceptions in touch with a changing world. Typically, the parodies begin with something real—the Dublin Corporation Fruit, Vegetable, and Fish Market, for instance—and swell beyond any resemblance to their source. Style becomes its own occasion, following its own dynamics, based not on the interaction between words and things but on the interaction between words and other words, multiplying on one another and finding their own rhythms.

More than anything else, 'Cyclops' expresses the need to make words, to fix personal, national and sexual identities once and for all. That the suddenly (and uncharacteristically) voluble Bloom should start defining his terms just after being displaced by Boylan is a matter of elementary psychology, as is the bigotry of Barney Kiernan's oppressed patrons. The comedy comes because the names are always off-centre, like the stock literary responses which they prompt. The more Bloom's martyrdom is examined according to the melodramatic expectations raised by what at first seems the most poignant parable of the book, for instance, the more correct the Citizen seems in calling him 'neither fish nor flesh'. Bloom is a persecuted Jew on an errand of mercy which he will fulfill by defrauding another Jew.[15] The effect of his martyrdom is greatly qualified when, recalling his masochism, we start wondering why of all sports to recommend before this avatar of the Gaelic Athletic League he has to choose the quintessentially British lawn tennis, or realise how much more robust he is than his antagonist. As clearly as anywhere else in the book, the facts of 'Cyclops' show that that is the way life is—a mess. Making it verbally coherent requires closing one eye at least.

'**Nausicaa**': Such awareness, of course, only deepens the movement away from 'life' towards an even blinder worship of self-made images. If reality does not fit, so much for reality. Gerty McDowell, the nun-like heroine of the next episode, is moved to tears by a poem entitled 'Art thou real, my ideal?'—the answer is always no. Clearly enough, she is the lace-curtain counterpart to the pub's aggressive maleness.[16] She, too, is a type, a 'specimen' (*U* 348). Joyce's notes to 'Cyclops' indicate that he once considered giving the Citizen a 'little niece' (*BM* 82) to play the part of Galatea, the nymph chased by Polyphemus, and Gerty's connection with the Citizen's canine friend Garryowen by way of her uncle continues to suggest a relationship at least metaphorically familial.

For allegorical commentators on the *Odyssey*, Polyphemus' island and Nausicaa's Phaeacia, land of song and games, represented barbaric and effete extremes for the polytropic Odysseus to negotiate. Now Bloom, having projected and confronted the picture of himself as naturally vicious, a 'wolf in sheep's clothing' (*U* 338), faces an equally reductive version of himself as over-tame and effeminate.

Gerty is the next projection from his depths, a female counterpart to the Frankenstein monster of 'Cyclops'. Gerty's vision of domestic bliss with the man of her dreams (*U* 352) is an early version of the bungalow and grounds described at length in 'Ithaca' (*U* 712-18), its acquisition being Bloom's 'ultimate ambition'. Once again, the narrative has made of Bloom's deepest longings a talking doll.

Most poignantly, Bloom wants a return to the happiness that he imagines he had during his first year with Molly, 1887, the year of bowling at Mat Dillon and Luke Doyle's charade, those scenes which he remembers so warmly toward the end of his half of the chapter: 'Made me feel so young', he says, shortly after colouring 'like a girl'. It is not likely a coincidence that his age then—twenty-one—is Gerty's age now, or that her thoughts should reflect his in all major and many minor ways.[17] Joyce's Linati schema lists 'The Projected Mirage' as the 'meaning' of this episode, and that is exactly what Gerty is in relation to Bloom—a projection of some of Bloom's least original fantasies. For instance,

> No prince charming is her beau ideal to lay a rare and wondrous love at her feet but rather a manly man with a strong quiet face who had not found his ideal, perhaps his hair slightly flecked with grey, and who would understand, take her in his sheltering arms, strain her to him in all the strength of his deep passionate nature and comfort her with a long long kiss (*U* 351-2).

Now, of course I cannot say for certain, but I strongly suspect that this is not a typical female fantasy, and that the man who wrote 'Penelope' knew it. It is a picture not of what attractive young women think, but of what many middle-aged men would like to think they think about their grizzled ('flecked with grey'), paunchy ('manly'), slow ('deep') selves. Gerty's 'ideal' takes its outline from Bloom's wishful notion of female fantasies as they might apply to him, and its details from his limited knowledge of what women like in men: Molly said she chose him because he was 'so foreign from the others' (*U* 380) and Milly has been carrying on about matinee idol Martin Harvey (*U* 767); so Gerty looking at Bloom sees 'a foreigner, the image of the photo she had of Martin Harvey' (*U* 357).

Joyce being Joyce, it is likely that the 'Galatea' listed in his schema and included in his notes embraces both the nymph chased by Polyphemus and the ivory statue sculpted by Pygmalion, in Ovid's version, as an alternative to the lewdness of the surround-

ing women. (When the 'stonecold' Gerty-nymph of 'Circe' chas-
tises Bloom, he answers, 'O, I have been a perfect pig' (*U* 551).)
Bloom's thoughts in 'Nausicaa' are especially rich in Ovidian
stories of people changing form with flora and fauna, as are Gerty's
of icons and animals that are, as she says, 'almost human'. And it is
not all that remarkable that this modern Galatea should talk, as
well as come to life, given the technical advances since Ovid's time
in the manufacture of automata: 'Press the button and the bird will
squeak' (*U* 370).

Whether or not Joyce had the Pygmalion story specifically in
mind (and it seems likely that one Galatea would have suggested
another), this female effigy, like the male Cyclops, is Bloom's
creation, his 'projected mirage', up to the point of revealing her
lameness as soon as he goes limp (*U* 367)—up to the point, in fact,
that she not only acts out his fantasies but mirrors his engendering
of them. She is the fulfillment of Bloom's wish to 'see ourselves as
others see us' (*U* 376), although at the same time she proves his
maxim that 'When you feel like that you often meet what you feel.'
(*U* 369). She also has her projected mirages, the main one being her
image of Bloom. Having been jilted by the boy on the bicycle, for
instance, she imagines that Bloom has been wounded in love by
some female cyclist (*U* 358).

In other words, a personified mirror-reflection of Bloom's
longings looks back at her begetter as a reflection of her own
fantasies, themselves deriving from Bloom's. 'Nausicaa' is a hall
of mirrors (etymologically identical with mirages) reflecting off one
another and producing an elaborate web of criss-crossing correspondences hypothetically governed by what Gerty thinks of as
magic (*U* 351) and Bloom thinks of as magnetism (*U* 374). The sun
has set, its red orange yellow rays split by the atmosphere's
prismatic effect from green blue indigo violet (as outlined by
Bloom on 376), and the 'evening influence' (*U* 376) sensitises both
Gerty and Bloom to the correspondences of the seven colours, to
the moon (Gerty begins menstruating and Bloom knows it) and to
one another. Blue, for instance, stands for Gerty's Virgin Mary
pose, red—she is forever 'crimsoning' or 'flushing' at intense
moments—for its opposite. She has four different colours of lingerie
ribbons which, when worn on different days, are supposed to
produce different kinds of good luck according to established
principles of sympathetic magic; for his part Bloom hopes for

similar results from the violet garters he has bought Molly. (Both reflect their creator, who dressed himself in the colours of glaucoma in hopes of warding it off.) They both believe in such things because they both feel, at this hour of evening influence, intimations of the central doctrine of hermeticism and its necromancers, that above and below are attuned.

The corollary is that every appearance has something behind it. About every one of the *tableaux* comprising this 'pictorial' chapter, one can confidently say what Gerty says of the picture hanging in her privy: 'You could see there was a story behind it' (*U* 355). So Gerty and Bloom pride themselves on their skill in hermeneutics, Gerty for instance on her knowledge of nose-types and what they mean. Appropriately, their consummation is witnessed by a bat, bats being known, even before the discovery of their sonar-like echolocation, for their extreme sensitivity to sound waves. The two of them can pick up one another's 'waves' because of the evening influence and because they are posing for one another, not only as pictures but as hieroglyphs. Both believe in an incarnational world of fabulous artifice, of emblems which can mediate between one sphere and another, just as the Virgin Mary can 'intercede' (*U* 354) between man and God. The gathering black of dusk is a 'Good conductor' (*U* 374) which mediates the waves from moon or bell-chime; perfume, incense, and the efflorescing semen-smell of celibate priests mediate the respective messages of their sources; even Gerty's ex-boyfriend Reginald Wylie, trying to get into (suggestive name) Trinity, is studying for his 'intermediate'. The theology implicit in 'Nausicaa' anticipates the Druid-St Patrick debate of *Finnegans Wake,* itself a re-casting of High Church—Low Church disputes over ritual and symbolism: 'The light of the spirit [according to the Puritans] should reach the individual directly, like sunlight through pure glass; it should not be contaminated by "externals", as sunlight was coloured by the pictured windows of Papists.'[18] Like *Finnegans Wake,* 'Nausicaa' is thoroughly on the 'Papist' side. Gerty herself becomes a rose window, 'her face . . . a glorious rose' (*U* 360), 'suffused with a divine, an entrancing blush' (*U* 366), wearing diaphanous stockings that glow in diaphanous twilight.

Paradoxically, then, this 'pictorial' chapter, with its themes of masturbation, fetishism, and voyeurism, of unreal ideals and a sacrament viewed but not eaten,[19] is a sequence of intimacies. The magic works. It is the opposite of, and perhaps the answer to, the segmented and cubicled landscape of 'Aeolus'. The masturbation involves not only telepathic communion between Gerty and Bloom but the sympathetic participation of the heavens and the Roman Catholic liturgy. The Benediction of the Blessed Sacrament taking place throughout the episode is not a substitute for Communion but a 'spiritual' enactment of it so affecting that the Church has long been uneasy about its tendency to replace the Eucharist, and especially about its legendary effectiveness as charm and worker of miracles.[20]

The first recorded champion of the practice which eventually became the Benediction was St Gertrude of Helfta, a mystic whose life seems to an extraordinary extent to be the model for the mystical Gertrude of 'Nausicaa'.[21] Like Bloom in his half of the episode Gerty believes in telepathy, metempsychosis and all that. She has a mistily neo-Platonic idea of her true home as being 'aloof, apart in another sphere' (*U* 194), from which she has been excluded by 'accident' (*U* 364)—the word carries its Aristotelian meaning—and to which it is the business of her magic to return her. The best-known English language representative of her kind of Christian mysticism is the Wordsworth of the 'Immortality Ode', the imagery of which—sea, twilight, foster mothers, mountains, four-year's darling—drenches the chapter. Joyce's acknowledged source of 'Nausicaa', Maria Cummins's *The Lamplighter,* is a pretty pure confection of Victorian Wordsworthianism. It tells the story of the 'Immortality Ode', translated into fairy tale: a poor foundling is rescued from her cruel stepmother and turns out to be of noble birth. The lamplighter of the title functions as her intercessor with his linstock, which leads her eyes to the heavenly lights. It is the main story of Gerty's imagination, the Cinderella story,[22] versions of which have also been behind 'Sirens' and 'Cyclops', here bringing to the fore the formative neo-Platonic myth which will in turn control the next episode, 'Oxen of the Sun'. It is the myth of twilit humanity sunk from a higher sun-bright realm. It teaches of occult sympathies, both cosmic (moon to woman) and mental, of the sort that Bloom has experienced with Molly (*U* 380) and that Gerty imagines between women and female priests, (*U* 366), and that proverbially exists between twins—which perhaps explains the presence of the Caffrey twins. It teaches of reincarnation in recurring cycles, and both Gerty and

Bloom think about cyclists and migrating birds, lovers, and so forth, and at their climactic moment together bring forth onto the scene a bat, which Bloom calls a 'ba', thus linking it with both Baby Boardman (who goes 'Habaa baaaahabaaa baaaa' (*U* 357)) and the Egyptian word for both the prophetic cry of a newborn child and the soul of the dead.[23] Watching the bat, Bloom reintroduces the word itself, 'metempsychosis' (*U* 377) and adduces Ovidian examples which show that, as always, he has it muddled up with 'metamorphosis'. The muddle is, as always, right in its way: doctrines of transmutation easily lead to doctrines of transmigration, figures drawn from the tide and moon to figures drawn from the planetary orbits.

The mysticism shared by Bloom and Gerty is reflected in the chapter's extrasensory events. It is no great trick, at an hour when watches stop and rockets explode according to telepathic cues, for Bloom to project a mirage of his own wishes. Nor is it suprising that his mirage should itself be able to view him from an independent perspective. She is simply, again, mirroring his mind, undergoing what parapsychology enthusiasts call an 'out-of-body experience'. She can describe herself from without ('her face was suffused with a divine, an entrancing blush') by virtue of the same powers that enable her to see into the church and the rectory. As a self-styled mystical 'rose', she may be experiencing, at this heated moment, the phenomenon of *Palingenesis* described in Sir Thomas Browne's *Religio Medici,* tried out by the Yeats circle and recorded in Joyce's notes with the phrase (from Browne) 'ghost of a rose' (*BM* 217), the supposed reappearance of a flower's 'ghost' hovering over the original when it is burnt. Certainly, her 'ghost' has left her body. Throughout she is in a self-induced trance, 'lost in thought', 'wrapt in thought' (with a play on 'rapt'), in literal *ek-stasis* at the climax, and her irritation at being addressed recalls the reaction of a practitioner of Transcendental Meditation interrupted in mid-mantra (Gerty's is the *Tantum ergo*).

The method for inducing trances is well known: prolonged concentration on one sound or object. Its most ancient implement is the crystal ball, which has earned its popular reputation for fortune-telling because it can often induce hallucinations. Twentieth-century crystal gazers generally admit that the hallucinations are the viewer's projections, but projections deriving from the collective unconscious or *anima mundi* or some such, and therefore evocations of what is past or passing or to come. Their lore is rich with theories of cosmic or animal magnetism and stories of thought transference. Crystal balls being expensive, the two recommended substitutes are a mirror—whence our legends of 'magic mirrors'—and a shallow pool of water. The best-known magic mirror of course is the one in 'Snow White', a facsimile of which (twenty lines later comes a reference to 'prince charming') has, in effect, told Gerty what the stepmother's magic mirror had originally told her: 'You are lovely, Gerty, it said' (*U* 351). For the most part, the magic mirrors of 'Nausicaa' are the eyes, both Bloom's and Gerty's, to which are attributed all sorts of special powers by virtue of the old saying that eyes are mirrors of the soul and the metaphysical conceit that they mirror the beloved. Gerty and Bloom, their eyes 'gazing' at one another as the climax approaches, are actually gazing in mirrors, each being the projected mirage of the other, and it is nearly impossible to do that for very long without falling into something resembling a trance.

All these extrasensory phenomena constitute a disarmingly straightforward expression of Joyce's narrative technique. After 'Wandering Rocks', *Ulysses* becomes Joyce's most sustained experiment so far in the sort of narrative extension forecast in *Dubliners,* a study of characters leaving their bodies and returning to view, judge, or commune with themselves, and it seems inevitable that at some point it should gather up among its major themes the traditional vocabulary of such extensions, of thought transference and psychic doubles. Gerty believes in telepathy as fish believe in the sea: if it did not exist, she would not exist. She feels that Bloom is her dream come true (*U* 358) because she is in fact his. When she leaves the scene, the spell is broken for a while and Bloom's thoughts on magnetism and cyclists follow hers in the book's last stretch of monologue until 'Penelope', as an expositor's commentary might follow a sacred text, but at the end of his meditations Bloom drifts into a trance of his own, the expressive extension of which will be considered in the next three chapters. From 'Oxen of the Sun' through 'Eumaeus', *Ulysses* makes most sense as the telepathic journey of a mind, predominantly Bloom's but often blending with another, liberated by the trance induced in 'Nausicaa'. Bloom is sitting in the approved position, his back to the sun, at the approved time, dusk, with the clouds drawn across the sky like curtains, and in the prescribed manner scratches occult inscriptions next to a 'dark mirror' with a magical stick which should suggest the owner of the second best-known magic mirror of legend, Merlin. He then sinks into a hypnagogic reverie, a 'half dream', during which the voice, like Gerty's earlier, can all at once see its origin from without, as 'Mr Bloom'.

'**Oxen of the Sun**': Descriptions of visions induced by 'scrying' in crystal, mirror or water agree on three main stages after the initial trance: first, the glass or water appears to become grey in what is called 'clouding'; second, it turns black for a brief period; third, the hallucinatory pictures appear. This describes *Ulysses* from the end of 'Nausicaa' to the end of 'Circe'. Bloom sits dreamily watching the dusk and the clouds gather, then, in 'Oxen of the Sun', the mood darkens into a phantasmagoric chapter of palpable 'tenebrosity' and murkiness, and at the end everyone is plunged into turbulent darkness ('Night. Night'—*U* 427) just before the hallucinations start in 'Circe'. In 'Eumaeus' the images subside and the 'clouding' returns.

Like Gerty, the apparitions of the episode following 'Nausicaa', 'Oxen of the Sun', originate in Bloom's mind. The style and technique change because he changes. After his orgasm, he has drifted by degrees into depressed lassitude, finally dozing off. It seems that the 'aftereffect' is 'not pleasant' (*U* 370), both because of the unseemliness and because of the chain of associations: that Bloom masturbates, it appears habitually, because of the cessation of his sexual relations with Molly, which cessation began '10 years, 5 months, and 18 days ago' (*U* 736), evidently as a result of Rudy's death. This was the beginning of the Blooms' most difficult period. It is associated in Bloom's mind with Holles Street, their principal address at the time, where they were (as Bloom and Gerty are, literally, in 'Nausicaa') 'on the rocks'. In moving to the Holles Street Maternity Hospital and turning it into a scene of misbirths, abortions and perversions, *Ulysses* continues to follow the drift of Bloom's mind, here into a dark period of which the main remembered features are a dead infant, a state of constant frustration, sterility and failure, and a series of compensatory sexual aberrations[24] enacted in the shadow of a building whose presence was a bitter reminder of how far 'inverecund habit' had taken Bloom from the 'honourable by ancestors transmitted customs' and 'evangelical' command to fulfill his race's 'prophecy of abundance' (*U* 385).

So the beginning of 'Oxen of the Sun' follows the end of

'Nausicaa' according to elementary dream logic. 'Cuckoo Cuckoo Cuckoo' three times fades into 'Deshil Holles Eamus' three times,[25] trochees begetting trochees, then expands into the more complicated but similar metrical patterns of the next two paragraphs. The loose run-on writing of Bloom's trance, which on p. 382 separates the 'Cuckoo' sounds, expands on p. 383 into two enormously periphrastic sentences of which the gist and efficient cause is Bloom's self-reproach in combination with his wish to evade reproach. The triple 'Cuckoo' will continue to reverberate: Joyce's letter on the chapter (*L* I, 140) ascribes the recurring strong-stress passages to the Anglo-Saxon heritage, but it is a peculiarity of these passages that the stresses come in threes at least as often as they come in fours. The other style, of long, relatively unpunctuated sentences, will dominate the various voices to such an extent that differences are often blurred and Joyce's unquestionable gift for mimicry attested to by many friends, not to mention *Finnegans Wake,* is undercut. The substance of Bloom's self-reproach, that as 'his own and only enjoyer' (*U* 409) he has become one of those who 'impossibilise' 'Godpossibled souls' (*U* 389) and so have 'Sinned against the Light' (*U* 428), is the theme of the whole episode.

Probably the most complicated chapter of the book, 'Oxen of the Sun' works on many levels, including a literal one involving Bloom's visit to a hospital. But the primary level, the tonic chord from which the others progress, is the trance into which Bloom has fallen at the end of 'Nausicaa'. The first two people he meets, Nurse Callan and Doctor Dixon, are just the people he would naturally think of first when he recalls Holles Street and the hospital—first, Miss Callan because he remembers her from his days there (*U* 373) and because as a young virgin she would be recalled to him by the sight of Gerty, and second, Dixon because thoughts of hospitals naturally lead Bloom to the memory of his recent visit to the Mater, where Dixon treated his bee-sting (see p. 163). The chapter makes most sense as a sequence of ghosts conjured up one after the other by the visions of a man in a state of melancholy meditation on childbirth and related issues, especially if that man has been recently reminded of his unhappy experiences with birth and sex by an anthology of misbirths and monsters called *Aristotle's Masterpiece* and the sound of a cuckoo clock. That is why, for instance, Alec Bannon puts in his improbable appearance with his picture of Milly, and for that matter why Stephen says, 'Return, Clan Milly': thinking of childbirth, Bloom thinks of his child. Even on the literal level, throughout most of the chapter Bloom is in a sort of daze, 'in a strange humour', 'passing grave', 'shut up in sorrow', 'ruminating', falling for awhile into a trance, or trance within a trance, while staring at a beer bottle. As for the 'Homeric' level, the slaughter of Helios' oxen occurs while Odysseus is asleep. As for the 'obstetric' level, Mrs Purefoy has probably been anaesthetised into 'twilight sleep' (*U* 410), the pharmacological equivalent of Bloom's beach-side snooze, and the chapter consistently recommends that expectant mothers be freed from distraction by meditation or drugs.

Of course the chapter's erudition is beyond Bloom's reach. That is where Stephen comes in. According to Joyce (*L* I, 140) he stands in relation to Bloom as egg to sperm, *succubitus felix* to *nisus formativus* (*U* 418). He gives substance, flesh, to the impulses of Bloom's spirit, and supplies the words that express Bloom's moods. To the observation made by Albert Goldman, David Hayman and Marilyn French[26] that the styles reflect the stances being struck, becoming Swiftian when the conversation becomes satirical, for instance, it should be added that the stances themselves reflect the changes of one mind variably receptive to the society around it. It is not that 'Junius' appears when Joyce's time-table calls for him and attacks Bloom according to form, but rather that Bloom, having just censured the young men for their mockery of the Purefoys' blessed event, suddenly realizes that for private reasons 'It ill becomes him to preach that gospel', and with that realisation begets the voice of someone famous for knowing secrets and exposing hypocrisy.

As that reversal illustrates, the Bloomian trance is far from uniform. It begins as a state close to sleep and ends as a state close to delirium, and in between drifts back and forth between poles of abstracted consciousness and near-total obliviousness, depending on how much the subject interests Bloom or how absorbed he is in his own musings. The introduction of Mulligan in the style of Addison (*U* 401), for instance, shows that Bloom's attention has been caught by this engaging character and that he sees him quite clearly, Addison being for Joyce an early incarnation of Gogarty.[27]

At the other extreme, the 'De Quincy' sequence doubles back on another parody voice and takes what is being said yet another remove into abstraction. Here, Bloom is staring at a red triangle on a bottle of Bass ale which, as Fritz Senn points out,[28] fuses in his imagination with the 'Alpha' scratched in the sand earlier, just before the beginning of his trance. To be even more precise, it brings together that triangle with a memory of the 'redlabelled bottle' (*U* 97) containing the poison with which Bloom's father killed himself. The two associations combine and act on the events and conversation in the hospital, first, to turn Haines into a suicide in a Gothic novel (many of the details come from Bloom's 'Hades' memory of his father), his bottle of Bass transformed to laudanum (*U* 412), then send Bloom off on a reverie about Rudolph and his own failed fatherhood (*U* 413), and finally transform details from the mingled talk recorded on pp. 414-16 to the prolonged reverie of p. 414, as follows:

414-16:	414:
'Francis was reminding Stephen of years before when they had been at school together in Conmee's time. He asked about Glaucon, Alcibiades, Pisistratus. Where were they now?''	' . . . the soul is wafted over regions of cycles of cycles that have lived . . .'
—	
Background talk between Lenehan and Madden about horserace	Bloom envisions horses.
—	
'You have spoken of the past and its phantoms . . .'. '. . . can call your genius father.'	Horses become 'Twilight phantoms', Bloom's wife and daughter.
—	
Lynch remarks on Stephen's literary sterility; Lenehan says, 'He would not leave his mother an orphan.'	A wasteland vision.

Background talk about horserace comes to the fore, with a report of Sceptre's running.

A stampede of 'beasts' across the wasteland. 'Sceptre' conjures Blazes Boylan, who becomes 'the bulls of Bashan and Babylon . . . trooping to the sunken sea, *Lacus Mortis*'— Molly, by way of Bloom's earlier wasteland vision (*U*61) of 'a dead sea, the grey sunken cunt of the world'. The evocation of Boylan as 'the lionmaned and giant antlered, snouter and crawler, rodent, ruminant and pachyderm' is one of the chapter's nicest touches.

—

' . . . all hearts were beating. Even Phyllis could not contain herself.'

They 'murder the sun' amidst 'unslaked and horrible gulpings'. The mediating association here is Boylan's activities with his own Phyllis.

—

' . . . the dark horse Throwaway drew level . . . All was lost now. Phyllis was silent.'

The 'equine portent' returns, first as Molly ('the house of Virgo', Molly's sign) then because of the 'All is lost' tag, as 'Martha, thou lost one'; then 'Phyllis' dilates into 'Millicent'.

—

'Juno, she cried . . . '

' . . . a queen among the Pleiades . . . '

—

' . . . a bright casket of gold . . . '

' . . . sandals of bright gold . . . '

'The sweet creature turned all colours . . .' '. . . emerald, sapphire, mauve and heliotrope'. It is notable that Bloom blocks out about twenty sexually suggestive lines once Phyllis is identified with Milly. Just the opposite happened when the identification was with Molly.

Stephen, who in the above passage is talking about summoning ghosts while Bloom is doing it, provides the kind of precise and curiously learned mind needed to arrange these shifting levels of Bloom's trance in (more or less) a scheme. (The parodies have him speaking in the voice of Browne, distinguished by his labyrinthine syntax.) He is responsible for the chapter's best-known feature, the ingenious parallel between the growth of an embryo and English literary history. He not only puts Bloom's mental wanderings into words: he puts them into order. In fact the arrangement is much more intricate than we have realised. Joyce's description of the episode says that in addition to embryonic and literary ontogeny, it embraces 'faunal evolution in general' (*L* I, 139) by which he seems to mean the phenomenon of growth on all levels, or, even more grandly, any periodic movement through time toward a predetermined destination. So far I have found six parallel journeys, aside from the histories of the embryo and English prose: 1. linguistic (from Latin unity to a modern Babel); 2. literary (a history not as a succession of authors but as a decline-and-fall from universal myths and univocal poetry to modern eccentricity); 3. political (from imperial unity to modern anarchy); 4. biblical (from *fiat lux* to Armageddon); 5. cosmic (from the sun past the planets toward the Milky Way); 6. biographical (from conception to death and judgment).[29] What holds them in suspension, aside from verbal ingenuity, is one great overriding myth, the Plotinian representation of all existence as a series of emanations from one 'omnipollent', 'incorrupted' source, usually symbolised as the sun. The Stephen-spirit has simply systematised a philosophical tradition inherited from the previous chapter's resident neo-Platonist, Gerty McDowell, like Stephen a self-styled 'Greekly perfect' Cinderella who considers herself displaced from 'another sphere', and who envisions ecstasy—' . . . a light broke in upon her. Whitehot passion . . . ' (*U* 365)—as a sunburst.

Gerty turned Bloom's ideas into a Wordsworthian ideal; Stephen takes Bloom's Hebraic self-admonition to increase and multiply and Hellenises it, makes it philosophical and abstract. The essential connection, on which the whole endeavour turns, is between conception and the sun.[30] Intercourse is a Plotinian return to the sunbright source and begets the 'sunnygolden babe of day'; (*U* 413) contraception is darkness, deprivation, a flight from the sun past the orbits of the most distant planets. 'Oxen of the Sun' takes this one idea and works it out through so many different parallel journeys that it necessarily calls on the author's daedal skill for making many little wheels and gears all fit together in one enclosed space. One way of fitting them together is with numbers, the 'law of numeration' that, as Lynch suggests (*U* 419), may govern everything. The chapter is of course full of nines and threes, the numbers of gestation and God, one dividing nicely into the other, and there are other similar tricks with numbers. We are no doubt meant to take the 'two pound nineteen' in Stephen's pocket (*U* 391) as a sign that he has fallen short of Holiness by the amount of the 'bare shilling' (*U* 413) charged by a whore; Mrs Purefoy is pregnant nine months out of twelve in a rhythm both seasonal—Purefoy gathers his 'homer of ripe wheat (*U* 423)—and musical, three-four time having been considered God's tempo by the mediaeval church. More important are the numerical correspondences that become apparent if one numbers the chapter's paragraphs from one to sixty-two and notes which events occur where along the sequence. Hugh Kenner has already observed that there are forty paragraphs between the 'lightning flash of conception' and the 'outflinging' of the word (10, 385; 50, 422)* corresponding to the forty weeks of gestation,[31] and we can add as well that twelve paragraphs remain, so that Mrs Purefoy's three-month period of fallowness is recapitulated in a new key—twelve barren weeks following forty of fertility. Forty is also the number of days and nights in the Flood—and sure enough the Purefoy birth is also a downpour (50, 422) begetting a menagerie that Dowie invites into the ark. Purefoy, the 'old patriarch' and 'remarkablest progenitor', is Noah, 'all their daddies'. ('Pepys-Evelyn' has adumbrated the correspondence when he reports Purefoy 'dapping on the sound' with a 'pair of his boys'.)

Historically, this sort of thing evidently began when Julius

*For the sake of precision, I list both page and paragraph number.

Africanus, one of those Church fathers in whom Stephen specialises, took literally a verse from Psalm 90, 'A thousand years in Thy sight are but as yesterday', and conflated it with the seven days of the Creation recorded in 'Genesis'. So God's working week is 6,000 years long, and the Millenium will arrive on his thousand-year Sunday. 'Oxen of the Sun' is tied together with this sort of numerological baling wire. An apocalyptic fire [32] arrives exactly when Julius, and many prophets since, claimed it would, at the very beginning of paragraph 61,[33] the sixty-first century after the Creation: 'Hark! . . . Blaze on. There she goes. Brigade!' (61, 428). (Two paragraphs previous, someone has been making the very serious mistake of praying to Allah.) As prophesied, incidentally, it is preceded by the conversion of the Jews: Bloom mixed up with Pope Leo XIII,[34] drinking 'Rome boose' and—I think—being addressed as 'Kind Kristyann' (58, 427). (There are also suggestions of Satan's brief escape and reincarceration, and, with M'Intosh's appearance, the resurrection of the body.) Previously, the three major events of biblical history intervenient between the Creation and the Apocalypse are reflected in the chronologically correct paragraphs. The Flood is dated 1,565 years after the Creation, and so in paragraph 16 we find a bunching-up of Noah's attendant images: a wooden structure, shelter from the rain, 'buffaloes and stags', 'vessels', sea as in 'seasand', 'olive', brewing, 'Chaldee', 'angry spirits', 'a vast mountain', and (reported by the credulous 'Mandeville' as 'serpents') vine cultivation for the production of alcohol. Paragraph 24 draws its biblical language mainly from the 'Deuteronomy' and 'Exodus' accounts of the sojourn in Egypt, which traditionally had begun by the twenty-fourth century after the Creation, and in paragraphs 26 and 27 the exodus itself, dated between 2,666 and 2,706 years after the Creation, is important: God rebukes the people for their 'hellprate and paganry' (26, 394) (cf. Jehovan on Sinai), and Stephen is not to reach 'the land of promise' (27, 395) (cf. Moses on Pisgah). The central event of the Old Testament is followed by the central event of the New, the Crucifixion, dated 4,037 (4,004 + 33) years after the Creation. In paragraph 39 Haines is Judas, haunted by guilt, pursued by the 'black panther', Christ, confessing the Childs Murder, and attempting suicide. In paragraph 40 Bloom denies the 'sunnygolden babe of day' at whose conception 'light flood[ed] the world', and in paragraph 41 come the 'murderers of the sun'.

This may make the whole thing sound neat and easy, but of course it is not, because none of the co-ordinates will stay still: they make echoes which blend with other echoes and become difficult to distinguish from one another. The Nativity alone has reverberations in paragraphs 3, 10, 33, and 50, and the repetition of this one event suggests the number of possible 'beginnings' and 'endings'. Joyce's declared 'headpiece and tailpiece' (*L* III, 16) for instance, mean that there are at least three possible beginnings (1, 4, 10) and two possible ends (52, 62) to the episode's 'foetal' growth; any attempt to settle on one point or other is likely to resemble a theologians' dispute over the borders of life. The echoes never die out completely. The episode is fitted together out of a system of typological correspondences similar to those discovered by biblical exegetes between the events of the Old and New Testaments, operating on the assumption that all the significant events of history are, in the words of M. H. Abrams, either 'echoes or prophecies of the nodal episodes', and producing what he calls the 'drastic condensation and displacement of metaphor in Christian devotional literature'.[35] Here is one spectacular example:

> The air without is impregnated with raindew moisture, life essence celestial, glistering on Dublin stone there under star-shiny *coelum*. God's air, the Allfather's air, scintillant circumambient cessile air . . . See, thy fleece is drenched . . . Mother's milk, Purefoy, the milk of human kind, milk too of those burgeoning stars overhead, rutilant with thin rain-vapour, punch milk, such as those rioters will quaff in their guzzlingden, milk of madness, the honeymilk of Canaan's land . . . To her, old patriarch! Pap! *Per deam Partulam et Pertundam nunc est bibendum* (424).

A great number of journeys all end here, and 'Carlyle's' 'raindew moisture' is the node where they come together. It is afterbirth (the end of gestation), ejaculate (the end of intercourse),[36] Canaan's 'milk and honey' (the end of God's wrath), the morning dew on Gideon's fleece (the end of subjugation), the milk of the Milky Way (the end of the cometary journey from the sun), the infant's first taste of mother's milk (the end of the child's birth agony), a toast to the goddess Pertunda (the end of virginity), a toast to the goddess Partula (the end of the mother's birth agony), the reward for

Purefoy's labors (the end of a hard life; the end of a hard day's work), a nightcap (the end of a day), and the 'milk of madness' (the end of reason). The whole passage, of course, represents the end of the literary tradition. Finally, all this occurs in paragraph 52, corresponding to AD 1200-1300, the period when, according to Stephen's favourite prophet, Joachim of Floris, the era of the Son was to end and the era of the Holy Spirit begin, ushering in a final period of 'perfect liberty'.[37] Theodore Purefoy, here, is both patriarch and babe, grotesquely guzzling his own seed; 'Pap!' denotes both paternity (he is a 'Pap') and his infancy (at his mother's 'pap'). It is also probably a comment on most post-Carlyle prose.

In such a typological thicket, the basic allegory of the episode is first, qualified, and second, obscured. Qualified because the over-all decline-and-fall pattern is counterbalanced by the suggestion of hidden beginnings. The dwindling patriarch becomes, at death's door, a newborn baby. The end of the Flood is the beginning of a new covenant. The babble of the last pages is the death rattle of English, but can also be seen as 'a recapitulation of the whole process of the birth and renewal of language.'[38] The concluding sentence can suggest a corpse being fitted for a shroud,[39] or the soul 'trying on' a new incarnation. We are reminded at the junctures that the end of one history may be a re-beginning as well, or may be crossed by other histories occurring on other levels. The whole episode is Plotinian, and for Plotinus and his commentators the journey away from the sun-bright One is ultimately circular, as exemplified by the journey of Odysseus, here incarnated first in Bloom, 'who over land and seafloor nine years had long outwandered' (*U* 385), and then in Purefoy, a successful father who after 'twenty years' (*U* 425) is allowed to rest.

As for the tendency of the parallels to obscure the basic pattern, surely that is the single most obvious thing about the episode. Stephen and Frank Costello both comment on the 'tenebrosity' of the whole enterprise, and readers often echo their criticism. [In 'Proteus', Stephen anticipates this comment on his maze-making: 'You may find my words dark' (*U* 48).] The simple *thickness* of the writing shows the past as it has come to seem by now, as memories wrapped in memories, echoes of echoes, ghosts of figures who in their own time were neo-classicists or Gothic revivalists. When Harriet Shaw Weaver remarked that 'this episode might also have been called Hades,' Joyce suggested that she might have been on to something: 'Do you mean that the *Oxen of the Sun* episode resembles Hades because the nine circles of development . . . seem to you to be peopled by extinct beings?' (*L* III, 16). That was not what Miss Weaver meant, but it does suggest that the readers who have found this episode to be a rather hellish experience may have been righter than they realised. It is a chapter devoted to the dead, and its tenebrosity derives as much from their influence as from Bloom's gloom. Its thickness and obscurity result from the attempt to crowd them all in; its complexity results from the attempt to make them all fit.

The result is an equation between living and dead which is double-edged. It implies both the permanence of the defunct through 'metempsychosis' and the impermanence of the living through 'phenomenon'. From the thrice-repeated 'Let us go' of the first paragraph to the thrice-repeated 'Come on' of the last, the characters are 'wenders' and 'marchers' continuously arriving at doors and leaving by them in a journey which at the end accelerates to a headlong race: 'All off for a buster, armstrong, hollering down the street' (*U* 424). Their lives are like the programmed pilgrimage of the foetus from conception to birth. In fact the whole chapter is the exfoliation of one continuous forward movement, that of the spermatozoon, which according to Joyce's notes defies gravity, turns men and women into its instruments, and even 'obliges God to create' (*BM* 203, 222). So the allegorical spermatozoon, Bloom's entranced mind, determines the movement of the chapter from self-reproach ('Sallust-Tacitus') to wide-eyed observation ('Mandeville') through meditation to retrospective reverie (the romantic and late Victorians). Even the wild ending is attributable to the effect of two drinks (recorded on p. 452) and a sprint on the sedentary and abstemious Bloom: at his entrance in 'Circe' he is still sufficiently 'light in the head' (*U* 436) to bring back the memory of his one full-scale debauch. (He is also a crystal-gazer on the verge of experiencing hallucinations.) As entranced mind and as sperm, the traveller of 'Oxen of the Sun' has the same direction: deeper and deeper. The last few pages before the 'Carlyle' parody are full of romantic memories and female figures because the mind in charge has sunk as far as possible into its own deepest past, and the sperm is finally approaching the egg. As for 'Carlyle', he is pulled out of his proper historical place and saved to give the last word⁴⁰ because as an eccentric Calvinist Scotsman from the far side of Hadrian's Wall he is as far removed as possible from the traditional, orthodox, imperial Roman values invoked on the first page, and because his Teufelsdrockhian argument that we are all ghosts in transit is the chapter's own.

By the time it reaches 'Carlyle' the chapter has revealed a theory of history, of all movement through time, in fact, as a dynamic surge toward an apocalypse. Such theories are perforce prophetic: if you believe that history moves to one great goal you have to say what it will be.⁴¹ So it is simply of course that the delirium of the last ten paragraphs should be, among other things, a prophecy of The First World War, written at a time when to speak of it as the Apocalypse was to make the commonest of commonplaces. (Crystal balls, after all, are supposed to tell the future, and delirium traditionally attends the prophetic state.) The final section begins with a shelling by an 'Armstrong', a large cannon similar to Big Bertha, and after four pages of botched military manoeuvers, 'Digs', 'Tanks', soldiers dropping like flies, booziness (troops were given double rations of rum before battle) and polyglot obscenity, grinds to a stop when the Yanks have come in the person of Alexander J. Dowie, who doubles as John J. Pershing and Woodrow Wilson, with his ark-like League of Nations. As near as it is possible to tell, the whole thing ends at or about 11:11, not as a victory but as an armistice, a 'longbreakyet' (*U* 427). That some of those not already departed are getting sick reflects the 1918-19 influenza epidemic which killed more people than the war; in this light Dowie's brag that he has 'yanked to glory most half this planet' and has 'a coughmixture with a punch in it for you' makes him an especially chilling hangman God.

'Circe': A book that by its approximate mid-point has given us the history of the world must either repeat itself or somehow move outside the time it has circumscribed, or both. *Ulysses* does both. Bloom's trance, like Gerty's, takes him outside himself by taking him deep into and then through his past. The technique of 'Oxen of the Sun', that of expressing Bloom's mental journeying with Stephen's erudition, forecasts the method of the next episode, 'Circe'. The initial act remains the same as it was at the start of the book: seeing or hearing something, naming it, and thereby calling up a throng of ghosts. As in 'Sirens', 'Cyclops', and 'Nausicaa', those ghosts revealing the buried impulses of their conjurer, come to life before his eyes. Only now, in 'Circe' as in

'Oxen of the Sun', the memories are often partly outside the range of the person calling them up. Repeatedly, one character's memories blend with another's as if their psyches had taken leave of their earthly limitations and come together beyond the veil. For instance, the Shakespeare composite portrait formed on pp. 567-8 when Stephen and Bloom stare into a mirror is an optical illusion which can be envisioned only if we think of them as the two eyes of one larger person looking ahead and framing one unified stereoscopic picture. The 'paralytic' effigy that results is an example of this chapter's subject: the way the mind materialises its movements and their intersection with the shifting world by bringing memory to bear on sensation. (The large number of 'Bowie knives', 'Henry Clays', 'gladstone bags' and so forth sprinkled throughout the episode recall how much of our language is made in this way.) It is the culmination of the book's movement over the last four chapters, the same thing, but much wilder.

As usual, there is what Bloom would call a 'phenomenal' explanation for the wildness, and it is to be found mainly in the 'sicksweet' fumes from the 'birdseye cigarettes' being smoked in the vicinity (*U* 452), whether of cannabis or opium is not clear.[42] (Although neither Stephen nor Bloom take any drugs, they can still experience what drug-users call a 'contact high'.) That, along with the influence of drink, tobacco, fatigue, and recent exertion, is more than enough to account for the episode's dilations, suspensions, and distortions of sensation, enough to produce the 'hallucinations' which, on one level, correspond to the 'disturbances of the eyesight and bearing, paralysis of muscles, especially of the eye muscles' of locomotor ataxia,[43] and on another, the visions of crystal-gazing.

Since studies of 'Circe' have tended to treat the hallucinations as for the most part free-floating and self-contained, the following concentrates on the events and sensational or psychological processes which act together to generate them.

427-8: The 'stunted' forms are children, seen in silhouette.[44] 'Wafers of coal and copper snow' are ice cream sandwiches ('snow-cakes') illuminated by the 'rainbow' lights. The 'gnome' and 'pigmy woman' are also probably children. Everything jerks and spurts and staggers because of the stroboscopic effect of the fitfully flaring or flashing light in the south, either from the fire, a 'lighthouse' (*U* 429) or a 'Searchlight' (*U* 434).

431: Stephen is called a 'parson' because of his black suit and

Paris hat, and in response to the label and the rain-covered streets chants 'Vidi aquam', etc.

432: Stephen strikes the lamp post, causing the gas jet to flicker and irradiate ripples of shadow and light, 'shattering light over the world'. The impact stings his hand, as we will discover later.

434: The cyclists 'swim' because they cleave the fog and because their tires are splashing through puddles.

436: At an intersection, Bloom confronts his own shadow against a wall, a traffic signal, and a streetsign painted over in Gaelic by some enthusiast. The last of these reminds him of his alien status and recalls the Citizen; hence the Spanish and Esperanto. When the signal 'raises a signal arm' for him to pass, he plays Alphonse and Gaston with his shadow before collecting himself sufficiently to move on. The traffic signal reminds him of the fingerpost at Stepaside.

437: The dog begins its metamorphoses, described in chapter I.

438: Bloom's sprint with the medical students recalls an earlier sprint, and with it the parents who reproached him for it.

439: The cue for Molly's 'yashmak', and thus her harem outfit, is the sight of Edy Boardman with 'her shawl across her nostrils' (*U* 431)—both are positioned next to the bawd. Molly's reference to 'cold feet' comes because Bloom is standing in the wet. (Note that, not for the last time, he is 'spellbound'.) Reminded of his feet, Bloom bends down, 'stoops his back', perhaps thinks to tie a bootlace, then 'pats divers pockets' to be sure nothing has fallen out; most males who carry things in their shirtpockets will recognise the routine. Evidently the soap is dislodged: its 'perfume' rises to his nostrils and prompts a vision of Sweny the druggist as soap. If the flashes of light do originate in a searchlight, then the 'disc of the soapsun' probably results from a beam of light being trained on a low cloud.

441: The bawd's offer of a fifteen year old girl arouses guilty thoughts of the fifteen year old Milly and, through her, the young Bridie Kelly, who Bloom imagines may have carried his child (*U* 413). The connection is helped along because Bridie was the woman with whom Bloom had his first sexual experience, and because he thinks Milly may be about to have hers.

442-9: Posing as a slummer, flirting with vice but nothing more, Bloom evokes the unconsummated flirtation with Josie Breen. The supernumeraries coming and going mostly originate in the milling crowd. Richie Goulding's 'black legal bag . . . on which a skull and crossbones are painted in white limewash', has the same source (probably a dustbin, since it is filled with offal) as Bloom's memory of the plasterer's bucket which he once used as a toilet. (The woman urinating nearby nudges the latter memory.)

452: The 'Wet Dream' scrawl reminds Bloom of Molly's 'drawing on the frosted carriagepane' because he 'gazes ahead' at it through the fog.

453: The appearance of the murmuring Watch occurs because: (1) Bloom is in a dark corner, as he was when the Watch spotted him with Bridie Kelly; (2) he has just been reminded of Bridie; (3) he is in a center of prostitution; (4) the dog's growling sounds like angry muttering.

454-74: One of the Watch becomes Signor Maffei: brass buttons become diamond studs, the notebook for taking Bloom's name and address a paper hoop, the swaggerstick a carriagewhip. (Later he will become Rumbold.) Maffei's ferocity originates in the background sounds of the dog's growls. On the literal level, Bloom is in yet another trance, staring at a cluster of glowing and flashing lights becoming, in order, the buttons, the studs, and the 'breastsparklers' which along with the 'glint' of Maffei's eye ('I possess the Indian sign') so mesmerises Bloom that he forgets his own name (*U* 455). Glancing, in this state, into his hat, he recalls John Henry Menton (by way of the dinged hat of 'Hades'), then, because of the Henry Flower card inside it, conjures Martha Clifford and the fantasia of the next twenty pages. (The 'high grade ha' label begets his pretentions of gentility in the person of Philip Beaufoy, who mocks him with a high grade ha.) The drifting fog-banks stage-manage the setting, concealing or disclosing other characters. The corner's 'stalestunk' smell (*U* 453) keeps reminding Bloom of the incident with the plasterer's bucket: the accuser Mary Driscoll appears with a bucket (*U* 460), and through the next several pages Bloom is charged, among other things, with being a 'domestic animal' that needs to be house-broken. (Beaufoy, for instance, recalls his treatment of 'Matcham's Masterstroke'.) More generally, this fantasia reveals Bloom's uneasiness with the state and with women; the two anxieties dovetail when the Watch asks Mary Driscoll, 'What do you tax him with? (*U* 460), and later when the Watch accuses him of being Jack the Ripper. The spell starts to break when Hynes calls Bloom 'a perfect stranger', which is at least a step back to his real identity; two pages later John O'Connell's foghorn voice is really a foghorn.

475-7: Bloom approaches Mrs Cohen's through the fog; the sounds of the whore's kisses (cf. *U* 586) combine with the light glinting through the curtains from the 'lighted house' to form a synesthetic effect of twittering, 'giddy specks, silvery sequins'. The sound from the piano of Stephen's 'empty fifths', which, as we later learn from Stephen, are without musical character (*U* 504), seems like 'Church music' now because of the 'Overtones' (*U* 474) from the sepulchral foghorn; the sound itself has just reminded Bloom of a funeral and evoked Dignam. On the next page, when under Zoe's influence Bloom's thoughts become exotic, the music sounds 'oriental'. The brilliant transformation scene in which Zoe's clothes, make-up, and features become first a 'womancity' and then a tomb (cf. *U* 475, *U* 477) may have been anticipated, and to an extent programmed, when Zoe's rose perfume reminds Bloom of the similarly scented Gerty and thus recalls the experience with her: 'Sweet and cheap: soon sour' (*U* 374). (The main stimulus for the changed vision is Zoe's garlic breath.) The hallucination begins when Bloom 'gazes in the tawny crystal of her eyes'—another crystal ball.

478-91: The messiah scene is prompted by Zoe's call for a 'stump speech' and given its definitive character when the sound of bells 'from distant steeples' reminds Bloom of the Dick Whittington story, which he forthwith adopts as his own.[45] Images of himself as Lord Mayor recall the early courtship with Molly, when he was befriending the likes of Val Dillon and talking, insanely, of running for office (*U* 771). The nearest thing to a rival then was not Blazes Boylan but Molly's Gibraltar lover Harry Mulvey, here attacked as the Flying Dutchman (*U* 478) and bested as 'the hereditary enemy at Ladysmith' (*U* 484—see chapter 7, p. 150). Rumbold's 'bloodcoloured jerkin', coiled rope, and bludgeon (*U* 471), themselves transfigured from the watch's furnishings, become 'Late Lord Mayor Harrington's' 'scarlet robe', 'gold mayoral chain', and 'mace'. The maypoles and so forth are streetlamps; the 'streamers' with Gaelic and Hebrew messages are advertisements; the 'ladies' are whores; the soldiers are soldiers. The 'air perfumed with essences' of rosepetals (*U* 481) comes from Zoe's scent. The 'joybells' ringing (*U* 482) are the aftertone from the bells recorded on p. 478. Bloom's Koh-i-Noor diamond (*U* 483) shows that he is still staring into Zoe's crystal eye. The chaste 'princess Selene' who replaces the unworthy Molly wears the same outfit worn by Mrs Breen (*U* 445), Bloom's standard instance of the wife he might have had. The 'magnesium flashlight' (*U* 486) originates in another flare-up of flash from the south.

492-9: At the source of Bloom's failure as a messiah is his Jewishness. Having advocated 'mixed races', he is denounced by Dowie as 'a disgrace to christian men', which charge begets the mob, who beget the medical students (because mob=radicals= medical students; see *U* 163), who beget Costello's diagnosis of 'fetor judaicus', which occasions, according to stereotype, the 'gold and silver coins' collected on Bloom's behalf, which become his gold and silver children, with mainly Jewish names, which leads to his adoption of mainly Jewish identities (*U* 495), which leads to Brini's catalogue of mainly Jewish names, which leads, finally, to Hornblower (doubling as Gabriel, from his position at Trinity's gates),[46] Mastiansky and Citron, Mesias, Reuben J. Dodd and the final identification with another Jew, Jesus, perishing at the hands of the Fire Brigade whose presence is advertised by the fire to the south.

499-500: Bloom comes to; Zoe remarks, 'Talk away till you're black in the face.' The first two words evoke a gabby stage Irishman out of Synge; the last four words evoke the face of the dead father in the dark room.

501: Responding to Zoe's 'Babby', Bloom becomes the infant Milly, counting Zoe's buckles as Milly counted his buttons (cf. *U* 693).

502: All of the furnishings listed on p. 502, along with some not listed, will appear, transformed, during the next eighty-four pages.

503: Lynch's brass poker flashes because Zoe has turned the gaslight up; in shadow it looked like a wand.

504: Lynch's cap is cynical because, facing Stephen, it is perched on the back of Lynch's head—the 'animal' side, according to Joyce's notes (*BM* 294).

506: Looking at Bloom, Stephen sees the picture of another (supposed) Jew, Reuben J. Dodd, as presented in 'Hades'. Bloom-Dodd is clutching his spine because, as Bloom alone mentions later (*U* 528), he feels a 'twinge of sciatica' in his 'left gluteal muscle' and so is massaging it, and because in 'Hades' Simon wanted to break the hasp of Dodd's back (*U* 94). The 'pilgrim's wallet' 'across his loins' is Bloom's hat, which he has removed; the 'promissory notes and dishonoured bills' inside are his 'Henry Flower' card; the boatpole and 'sodden huddled son' are the hatrack with 'man's hat and waterproof' (*U* 502), seen over Bloom's shoulder. That the image comes mainly from Bloom's own thoughts (his identification with Dodd on p. 498), that the image itself draws on associations from Bloom's mind, that nonetheless the emblem takes shape in Stephen's eyes as he sees Bloom juxtaposed with the hatrack and catches the conversation (*U* 505) about Antichrist and the end of the world—all this illustrates Joyce's 'Circe' method of expanding his field of association beyond individuals while adhering to the essential model: one person with one set of eyes and ears responding to a limited and accountable set of stimuli.

506: As Dodd is to fatherhood, so Punch Costello is to sonhood: a grotesque parody. In the previous episode Bloom had 'nauseated' Costello as a 'cropeared creature of a misshapen gibbosity' (*U* 407) because his abnormally large head (*BM* 222—the source of his nickname, probably) had recalled the pictures in Aristotle's *Masterpiece* (*U* 235) and thus grisly thoughts about Rudy's corpse. On entering the doorway, Bloom: (1) sees Stephen and recalls him from 'Oxen of the Sun'. The memory of that scene combined with (2) a memory of Lynch's remark about 'hobgoblins' (*U* 503) evokes Punch Costello as hydrocephalic hobgoblin. As (3) the erratic gasjet sputters, whistles, and wanes (*U* 503,510), and (4) noticing it, Bloom notices the circling and batting moth, Costello becomes, in the gathering darkness, a whirling, shrieking misbirth born through his own legs (the *Aristotle's Masterpiece* association again), then, because of his irreverence and habitual gambling (as recorded on pp. 398-9), l 'homme qui rit and a croupier. The 'crepitant cracks' originate in (5) Florry's breaking wind, as does the 'female tepid effluvium' (*U* 507) which in turn causes the 'coughs and feetshuffling'—her friends are giving her a wide berth.

507: Which initiates another complicated sequence of events. Briefly: Florry's act causes someone to open the window wider, letting in the fog and the sound of a gramophone. The apocalypse of the next few pages combines the music ('The Holy City'), the rasping sound of the gramophone needle, the flickering, dimming and flashing of the gasjet, the fog drifting in through the window, the moth's reminding Bloom of cyclists (see *U* 376 for the association) and thus of Æ and the two-headed octopus with a

Scottish accent (see *U* 165), and someone announcing the time, 12:25.[47]

510: The 'green light' flares up and illuminates the corner by the fireplace, revealing the homely coalskuttle as John Eglinton, a 'plain man' lit up by his 'greencapped dark lantern' (see *U* 184 for the connection). Behind it are the twig broom, bellows, and tongs, which become, in order, Æ, his bicycle pump, and his crayfish. The combined sensations of clammy fog, 'whistling' gasjet, and green light metamorphose him into Mananaan MacLir, god of 'whistling seawind' and snotgreen sea.

511-23: Bloom looks 'desirously' at the alluring Zoe and then sees the bony, unappealing Kitty Ricketts. This stark juxtaposition of the flesh-as-romance and flesh-in-reality begets the juxtaposition of Bloom's complementary doubles, Virag and Henry Flower.[48] It becomes epitomised when Bloom, looking at Kitty by the mantel, sees the fireplace's peacock fan and coaly mouth: romance and reality. That life, especially female life, is a crow beautified with fake feathers is pretty much the burden of Virag's argument; he illustrates it by shedding his 'multitudinous plumage' and revealing his 'coal-black throat' (*U* 522). When they strut around on their gawky legs, Virag and Henry are the andirons come to life like the dancing tables of children's cartoons. The 'upstage entrance' is the chimney flue. Both wear feathers from the peacock fan between them. Virag, being the andiron nearest the hatrack, also wears raincoats (the hatrack in Bloom's hallstand is also remembered) and gets his flashing monocle from the mirror. Henry wears—a rare Joycean clue—a 'mantle'. The heads carried by both of them (Virag unscrews his) are the traditional animal heads decorating the andirons; my own experience is that, being of cast bronze manufactured separately from the iron frames, they can often be unscrewed.

515: Bloom hears the moth knocking against the lampshade and Virag immediately becomes a moth, playing back Bloom's 'Nausicaa' thoughts about night insects. His 'scooping hand' comes from the coal scoop.

520-1: Kitty's chatter about Mary Shortall and Jimmy Pidgeon elicits, for Bloom, Virag's retailing of some hoary scandal about Christ's birth, and for Stephen the Philip Drunk—Philip Sober crosstalk from Leo Taxil's anti-Christian book. The two Philips, of course, reduplicate, for Stephen, Bloom's 'Reduplication of personality' (*U* 518) in Virag and Henry. As Virag's chant of 'pretty pretty' had earlier elicited Henry Flower, so now his cry of 'Kok!' brings us the priapic Ben Dollard, presented with borrowings from five different episodes. (The 'Hik! Hek! Hak! . . . Kok!' in turn originates from Lynch's laughter.) The same kind of logic, probably with a little Freudian help, produces Simon Dedalus from Stephen's 'Monks of the screw'.

523-5: Simon, standing in the door, is Bloom, standing in the door; by his 'cardinal' manifestation we may gather (as Bloom confirms on p. 526) that the room's light is returning to mauve. The raised two fingers that become Simon's 'Easter kiss' are from a typical Bloom gesture (see *U* 170). The seven 'dwarf simian acolytes' seem to be nothing more than the sound of the 'creaking staircase' from behind Bloom, along with the simian overtones from 'Monks'. Simon's comical doubleshuffle offstage is an unflattering version of Bloom's movement: 'Bloom starts foward involuntarily.'

526-55: Zoe's teeth crack through her candy. The sound brings Bloom back to life, and he exorcises the imagined presence of Boylan. (The Dollard apparition was probably an alternate incarnation of the rampaging male libido, censored and displaced according to one of the best known tricks of dream logic.) Thinking of Boylan, then told to 'Do as you're bid', then hearing a 'firm heelclacking', then meeting a whoremistress who holds a fan that recalls *Carmen* and thus of course Molly-in-Gibraltar, usurpation, and an operatic idea of 'fate', Bloom is prepared for the hypnotic hallucination of the next twenty-seven pages. Focusing on the fan, he follows it first to Bella's face and 'falcon eyes', thence to the beryl eardrops, the latest—and most traditional[49]—crystal ball to send him into a trance. The fan's mesmeric tapping becomes the *Carmen* message, rapped out in monosyllables ('We have met. You are mine. It is fate') and conjuring Rudolph and Richie, both martyrs to back pain and so examples of the hereditary 'fate' forecast by Bloom's twinge of sciatica. Following the fan's direction down to Bella's foot, Bloom re-becomes a shoe salesman; looking up, he notices the 'superfluous hairs' of her sprouting moustache (527), and Bella immediately turns into Bello.

In addition to the obvious determinants of Molly, Bloom's masochism and the morning's memories, Bloom's late father-in-law, Brian Cooper Tweedy, is probably one of Bello's sources. He would of course go with the Gibraltar and early courtship memories. He also wore a moustache and smoked (though a pipe rather than a cigar), he shares Bello's initials for his first two names, his military pose is often Bello's own, and his only recorded words sound a lot like Bello's in his drillmaster phase: 'I rose from the ranks, sir, and I'm proud of it' (*U* 56). 'With brains, sir' (*U* 646). As a military type who knew Bloom, in the early courtship days, at his most ambitious and promising, Tweedy would logically personify Bloom's self-accusations over his failure as both husband ('Adorer of the adulterous rump!') and wave-maker (*U* 530, 542). Bello's single cruelest act is to lure Bloom's memory back to the time before his marriage when he was regularly visiting father and daughter.

Since Bloom's eyes are closed throughout most of the Bello Cohen sequence, his hallucinations have mostly non-visual origins. Bello's cigar originates in the cigarette smoke floating around, the sound of her 'uncorking' herself is from a bottle's being unstoppered in the background (some of the others are having drinks); when the bottle is poured, we have 'the sound of a waterfall' (*U* 547). (On p. 557, everyone is requested to drink up, but Stephen resists: 'No bottles!') The flatulence which follows, alas, is evidently Bloom's: just before Bello 'farts loudly' Bloom, 'Stifling', says 'Can't', (that is, hold it) he has just been 'squeezing' his legs together (*U* 534), and Bello will soon call him a 'skunk' (*U* 538). Despite Bloom's contribution, however, the overwhelmingly cloacal quality of these pages originates largely from the aura of the repellantly unhygienic Bella herself, as Bloom will make clear in a passage which should dispel any lingering illusions about gaslit sin: 'Take a handful of hay and wipe yourself' (*U* 554). As least as much as the sound of Bloom's popping button, Bella's sulphurous stench is what eventually breaks the spell, cracks the nymph's mold, and brings Bloom out of his fantasy world. Before that:

536: The 'medley of voices' of 'The Sins of the Past' comes from the background chatter, as do the 'Voices' on p. 544.

540, 544: The 'handbell' and 'passing bell' are the 12:30 chimes. They are four pages apart because time is moving very slowly during Bloom's trance: the whole hallucination lasts a few seconds.[50]

540-41: Bloom gets a second spasm of sciatica, in the same place as before: 'He brands his initial C on Bloom's croup.' When the twinge directs Bloom's attention on that area, the result is Bello's description of Bloom's 'provoking croup'. Then another spasm, and so another rude poke (*U* 541), this time with the fan.

544-5: 'From the suttee pyre the flame of gum camphire ascends. The pall of incense smoke screens and disperses. Out of her oak frame a nymph with hair unbound, lightly clad in teabrown art colours, descends from her grotto and passing under interlacing yews, stands over Bloom': Amidst the scents of the smoke and Kitty's henna (made with camphor) Bloom opens his eyes, and his sight clears gradually through blotches and pools of colour, as it does when one has had one's 'eyes shut tight' (*U* 531) for a spell. The nymph materialises from Bloom's memory of Milly, projected against the screen of Mrs Cohen's 'ivory gown, fringed . . . with tasselled selvedge' (*U* 527), which becomes the oak-framed canvas from which she descends; the yews are from the 'yewfronds' (*U* 502) on the wallpaper. Their 'whispering' leaves (*U* 545), the 'silversilent summer air' (*U* 550), the nymph's 'lascivious crispation' (*U* 551), the 'crackling canebrake' across which Virag strides (*U* 552) and the yews' 'silverfoil of leaves precipitating' (*U* 553) all originate in the noise from Kitty's fidgeting with the 'silver paper' (*U* 555). The winging 'grouse' (*U* 551) is a cushion being thrown. Bello's transformation into the solemn nymph is explained retrospectively when we learn that someone 'was playing the dead march from *Saul*' (*U* 555). Bella's 'You'll know me the next time' repeating Zoe's words earlier (*U* 476), shows once again that Bloom's dazed staring is excessive even by brothel standards.

559-60: The 'Parlour magic' of the materialised cigarette, Stephen's 'enigmatic melancholy', the blurriness and doubleness of his vision—leading to talk about two-backed beasts—are symptoms of Stephen's all-day drunk.

561-3: The figure of Father Dolan conjured by Lynch's slap and Zoe's comment about the 'eye' pops out of the pianola because Stephen's ashplant and hat, on top of it (*U* 503), remind him of Dolan's pandybat and head. The accompaniment by Father Conmee's head is another instance of Stephen's double vision. His mind on Dolan and his attention focused on his hand by the fortune-telling, Stephen becomes aware of a tingling in his palm, similar to the sensation from the pandying of sixteen years ago, from the time about twenty minutes ago when he smacked the lamp post with his ashplant: 'Hurt my hand somewhere.'[51]

563-7: As Bloom goes into yet another trance, the whores giggle, evoking the jingling of Boylan's car, and whisper in 'liplapping' plopslop' (*U* 566), evoking the sounds first of Molly in her bath and then of her lovemaking with Blazes. Boylan's part is supplied mainly by 'lecherous' Lynch, filling the role called up in Bloom's imagination by Zoe's line 'Henpecked husband', which brings us, oddly, a huge egg-laying rooster (its egg is Bloom's weal) from which the associative progression to Boylan is obvious and inevitable. Lynch, who is fooling around with Kitty and laughing, pooh poohs Zoe's pretensions as a fortune teller by holding up his hand ('mocks them with thumb and wriggling wormfingers' (*U* 564), laughing, and summing it all up, typically, as 'blatherskeit' (cf. *B* 183, *FW* 200.04) which becomes Boylan's peculiar 'Blazes Kate!' and, when repeated later, 'Gooblazqrukbrukarckrasht!' (*U* 567) I'm not sure, but I think his comments also include 'Flipping malarkey' ('Plucking a turkey'), 'mountebank' ('money back'), 'balderdash' ('gin and splash'), 'poppycock' ('Topping!') 'pshaw' ('pishogue') and 'your eye' ('your eye'). In any event, the sequence ends when he points to the mirror ('He [Boylan] holds out a forefinger') and makes the obvious remark that fortune-telling just reflects what people expect to see.

571-3: After his strenuous performance, Stephen feels light-headed, feels, in fact, that he is flying: 'My foes beneath me.' Trying to steady himself, he focuses on the gaslight and chandelier, where the sight of the moth begets the 'wheeling' Simon Dedalus on 'buzzard wings'. Simon's strange invocations ('Ho, boy! . . . Hoop! . . . Burblblbrurbbl!') originate in the mingling laughter (*U* 570) as it is gradually drowned out by the ringing in Stephen's ears which will in turn become the deafening 'clamour' of the race track. The effect of 'The fronds and spaces of the wallpaper [filing] rapidly across country' will be recognised by anyone who has ever been drunk enough to experience what a friend of mine calls 'the whirlies'. The hunted fox of the chase comes from the stuffed fox in the hall. The crowd's 'beaglebaying, burblbrbling' sound is a further metamorphosis of Simon's 'eagle' and 'brbl'. The whirling makes Stephen think of a whirligig, and so the fox evokes a racing ring of horses, including one whose 'eyeballs' are 'stars', from the gleams of light coming from the chandelier's prism and, probably, shining off the glass eyes of the fox. The same prism gives us Deasy's 'blue eyes flashing' ('prism light on GD's blue eyes'—*BM*

322) along with the yellow, green, and orange flashes which have produced his 'honey cap, green jacket, orange sleeves'. (The same prism produces the 'ORANGE LODGES' and 'GREEN LODGES'.) Like the checkered sunlight in 'Nestor', the spangles refracted from the prism become 'dancing coins'; when mixed together with the sound of the 'drizzle of rain' from outside they become sliced vegetables in a stew. All this sudden activity from the chandelier suggests that something, perhaps Stephen's acrobatics on pp. 569-70, has jarred it, causing it to sway back and forth; it may well be that Simon's uncertain swooping and whirling (*U* 572) owes as much to the chandelier as to the moth.

574-83: The determinants of Professor Goodwin defeat me. He seems to have something to do with some garment removed (it is getting warm) and thrown across the room, as seen in very slow motion. Maginni comes from Stephen, either his shadow or his reflection in the window between the curtains. His 'clouded cane' is Stephen's ashplant; his movements and affectation of French are Stephen's; his rainbow colours are from the prism, from the pianola's 'gold pink and violet lights', and from the multicoloured oilcloth on the floor (*U* 502); his dahlia is suggested by Zoe's 'fleshflower of vaccination'. The dance originates mainly from the rainbow colours twirling across the floor and walls, their source the revolving 'Wonderlight' atop the pianola. The 'Hours' dance from dawn to night because Stephen is coming close to blacking out, for obvious reasons. Beyond all that, the determinants of the sequence beginning when Zoe cranks up the pianola and culminating in Stephen's vision on his mother are—fittingly, one might suppose, for the climactic scene of the climactic chapter—the most complicated of the book. More than anywhere else in 'Circe', Stephen's consciousness is in control. So much so, in fact, that it can take the 'waltz time' of the song on the pianola, 'My Girl's a Yorkshire Girl', and transform it into the slow dance of the opening movement of 'The Dance of the Hours', in the process producing the Hours themselves and turning the music hall atmosphere of the song into the splendid masked ball of *La Gioconda*. (It becomes clear why Stephen should, for the nonce, turn into a French-speaking dancing master.) This particular transformation occurs because Stephen has just enthusiastically relived his nights in Paris, remembering, for instance, 'cocottes beautiful dressed much about princesses like are dancing cancan' (*U* 570), and the cancan happens to be most frequently danced to the rousing strains which, in 'The Dance of the Hours', follow the first movement and conclude the dance. So the pianola's melody is almost immediately drowned out, and the dance that follows is of the sort that simply could not be done to 'My Girl's a Yorkshire Girl': 'Stephen with his hat ashplant frogsplits in middle high-kicks with skykicking mouth . . . '. As for the scene that follows, it is simply Stephen's entranced re-enactment, now that he has *La Gioconda* planted in his mind, of the scene that follows 'The Dance of the Hours' in that opera. Here is a plot summary:

> This edifying spectacle no sooner ends than the guests are invited to witness a whole pageant of actual horror. The scoun-drelly Barnaba rushes into the palace, dragging Gioconda's blind old mother. At the top of his voice he charges her with practicing witchcraft. La Cieca [the mother] vows that she was merely praying for the souls of the dead. Enzo is among the masquers, and when a bell begins to toll solemnly, Barnaba whispers that it is tolling for Laura. Enzo throws off his mask and reveals himself as the nobleman Alvise had proscribed. 'My country and my bride you stole,' he shouts at Alvise. 'Now complete your crime!' The Duke, sensing the moment has come for the ghastly climax of his revenge, flings back the curtains of the death chamber, and a cry of horror comes from the crowd. Extended on a bier is Laura's body. Enzo rushes at Alvise, brandishing a poniard and shouting 'Hangman!' but before he can reach the man, guards seize him.[52]

The exactness of the parallel shows that Stephen knows *La Gioconda* well. Mrs Dedalus is both the murdered Laura ('I was once the beautiful May Goulding') and the blind old mother (she has 'hollow eyesockets'), a conjunction adumbrated by her full maiden name which suggests both springtime and, for Stephen, 'The ghoul' (*U* 581).[53] Both scenes feature a chorus, a tolling bell, a mocking, costumed villain (Lynch, here, is playing Mulligan playing Barnaba), and a final, futile attack. The language fre-quently matches:

> CIECA: 'I was praying for the dead.'   THE MOTHER: 'I pray for you in my other world.'

ENZO: 'Tears trickle down,   'A green rill of bile trickling from
drop by drop.'   a side of her mouth.'

ENZO: 'Already I see you,   '. . . in leper grey with a wreath of
still and wan/All wrapped   faded orange blossoms and a torn
in a white veil.'   bridal veil . . .'

Finally, Stephen's words on being reawakened later, 'Black panther vampire', show that he is still remembering this scene with its description of Barnaba as 'un vampiro fatal'.

As always, the scene is fabricated, esemplastically, from the materials at hand. When he stops dead, Stephen has been frightened by the 'glareblareflare' of lightning and the 'Baraabum' of the ensuing thunder; an hour or so later (*U* 667) he will tell Bloom that his collapse was caused by the 'reapparition' of the 'matutinal cloud' which had earlier evoked his mother. The vision occurs as follows: Stephen, stopping himself, trying to get his balance as the room continues to swim around, sensing the special kind of vacancy that follows the sudden cessation of a loud, boisterous melody, reminded of his 'mother's people' by Bloom (in the voice of Simon), reminded of his mother's corpse by the clamorous 'reapparition' of the cloud (*U* 10) associated with her death, fixes his eyes on the 'hearthrug of matted hair' (*U* 502) at his feet (his mother's 'scant and lank hair'), then lifts his gaze to his own reflection in the mirror over the mantle ('She fixes her bluecircled [Stephen's glasses] hollow eyesockets on Stephen'), then hears the bells ringing 12:45[54] ('Liliata rutilantium'), hears the drizzling rain ('Tears of molten butter', 'a green rill of bile trickling'), smells the moistened ashes in the fireplace, their odour wafted to him by Zoe's fanning ('breathing upon him softly her breath of wetted ashes'), feels, understandably, overheated ('O, the fire of hell!'), is distracted by Florry's pointing at him ('She raises her blackened right arm slowly towards Stephen's breast with outstretched fingers') and, on hearing another peal of thunder ('the agony of her deathrattle') tries unsuccessfully to put an end to his horrific vision by knocking out the light.

586-7: The renewal of the rain, signalled by the thunder and lightning, explains Bloom's 'caliph's hood and poncho', the envelopes 'drenched in aniseed', the harmless pelting Bloom gets from 'Helterskelterpelterwelter', and the fact that everyone is gathered 'beneath the scaffolding'.

589: Stephen 'waves his hand' and Dolly Gray 'From her balcony waves her handkerchief'. She is his mirror image,[55] reflected back from a window set behind grillwork of the sort one frequently sees in balconies. (The same grillwork probably accounts for the 'pentice of gutted spearpoints' on p. 596.) The many mirror-images of the following pages ('John O'Leary against Lear O'Johnny, Lord Edward Fitzgerald against Lord Gerald Fitzedward', etc.) have the same origin.

590-602: I wish I knew more about the paraphernalia of turn-of-the-century plasterers. (I also wish I knew what they are doing setting up operations outdoors.) In any event, it seems clear that their scaffolding is suspended by ropes and holds a bucket, perhaps the same bucket Bloom once disgraced. Together, these props engender Edward VII's bucket, Edward himself when levitating, the hanged Croppy Boy, Edward again, dancing and swaying back and forth (somewhat like an earlier false father-figure), and the elevated altar for camp mass; finally, the rope suggests the hanged Judas to Stephen. The scaffolding is lit up on either edge with lights ('Black candles rise from its gospel and epistle horns') and holds, in addition to the bucket (Mina Purefoy's chalice), a plasterer's apron (Father Malachi O'Flynn's chasuble) and a mortarboard (The Reverend Mr Hugh C. Haines Love's 'mortar board'). The blasphemous inversion of 'God' is prompted by the return of the dog; 'Doooooooooooog!' is probably his bay. The ensuing political struggles seem to be largely determined by alternately blinking green and red 'warning signals' of the sort mentioned at the beginning of the chapter: the Citizen wears an 'emerald muffler', the British are 'redcoats' and toss 'redhot' bombs, and so on.

604: The 'muttering' of the crowd may well be just that, or it may be Joyce's re-use of a phrase that forecast the kind of writing he has carried to such amazing lengths in 'Circe', the 'muttering rain' of 'She Weeps Over Rahoon' (*CP* 50).

609: Fittingly, the apparition of Rudy is a compound image framed as Bloom looks at his own shadow against the wall (or, possibly, a dim reflection in a window), watches over the sleeping Stephen, and remembers Rudy. Also fittingly, it is initiated by a characteristic moment of sympathy: 'Face reminds me of his poor mother'—and so from thoughts of dead mothers to thoughts of dead infants. Bloom holds a cane with one hand and puts the other hand to his lips, and so the shadow is holding a cane and kissing a book—a book because Stephen is Bloom's idea of a professor (*U*

589). The mauve face, like the diamond and ruby buttons, is an after-image from Mrs Cohen's, perhaps helped along by the glow from a red warning light. Rudy's Eton suit and precocious scholarship reveal Bloom's blighted ambition for his son and his idea of Stephen's accomplishments. The 'white lambkin' in the waistcoat pocket is the handkerchief which will be mentioned on the first page of the next chapter, here mixed up with the wool jacket in which Rudy was buried.

'Circe' is what everyone has said it is, the nodal episode of *Ulysses,* not just because it combines elements from all the rest of the book, but because at the same time it changes them, radically and for good. Readers discover that the early proportions were off and the early meanings partial: that the 'raincaped watch', for instance, which earlier had rated only a few lines in 'Oxen of the Sun', is part of a memory that can send Bloom into a panic for twenty pages. At least one major character, Virag, has never been heard of before. The metamorphoses all point outward and, especially, backward, to an imagined plenum in relation to which they were partial and second-hand. As clearly as he ever proclaims anything, Joyce proclaims, from the moment when Stephen and Bloom finally come together for good, that the book's source is himself, James A. Joyce, and that it is to be taken as another and fuller portrait of the artist, both young and not-young, done with Shakespearian 'reduplication of personality', musical harmonisation of tonic and dominant, and mirrors. It is not surprising that the entire episode strikes some readers as Joyce's own private joke.[56] The prevailing myth that the chapter's many subordinate myths compose, turns out to be, simply, James Joyce's life. The first important fantasia, Bloom's vision of himself as a triumphant Dick Whittington, was Joyce's own, as *Exiles* and the letters show: '. . . tonight I was in the Gresham Hotel and was introduced to about twenty people and to all of them the same story was told: that I was going to be the great writer of the future in my country' (*L* II, 245). Virag and Henry Flower juxtaposed are the Joyce of *Dubliners* and the Joyce of *Chamber Music* juxtaposed. Bello Cohen of course personifies the now well-known secrets of Joyce's bottom drawer by combining forbidden impulses involving the two most important people in his life, his father and Nora Barnacle. When Molly cuckolds Bloom, the source of her lover's apparition turns out to be Lynch, based in turn on Vincent Cosgrave,[57] whose supposed affair with Nora sent Joyce in tears to 7 Eccles Street and revealed him to himself as the hornmad Iago, which name, conveniently, is Spanish for 'James'. Likewise when Mulligan reappears to taunt Stephen about his own obsession, his origin is in Lynch.

Finally, the appearance of Stephen's dead mother and his fight with the soldiers recall two of the most important events in Joyce's life from around the Bloomsday period. As for the most important event, the meeting with Nora, Stephen has been wanting to meet some woman all day, ever since he started reciting 'Who Goes With Fergus', a poem transparently about some ideal woman with white breast and dishevelled hair. On the last page, dazed, he recites lines from it again, Bloom takes them as a reference to a certain white-breasted Miss Ferguson, and his conclusion, coming from the bottom of our uxorious author's heart, must be counted as the single truest sentence of the book: 'Best thing could happen him.' Bloom is always right when he's wrong, and he was never more right. And then what for Joyce was the most important single consequence of that meeting: a young boy, the shadow of Bloom's substance, framed as Bloom contemplates his own image against the wall, like a fulfilled Shakespeare, no longer paralytic, looking at a different image from the one in the brothel's mirror and seeing at once both himself and a son named after a father.

So the 'romantic' phase of *Ulysses* concludes by returning to Narcissus, to a man looking at his own image, except that as in Shakespeare's Sonnet Number Three the mirror has become a window as well, looking into past and future. Compared to the chapters preceding it, 'Sirens' through 'Circe' have been exercises in *ek-stasis,* in ideas and states, themselves not new, getting detached from 'the mind that has conceived them' and coming to life. In fact it is possible to read each of the five episodes beginning with 'Sirens' as corresponding 'romantic' extensions of the five earlier episodes beginning with 'Hades'. In the melancholy 'Sirens' Simon Dedalus plays Orpheus to the memory of the Eurydice whose grave he visited in the lugubrious 'Hades'; the 'Aeolian' cast of 'Cyclops' has been widely noted;[58] both 'Lestrygonians' and 'Nausicaa' are dialectical reactions to their predecessors, trying to re-establish occult connections and going overboard; 'Scylla and Charybdis' and 'Oxen of the Sun' are the book's two 'literary' episodes; both 'Wandering Rocks' and

'Circe' are studies in fragmentation with virtually identical assigned 'Meanings',[59] and if Joyce had said that one of the two had
'locomotor apparatus' for its 'organ' but he wasn't going to tell us
which one, it would be difficult to choose between them. Be that as
it may—and of course one can always find some connection
between any two chapters, and such exercises must always keep in
mind the evidence of Joyce's changing plans throughout his
composition—the main thing is that in its shift to the five 'romantic'
chapters, *Ulysses* shifts its centre of gravity completely from the
things being seen and the thoughts about them to the acts of
thinking and seeing, and the sometimes monstrous effects of these
acts, to the odd way the mind can elastically hold on to the world
and at the same time to something unearthly, and so to the nature
and history of the mind doing the thinking and seeing. 'Circe'
winds up as another portrait of the artist, this time with sixteen
more years of past to put into focus. In the remaining three
episodes 'Eumaeus', 'Ithaca', and 'Penelope', the focus on that
figure will become still sharper.

6

Under the Microscope

After the 'romantic' movement ending in 'Circe', chapters sixteen
to eighteen, in the spirit of Stephen's 'classical temper', acknowledge the limits of the intellect and its instrument, language. In
'Eumaeus' Bloom concludes that 'the odds were twenty to nil
there was really no secret about it at all,' 'Ithaca' dismisses a
radiantly mythopoeic interpretation of the firmament with the
remark that there is 'no known method from the known to the
unknown' and Molly, near the end of 'Penelope', says that she
'wouldn't give a snap' 'for all their learning', since it leaves
unanswered the kinds of questions that the young Stephen Dedalus
asked himself at Clongowes. With 'no known method from the
known to the unknown', the impulse to make language slackens,
and with it the kind of stimulus-response memory that culminated
in 'Circe'. 'Circe' shows words and images being made; the clichés
and dead metaphors that follow it were made long ago. They are to
the hallucinations of 'Circe' as a shell is to a shellfish. The
protagonists just want to put the day out of their minds, arrange
things in order, and go to sleep. The book, like a man stacking up
coins on his dresser before sinking into bed, follows them as
always in a three-stage subsidence: memories purged and language
anaesthetised; memories sifted and language systematised; then a
final recall of a new world in a new syntax.

The episode of the *Odyssey* corresponding to 'Eumaeus' begins
as Odysseus, deep in a death-like sleep, is carried home by night in
a pilotless ship. It has been interpreted by commentators as the

story of the soul's passage through oblivion after death, and something of the sort is evidently happening, to characters and perhaps reader, in the corresponding section of *Ulysses*. 'Eumaeus' is governed by Hypnos, brother of Thanatos, and at times their kingdoms coincide. (The son of Hypnos, Morpheus, is also present, as W. B. Murphy.) Like Homer's Phaecians, the inhabitants of the episode have been petrified by an angry Neptune. Joyce's note 'Daunt's rock petrified ship' (*BM* 406) connects the shipwreck on Daunt's rock, viewed by a crowd 'petrified with horror' (*U* 638) to the *Odyssey* story, and there is also the cab hailed by Bloom which shows 'no sign of budging' (*U* 636), the sugar clotted on the bottom of Stephen's coffee, along with a bun which is a 'brick', and so forth. Skin-the-goat says Ireland has had 'all the riches drained out of it by England' (*U* 640); something has done the same to the shelter's stony dozers. The same influence operates on the sentences and paragraphs which, typically, start off confidently but soon sink into confusion from their own weight.

According to the ever present nautical imagery, the result is a maritime graveyard, the ocean floor of consciousness covered with a congealed residue sunk from the world of daylight—and so much for dreams and visions. The Parnell-Kitty O'Shea story, for instance, is a 'kind of dream', which means it is a particularly thick pastiche of clichés, a story of a matrimonial goose being cooked, coals of fire heaped on a head, and a 'fabled ass's kick' (*U* 651). With sedimentation goes stratification: society, for instance, ranges from the 'upper ten' to the 'submerged tenth' (*U* 646).

The verbal equivalent is generalisation as in the first sentence: 'Preparatory to *anything else* Mr Bloom brushed off the *greater bulk* of the shavings and handed Stephen the hat and ashplant and bucked him up *generally* in *orthodox Samaritan fashion,* which he very badly needed,' (my italics). At its extreme, the writing seems likely to expand indefinitely into that vast vague realm, beloved of politicians and takers of essay examinations, in which everything is generalised to the point of featurelessness, and the whole becomes what Stephen thinks of as a 'synopsis of things in general' about 'nothing in particular' (*U* 644). No wonder there is so much uncertainty about everyone's bona fides, so much talk of impostors and mistaken identities. Names themselves—as the *Evening Telegraph* shows with its record of 'L. Boom' and M'Intosh (*U* 647)—are the petrified remnant of some mistake or deception.

The natural reaction is an impulse to look through or beyond the strata of words to something more real underneath. What one critic has called the 'reactivation of [Odysseus'] conscious efforts at reaching reality'[1] begins with the night passage back to Ithaca; the same is true for this stage of *Ulysses*. That is why, as for Stephen's Aristotle in 'Proteus', things touchable have a claim that verbal formulae do not, why Stephen can blandly tender Corley a handful of metal discs, for instance, without bothering about whether they go by the name of 'pennies' or 'halfcrowns' (*U* 618).

The result is of course frequently reductive. Bloom has an amateur psychologist's explanation for Stephen's prickliness (unhappy 'home life'—*U* 645—and an amateur anthropologist's explanation for racial differences, ' . . . climate accounts for character'—*U* 637). The device he singles out as the summit of human genius is the X-ray machine, the enemy of mystery, the exposer of the soul as 'convolutions' of 'grey matter': ' . . . it is one thing for instance to invent those rays Rontgen did . . . but it's a horse of quite another colour to say you believe in the existence of a supernatural God' (*U* 634). Bloom sees a whore and wants her 'medically inspected', thinks of food as a subject for 'medical analysis' and in general fancies his X-ray way of getting to the bottom of things, for instance here the 'submerged tenth' 'very much under the microscope lately' (*U* 646-7). (He likes microscopes and telescopes too.) His cynicism in this chapter about society, government, the people he meets, history, and his own motives for befriending Stephen is simply the X-ray's reductivism, affecting to see 'through' appearances to 'the money question which was at the back of everything' (*U* 643).

Not absolutely everything, perhaps: there are also sex, age, race, and climate. But at most a very few primal causes are 'at the back of' a very limited number of types, and Bloom thinks that he's really said something when he's boiled something down to, for instance, 'the female form', or a 'Spanish type'. The Parnell tragedy, for instance, is the old story of 'woman', 'a magnificent specimen of manhood', and the 'usual *farewell, my gallant captain* kind', tipped off by the 'usual boy Jones' (*U* 655). Following Bloom, 'Eumaeus' petrifies, congeals and stratifies particulars into types and levels, and invites the reader to notice congruences—of one adulterous 'Spanish type' with another, Kitty O'Shea with Molly, for instance. If we can muster the will to pay attention to these types, then one by one they will all fall into place like tessera in one single emblem: the Ulysses theme of the returning voyager—his journey (the maritime motif), his perils (the motifs of rocks, shipwrecks, sirens and sinkings), his problematic recognition on return (the disguise and deception motifs) and his possible displacement (the change and betrayal motifs). The whole episode is a static emblem composed of lesser emblemata which, uniquely in *Ulysses,* do not refer elsewhere in the book, but simply mean what they say. For instance: 'I seen a Chinese one time, related the doughty narrator, that had little pills like putty and he put them in the water and they opened, and every pill was something different. One was a ship, another was a house, another was a flower' (*U* 628). This is a 'miniature cameo', as Bloom says elsewhere, of the 'whole galaxy of events' (*U* 646), of a man named Bloom returning like the sailor Odysseus to his house.

So is the 'doughty narrator's' tattoo, in blue ink, of an anchor, 'a young man's sideface looking frowningly rather', and the number 16 (*U* 631). It can be read in one of two ways. First, it is a complete and self-contained epitome of the book *Ulysses,* a three-part story, its cover inscribed in blue ink, about a gloomy young man and a latter-day Odysseus sixteen years his senior who meet on the sixteenth day of the month. Or, second, it means something else, private to the author, not referrable—and this is something new—to the previous pages. James Maddox, sensing this, thinks that Murphy is Joyce,[2] and I myself have come to the conclusion that he is a window on an autobiographical, extra-textual story so large that it will require my next chapter to handle it. In either case, the sailor Murphy arrives for the first time in the book, delivers his message, and is then left behind for good. About no other significant character in *Ulysses* can that be said with confidence. His signification is totally vertical: we read down through it to something altogether outside the book we have come to know. Wherever the reader looks for the answer to his puzzle, it will not be to the surrounding pages.

That is odd, because working out the rest of the book's puzzles generally involves a good deal of turning back and forth between one page and another, more often than not with the help of Myles Hanley's *A Word Index to James Joyce's Ulysses.* It involves, more than anything else, remembering. By contrast, reading 'Eumaeus' involves forgetting. In the *Odyssey,* Odysseus does not recognise Ithaca when he wakes up on its shores, and the memories of Stephen and Bloom are similarly fogged. That is why, paradoxically, the chapter is full of names (hundreds of them, about ten to a page) and the kind of show-off words memorised in secondary school from vocabulary lists. It all illustrates a principle familiar to teachers of undergraduate exposition, that diction is stressed in inverse proportion to control of syntax, that the more at sea a writer is about how things fit together the more likely he is to rely on certain impressive-sounding expressions and names as talismans of meaning or signatures of—for instance—'expertise'. The undistinguished prose of 'Eumaeus' is the work of a writer trying very hard to sound distinguished, and its sound is the thoroughly familiar modern sound (Joyce was a prophet in one way at least) of someone with nothing to say saying it, heading from one formula to another like a drunk lurching from one lamppost to another or—and this is Joyce's main analogy—a night-sailing mariner dead-reckoning from buoy to buoy. There is, typically, a sense of relief when the phrases or names are found, coming from the awareness that without them to head for and hold to, everything would sink into oblivion.

In his schema, Joyce designated 'nerves' as the 'organ' of the episode, not, it should be stressed, the nervous system: concentrated points of attention, not the network connecting them. Bloom's brainstorm, for instance, shows how they operate in the place of their greatest concentration: 'All kinds of utopian plans were flashing through his [Bloom's] busy brain. Education [the genuine article], literature, journalism, prize titbits . . .' (*U* 658). According to the level of stimulation, sensations and thoughts either 'flash' or drift from one concentrated bundle, one ganglion of name, phrase or 'utopian plan', to another. What has been called the chapter's 'nominalist'[3] cast reflects how central those bundles are now, how completely the matter of *Ulysses* has been changed from perception to sensation, from syntax to diction (four pages from the end of the book, Molly begins remembering her Spanish except 'for the grammar'—*U* 779), from patterns of imagery, echoes and foreshadowings to emblems. Having ceased to go anywhere, the book requires the reader to focus on concentrated centres of meaning.

'**Ithaca**': In the study of scientific phenomena forecast by Bloom's 'Eumaeus' references to microscope and X-ray, the equivalents to these nodes of meaning are the essences and strata formed by distillation, condensation and sedimentation, the processes by which are produced the 'stratifications of the earth', the 'cohesion' of trillions of molecules in a pinhead or trillions of integers in 'the nucleus of the nebula of every digit of every series' (*U* 699), the 'condensation of spiral nebulae into suns' (*U* 700), and 'continual production of semen by distillation' (*U* 734) recorded throughout the next episode, 'Ithaca'. One reason that Joyce in his schema designated 'comets' as the 'symbol' of 'Ithaca' was almost surely their 'almost infinite compressibility' (*U* 700), the belief, recorded in his notes, that one can 'put comet in thimble' (*BM* 460), distill or contract a body of galactic proportions down to next to nothing.

At the very end, 'Ithaca' does just that, congealing all of Bloomsday by degrees into a 'square round egg' (*U* 737)—which symbol stands in relation to the comet symbol as potential to actualisation, small ellipsoidal solid to airy expanse describing an elipse through and beyond the solar system—and then a final dot. Before then, the action of 'Ithaca' is a series of radical condensations, like a movie of explosions shown in reverse. Having reached the peculiar lucid plateau that one sometimes settles on two or three hours after one's normal bed-time, on the other side of the 'fatigue barrier', Bloom observes things carefully, attentively and blankly, and his main concern is to put them in comprehensible order. Near the end, he puts the desideratum, appropriately, into a nutshell:

What were habitually his final meditations? Of some one sole unique advertisement to cause passers to stop in wonder, a poster novelty, with all extraneous accretions excluded, re-reduced to its simplest and most efficient terms not exceeding the span of casual vision and congruous with the velocity of modern life (*U* 720).

'Ithaca' enacts the ideal that was occasionally visible through the murk of 'Eumaeus'. It is a chapter of self-sufficient emblems, condensations of meaning each 'reduced to its simplest and most efficient terms' (*U* 720), simple signs: the rearranged furniture, the stars in their Bloomian and Mollyish and Dedalusian configurations, Bloom's top and bottom drawers, male key in female lock, Molly's lamp. Stephen and Bloom communicate almost exclusively in the sign language of Hebrew and Gaelic letters, gestures to one another, song, and so forth. In fact when in their final parallel act they urinate side by side (*U* 702-3), they literally spell things out for us. Bloom's stream is visually the letter Y; Stephen's is audibly 'more sibilant'—the letter S. When Molly comes out from behind the machinery the first word of her monologue will already have been completed: YES. Nothing could be simpler. All of these emblems are precise, sharp-edged, as if made by an engineer for whom language is a set of precision instruments. When he lists thirty-four different attributes of water, for instance (*U* 671-2), it is with the implicit understanding that that is *it;* there is no 'etc.' at the end. The standard symbol of limitless flux has had a line drawn around it—not surprising considering that about a third of the scores of instruments mentioned throughout 'Ithaca' have to do with its control. This narrator's vision of paradise is similar to Bloom's pipe dream, Flowerville: at its center is a 'toolshed' and sublime potterer-gardener-handyman, a *homo instrumentus,* trimming the 'topiary hedges' and 'oval flowerbed in rectangular grassplots set with eccentric ellipses of scarlet and chrome tulips', similarly pruning and cultivating the social orders after rising 'in ascending powers of hierarchical power' to justice of the peace (*U* 712-16).

Many of the instruments have to do with extending and delimiting perception. Everything is seen according to certain set principles. When the narrator describes Stephen 'raising his gaze to the height of a yard' to see Bloom's clothesline (*U* 670), for instance, he sounds as if he is describing a telescope. Moving from one discrete exhibit to another, the spaces between each entry defining the borders of the lens or limit of the microphone's range, the episode presents a synopsis not of 'things in general', as in 'Eumaeus', but of one thing at a time. Like Bloom and Mrs Riordan, it scans its material through essentially the same instrument, over and over:

Had he [Bloom] performed any special corporal work of mercy for her [Mrs Riordan]?

He had sometimes propelled her . . . in her convalescent bathchair with slow revolutions of its wheels as far as the corner of the North Circular Road . . . where she had remained for a certain time scanning through his one-lensed binocular field-

glasses unrecognisable citizens in tramcars, roadster bicycles
. . . passing from the city to the Phoenix Park and vice versa.
Why could he then support that his vigil with the greater
equanimity?
Because in middle youth he had often sat observing through a
rondel of bossed glass of a multicoloured pane the spectacle
offered with continual changes of the thoroughfare without,
pedestrians, quadrupeds, velocipedes, vehicles, passing slowly,
quickly, evenly, round and round the rim of a round precipitous
globe (*U* 681).

The instruments of the house repeatedly deploy things into sym-
metrical, self-contained images: rondels.

Of the narrator's instruments, the two fundamental are parallel
and antithesis, the applications of the two fundamental categories
of same-ness and other-ness. Everything is put in relationship to
everything else according to whether it is similar to or different
from, in the same frame or outside it. The first five questions of the
episode about the 'parallel courses' of a 'duumvirate' joined by
'common factors', separated by 'unlike reactions', 'divergent'
views, and one 'equal and negative' view, establishes the operation. (The final image of 'Eumaeus' was of 'two figures . . . both
black—one full, one lean . . .'.) Everything can be placed this way,
for instance, Bloom's range:

What did Bloom see on the range?
On the right (smaller) hob a blue enamelled saucepan: on the
left (larger) hob a black iron kettle (*U* 670).

Similarities: both kitchen utensils; both on the range. Differences:
one black, one blue; one iron, one enamelled; one a kettle, one a
saucepan. Likewise the hobs are similar: both are hobs. And
different: one larger than the other; one to the right of the other.
The picture is computed on a grid of like and unlike. Anything can
be defined by being placed in apposition to something in some ways
similar; even infinity is 'renderable equally finite by the suppositi-
ous probable apposition of one or more bodies equally of the same
and of different magnitudes' (*U* 701). Milly Bloom and Bloom's
cat, for instance, share 'similar differences' in four 'respects' (*U*
693).

The 'rondels' are generated out of this operation. Two subjects are brought together on one round specimen plate and with X-ray and microscope analysed into their constituent atoms, which are then ordered according to a binary code. The similarities which distinguish them from everything else define the border of the composition they form, the circumference; the differences which qualify their identity with one another define its dimensions, the diameter. Internally, they are ordered according to a progression of degrees of similitude, as when Bloom's unchosen careers are ordered in a range from church (ranging from Roman Catholic to Non-conformist) to stage (ranging from 'modern' to 'Shakespearian') (*U* 690); externally, they are all equally unconnected from anything outside the range. Step by step, in a series of mental exercises which may remind us that Wittgenstein's *Tractatus* is being produced at just about the same time,[4] reality is defined from within by separating whatever comes within the scope of the knowable from what does not, 'ipsorelative' from 'aliorelative' (*U* 708). The final distinction to which all this leads is, simply, between what is and what is not.

This final stark opposition has affinities with the corresponding scenes of the *Odyssey*. One critic of Homer, noting the 'dramatic chiaroscuro quality' conveyed by Homer's use of light and dark in the homecoming episodes, suggests the main contrast is between 'the life-giving hero' as 'force of light' and the 'fabulous, formless darkness' of his hostage land.[5] Likewise Bloom, fire-lighter and candle-bearer, is the 'light of reason' (*U* 720), which in 'Ithaca' is to say that his world is 'artificial' in comparison to the 'natural obscurity' surrounding it (*U* 729). Flowerville, for instance, is thoroughly artificial in a genteel, old-fashioned sort of way (its topiary hedges, its 'fingertame parrot' with 'expurgated language'); so is the narrator (he calls the chamberpot a 'night article'). Epitomising Bloom's 'light of reason' is his plan for an educational kindergarten complete with a toy chest of 'astronomical kaleidoscopes exhibiting the twelve constellations from Aries to Pisces, miniature mechanical orreries, arithmetical lozenges, geometrical to correspond with zoological biscuits, globemap playingballs, historically costumed dolls' (*U* 683). This is one of the episode's moments of self-reflection, an epitome of what its systematic condensations and dispositions of reality have made of reality. Between the 1904 plans for self-improvement and the writing of this book, a number of things have happened, the First World War for instance, which have made clear to what extent all mental constructions are toys. Consequently there is a growing sense of littleness that comes over the reader of 'Ithaca', and with it the cold isolation from the vast realm not picked up on its instruments. Since the episode's epistemology is totally atomistic, there can be no indication of contiguous membranes connecting its discrete arrangements. The only relationship is through exclusion. When Stephen and Bloom commune over their cup of cocoa, it is as 'Blephen' and 'Stoom', fused into one entity by their isolation from the area of everything not-Stephen not-Bloom surrounding them. Their communion is a 'solution' according to the chemical definition ('A homogenous molecular mixture of two or more substances'), as their separation from everything outside them is an instance of chemical 'hypostasis' (*U* 689) ('A settling of foreign particles in a fluid'). (They are drinking 'soluble cocoa', 'allowing for subsolid residual sediment of a mechanical mixture'—itself an emblem of how the emblems of 'Ithaca' have congealed from the sedimentation of 'Eumaeus'.) The two can combine completely in one homogenous 'solution' or separate completely into hypostatised strata or suspended colloids, come together as one 'reciprocal flesh' or fly apart as 'centripetal remainer' and 'centrifugal departer' respectively (*U* 703). Anything between is simply an excluded middle: Stephen's 'another now and yet the same' from 'Telemachus', for instance (*U* 11), would translate simply as the logically absurd 'x and not-x'.

Disqualified from making connections, from linking x with not-x, the maker of 'Ithaca' instead presents the reader with a field of congruent figures and by his very silence invites him to find analogies—between cocoa-drinking and communion, chairs and people, stars and people—always with the understanding that like the correspondences of astrology they may be 'as attributable to verifiable intuition as to fallacious analogy' (*U* 701), and vice versa.[6] Increasingly, the congruences are less between one person or object and another than between replicas of one model, at different levels and of different magnitudes, the whole symbolised by the final light of the episode: 'The upcast reflection of a lamp and shade, an inconstant series of concentric circles of varying gradation of light and shadow' (*U* 736). What is real is not any one level of existence, but a single pattern, much closer to 'Blephen'-'Stoom' than to Stephen or Bloom, formed out of the systematic application of the categories same-ness and other-ness, infinitely extendable through gradations of analogy, informing all the episode's intermediate emblems. It has two determining properties. First, of course, it is round, like the rondel, the concentric lamp image above Molly's bed, and so forth. Second, it occurs in parallels, like the double urination of Stephen and Bloom, the 'parallel courses' mentioned in the episode's first sentence, and the episode's many doublings-back (for example, Bloom 'reentering the passage, reclosing the door,' etc.), mirror images, and reciprocal exchanges.

Now, there is a problem here. It is impossible to envision a figure simultaneously circular and parallel, because curves and straight lines are geometrically incommensurable. Still, our author, with a kind of heroic literal-mindedness, comes as close as he can: his proposed resolution is, again, the episode's designated 'symbol', comets. The comet's orbit is the nearest possible equivalent to a pair of parallel lines that at some point finally connect and close the circle. Literally, this point is at the end of an enormously elongated elipse beyond the solar system's concentric orbits; in 'Ithaca', it is also the 'extreme boundary' of existence (*U* 727), way beyond the concentric rondels of the knowable world. It is in the realm of the 'unknown' to which human life progresses from the 'known' (*U* 697), and since that progress is also, according to the narrator, from mother to father (*U* 708), that is from 'the only true thing in life' to 'the incertitude of the void' (*U* 207), it is also in the realm of Stephen's idea of spiritual paternity—in fact, the problematic point where begin the returns of metempsychosis. That is why Bloom, looking at the sleeping Molly's face and seeing traces of her father (as he had earlier (*U* 609) been reminded of Mrs Dedalus by the face of the younger Stephen when unconscious), imagines the 'parallel lines' of railway tracks receding, 'meeting at infinity', and returning (*U* 730). And that is why the chapter's intimations of consubstantiality between Stephen and Bloom invariably wind up running us off the charts, to the problematic convergence of Irish and Hebrew before the dawn of history (*U* 688) or the problematic convergence of their ages in some incomprehensible googol-googol reached through parallel geometric progressions (*U* 679).

The geometry of 'Ithaca', then, proves to be asymptotic. The circles and parallels, no matter how far their diameters and lengths are extended, never quite meet on the page. So, too, for language, which by expanding the sphere of the expressible to its limits diminishes it in relation to the more rapidly expanding field outside it. As the comet contracts, as the matter of *Ulysses* is condensed into the minimal microcosms of bed, seed, womb, egg, and dot, all-father Shakespeare shrunk to the 'snakespiral' springs (*U* 731) of a second-hand bed, language also approaches its minimal point, muteness. Bloom finds his 'final satisfaction' in Molly's 'female hemispheres', which are 'insusceptible of moods of impression or of contrarieties of expression, expressive of mute immutable mature animality' (*U* 734). (The one place 'where we havent 1 atom of any kind of expression', Molly indignantly confirms (*U* 777).) Behind all these coalescences is one destination, the coextensiveness of the greatest and the least, the 'minimum' defined by Giordano Bruno and illustrated with geometry:

> Between the smallest arc and the smallest chord there is no difference, just as there is none between the largest arc and the largest chord . . .
> From this it follows that the infinite circle and the infinite straight line, as well as the diameter, the center and all the rest of the infinite do not differ in anything, just as they do not differ in the point which is the smallest circle.[7]

When 'Ithaca' begins with the observation that 'the chord in any circle is less than the arc which it subtends' (*U* 666), it sets itself a challenge which Bloom provisionally meets when he frames the 'square round' egg of the ending, and begins directing the reader to the cometary point, beyond the page, of spiritual paternity and the intersections of metempsychosis.

At the end, the sense conveyed is that everything has been said about absolutely nothing, a paradox engineered by an author who keeps seeming to record all there is to note about any given fact but who actually keeps leaving things out. An early and easy example is the 'lapse of four minutes' between Bloom's disappearance from the kitchen and his reappearance in the hall, one flight up, a trip that should have taken, perhaps, fifteen seconds (*U* 669). What was Bloom doing? Does the 'lighted crevice of doorway' leading into the bedroom (*U* 669) indicate that he stopped to look in on Molly, that he gazed at her in the lamplight for minutes on end? Maybe, or maybe he stopped to unbolt the back door and had trouble with it, or maybe he barked his shin and sat down to rub it.

So many unanswered questions of this sort are there in 'Ithaca',[8] the conclusion seems unavoidable that the book, on the brink of 'Penelope', intends to leave the reader puzzled, that the final dot in answer to the last question is the equivalent of the Ouija board's 'Good-bye'. First the befuddlement of 'Eumaeus', and now this. When what at first seems an encylopedic synopsis opens so many spaces, the point is clear: close the encyclopedia and look elsewhere. In its own way, 'Ithaca' tells the reader where to look. First, by indirection: the most prominent absence from its text is the name 'Molly Bloom',[9] and sure enough the next chapter is hers. Second, by narrative nudging: the 'Technic' of the episode, 'Catechism (impersonal)', indicates a dialogue between a younger and an older man, and *Ulysses* in a number of ways, especially in 'Scylla and Charybdis', has taught the reader to expect such a dialogue between its two principals and, when he sees it, to look for a portrait of the artist. Third, by signs, for instance the 'Y-S' spelled out in the light from Molly's lamp, or (with the help of some inside knowledge) the episode's last intelligible image, a 'rok's auk's egg'. Most likely, this is the author's private reference to the 'Joyce egg', a smooth egg-shaped stone supposed to have been dropped by an eagle into the lap of Margaret Joyce of Galway and passed down through generations of Joyces. (A variant of the legend has her getting the original Claddagh ring, by the same means; hence Bloom's dream of an 'antique dynastical ring . . . (dropped by an eagle in flight)'—*U* 717.)[10]

According to these indicators, whatever follows 'Ithaca' will consist entirely or almost entirely of material left out of the previous episodes, and will be the most private piece of the book, parts of it in fact inaccessible to all but adepts in such mysteries as that of the Joyce egg. It was not out of laziness that Joyce wrote 'Penelope' in the style of his wife's letters. Since the last thing Bloom sees is a pattern of rings from the lamp's 'upcast reflection', and since the last phrase to rumble around his conscious mind is 'Sinbad the Sailor', we can expect 'Penelope' to move in circles (it does) and feature a roving sailor (his name is Mulvey). Finally, in a letter Joyce says that 'Penelope' has four 'cardinal points', the 'female breasts, arse, womb, and cunt' (*L* I, 170) and since of those four it is Molly's bottom that is singled out for 'contemplation' (*U* 735) at the end of 'Ithaca', we may suspect that the order of 'points' in Joyce's letter is misleading, and that 'Penelope' will begin not with 'breasts' but with 'arse'. In fact, if you were to draw a geometrically abstract picture of the object of that contemplation, you would have the outline of 'Penelope': upright, a figure 8, horizontal, the symbol of infinity.

'Penelope': To a great extent, then, 'Penelope' is determined by its predecessor, made by the same Bloomian shaper who swamped around in 'Eumaeus' and found his feet in 'Ithaca'. Man and wife are indeed one flesh. It is the last extension of a single evolving intelligence, the last of the book's 'rondels', 'passing slowly, quickly, evenly round and round the rim of a round precipitous globe' (*U* 681), 'the huge earth ball slowly surely and evenly round and round spinning', (Joyce's description of the episode—I, 170), encompassing a universe—this is its main advance over the epitomes of 'Ithaca'—with both men and women in it. It is the most intricately organised episode of *Ulysses*, seemingly chaotic[11] only because its logic is endogenous, uninfluenced by earlier rules or associations. It is, in fact, a whole new voyage, what Joyce in his notes calls the 'odyss of Pen' (*BM* 502) the Odyssey of Penelope. Its Penelope is a woman who grew up at the intersection of Atlantic and Mediterranean, Europe and Africa, north and south (Joyce romanticised the Spanish connections of Nora's native Galway), land, sea and sky ('the Atlas mountain', holding up the sky (*U* 762)), the meeting place of 'the Greeks and the Jews and the Arabs and the devil knows who else' (*U* 782), whose entire reverie is consequently a search for re-convergence. It circles around twice in eight sentences, describing a figure 8, (the pattern of *Finnegans Wake*, according to Clive Hart)[12] following its 'cardinal points' in the following order: arse, cunt, breasts, womb; arse, cunt, breasts, womb. Each group of four subdivides into two pairs, the first emblems of profane love, the second of sacred love, and the second sequence of four parallels, in detail, the first.

Following are some of the major co-ordinates of Molly's Penelopiad.

Sentence 1 (738-44): 'Bottom' is the cardinal point of the beginning. Since Boylan has recently slapped her and Bloom has just embraced her there, she connects it with Dublin men. That is why, to answer her question, Mrs Maybrick, a 'downright villain', killed her husband with 'Arsenic' (*U* 744). She begins her Odyssey at the bottom of the pit—Dublin. Whereas Gibraltar from the first is associated with thunderbolts and the fear of God (*U* 741), Dublin bores her 'to extinction'. Her opening words begin a survey of her life in Dublin, a place that has blighted all the traditional symbols of regeneration: Christ ('the first socialist', says Bloom), flowers ('the worst ones she could find at the bottom of the basket'), and sex ('its just the ordinary do it and think no more about it'). Her geographical review is also a roughly chronological survey of her eighteen years away from Gibraltar, with the last two memories, of her meeting with Bloom in 1887 and her meeting with Boylan this afternoon, defining the borders of her Dublin life. She feels trapped by Dublin men, and her last thought, concluding what among other things has been a catalogue of women sick, dying, withering, bored to extinction, or killing others or themselves, is of a drastic solution: Mrs Maybrick, the husband-poisoner. Like the other wives mentioned in this sentence, Mrs Maybrick was younger (by twenty-three years) than her husband, an unnatural state of affairs that greatly exaggerates Molly's own and will be counterbalanced at the end when she imagines an affair with the younger Stephen and remembers her romances with the young Bloom of sixteen years ago and the boyish Mulvey.

Sentence 2 (744-53): 'theyre all so different', Molly begins. 'They' are the men she has known since Gibraltar, the 'unlucky man' Henry Doyle, the 'little man' Arthur Griffith, the 'finelooking men' killed in the Boer War, 'a marrying man' (what Boylan definitely is not), and numbers of others. The earlier survey is widened and particularised. Consequently the most striking feature of this sentence—its scores of references to clothes. Their main significance is obvious: 'Ive no clothes at all . . . the men won't look at you and women try to walk on you because they know youve no man' (*U* 751). Clothing distinguishes people, makes men, for example, 'so different'. At least it does in Dublin; in Gibraltar the girls are 'naked as God made them' (*U* 750). It also imprisons. Getting her menstrual period at the Dublin Bakery Company, for instance, Molly was imprisoned, as usual by 'man tyrant', in 'that black closed breeches he made me buy takes you half an hour to let them down' (*U* 745). The ultimate example, of course, is Lily Langtrey's fabled chastity belt (*U* 751). Edward VII is supposed to have foiled it with an oyster knife, and it seems that any escape will have to be similarly rough—breaking and entering, breaking and exiting. Sexual intercourse is an instance of the former, which is why Boylan's erection reminded Molly of a crowbar, a burglar's tool (*U* 742). Since most sexual encounters stop short of anything so violent, they are mostly incomplete. Caged in their clothes, people do a lot of staring at one another but not much else. The sentence opens with Boylan staring at Molly's feet and closes with Mr Cuffe staring at her breasts; the courtship with Bloom is remembered as a fetishistic rite, all looking and showing, raincoat and muffler and petticoat and drawers (*U* 746). The cardinal point is the cunt, which is approached almost exclusively through fetishes—drawers, pictures, words. Although Molly does recall having seen 'a picture of a womans' in Gibraltar, even that was accompanied with 'a word I couldnt find anywhere' (*U* 747). (She can find it hidden in 'couldnt'.) The distinction is between words, the clothing of things (dictionaries, Dublin, males) and her own naked female reality. It is one example of 'the way the world is divided'. Of all such divisions (even her clothes are 'pleated'), two are critical: between past and present, between men and women. Her skin symbolises both: 'I thought it was beginning to look coarse or old a bit the skin underneath is much finer where it peeled off there on my finger after the burn' (*U* 751). It is itself a kind of clothing, making her yearly less attractive to men and taking her further from the young girl of Gibraltar. (It was at Gibraltar that she 'near jumped out of my skin' when she got Mulvey's note—*U* 759.) To go back in time she must literally burn it off; her re-baptism on the last page will be in a sea 'like fire'. As for the division between men and women, the best kind of connection possible she can imagine is a love-letter, a token sent across space. She was first attracted to Bloom because he looked (she thought) like Lord Byron, that great lover and writer of letters. Byron began his most famous liaison by sending Lady Caroline Lamb a rose and a note, and Bloom, who began his courtship with a gift of Byron's poems, is here similarly-differently remembered for sending Molly poppies, along with an improper letter. His Byronic pose has passed, of course (at thirty-eight, he has now outlived Byron by one year), but Molly still wants what it signified, still hopes to receive something from Bloom which will make her 'like new'—the face lotion he has forgotten to pick up.

Sentence 3 (753-4): Desiring escape, Molly composes an escapist interlude, moving from the 'differences' of clothing to the pornographic abstractions of Man and Woman. Though not quite what she had in mind when recalling the natural naked simplicity of Gibraltar, it is at least a start. Boylan is seen as such an abstraction:

'the savage brute', 'a big infant'. (In both capacities, men 'always want everything in their mouth'.) The cardinal point is the breasts, associated with two kinds of envisioned escape, regeneration through maternity (men become babies again) and through art (they make her a symbol of beauty 'placed up there like those statues'). The more mundane regeneration, or at least rejuvenation, which she hoped for from the skin lotion is also suggested by her breasts, which have become 'so much smoother' because of Boylan's attentions.

Sentence 4 (754-9): Hearing the train whistle and recalling her future trip with Boylan, Molly continues her fantasy of escape. In preparation she imagines discarding Bloom's old overcoats and copies of the *Freemans Journal* and *Photo Bits,* two symbols of Dublin. ('Wheres last Januarys paper?' her husband will ask (*U* 755)—typically, as he is associated with cold, newspapers, and time-in-Dublin.) Gibraltar by contrast is fiery and primal, its sun 'weltering down on you' (cf. Boylan's 'scrooching down on me'[13]), where at her first flirtation she 'hardly recognized myself the change I had a spendid skin from the sun and the excitement like a rose'. What she hoped for from her lotion and fitfully achieved with Boylan was a reality in the place of roses. She kicks off her blanket, symbolically rejecting the 'clothes we have to wear whoever invented them'. For a spell, however, her Gibraltar reverie clashes with the unromantic facts which start coming back to her as soon as she tries to remember what things were really like. That sun was oppressive, for instance, and the sea made her seasick. As in Dublin, boredom could make 'the days like years'. Realising that things were 'as bad as now', she sees that 'were never easy where we are'. No doubt the Spanish music halls of her youth featured skits about leprechauns and colleens and rollicking roistering Irishmen, as here she likes to sing a song called 'In Old Madrid'. Anyway that's all vanished irrevocably into the past, 'through a mist', and thinking about it only 'makes you feel so old' (*U* 756). Her hope for some kind of escape shifts to the second sentence's idea of letters as signals sent across space from outpost to outpost. Her bitterest memory of Gibraltar is that she received 'not a letter from a living soul', just as in Dublin she gets 'no visitors or post ever except his cheques or some advertisement' (*U* 758). Letters are what she needs and doesn't get from men, those dealers in cheques and advertisements who 'never understand' anything unless you 'print it up on a big poster for them'. (Her husband canvasses for ads; her lover is a billsticker.) Her letter from Boylan this afternoon ('yours ever Hugh Boylan'), which certainly 'wasn't much', was typical. If her contemporary Freud were to ask her his famous question about women, she would answer loud and clear: 'I wish somebody would write me a loveletter' (*U* 758). Approaching the fourth 'cardinal point', the womb, place of origins and creations, birth and rebirth, she frames an idea of art similar to that of the author of *Finnegans Wake:* it is a letter, ideally a love-letter, connecting writer and reader, reconciling the estrangements of time and space, redeeming a world deadened by the false, provincially male, Dublin art of posters and newspapers, achieving regeneration. A love-letter brings things together and so 'fills up your whole day and life always something to think about every moment and see it all around you like a new world' (*U* 758).

Sentence 5 (759-63): 'Mulveys was the first', begins the fifth sentence; the missing word is 'loveletter'. He was the first to send her one, and later to show her 'what kissing meant'. Paradoxically, he introduced her to the non-verbal reality she continues to associate with Gibraltar. (She has prepared for her return to it by burning old newspapers.) In Gibraltar the escape was from Mrs Rubio and her 'religion domineering' (*U* 759); in Dublin it would be from 'Kathleen Kearney and her lot of squealers . . . talking about politics' (*U* 762). Both prefer words over reality: Mrs Rubio would not hand Molly a hairpin 'staring her in the face' because she could not think of the Spanish word for it (*U* 759); Kearney and her friends like to call her names like 'soldiers daughter'. Molly has more than the usual amount of trouble with words in this sentence—'viaticum', 'stalactites', 'Blackwater River', Mulvey's first name, and the 'itsbeg' tongue-twister from her song all elude her—but with Mulvey 'everything was whatyoucallit'. It did not matter that he could not read the Spanish currency or that neither of them understood the Hebrew on the Jewish tombstones. The bottom, which started becoming important at the end of the previous sentence, is the cardinal point here, bottom in the sense of 'true at bottom', the reality underlying language. Kathleen Kearney and friends, for instance, know as much about politics as 'my backside' (*U* 762), which as we recall is notable for its absence of any expression. All names and labels are on the 'Miss This Miss That Miss Theother' level of male society, of lines of type in newspapers, in contrast to which the world of women is, as Stephen said of *amor matris,* the only true thing in life. By making

her a woman, Mulvey showed her the 'new world' and disentan-
gled it from the visions she had previously got only from books.
Literally, the two of them undressed, and what Molly remembers
most vividly is a moment of revelation, a sight of the world 'so
clear', as it once was 'ere oer the world the mists began' (*U* 762).
The sentence that begins with Mrs Rubio's word barriers culminates in mutual exposure committed 'in broad daylight too in the
sight of the whole world', 'the straits shining I could see over to
Morocco almost the bay of Tangier white and the Atlas mountain
with snow on it and the straits like a river so clear' (*U* 761, 762). The
mists part, and the comprehensive vision she has been groping for
is there, at the intersection of everything. Her cunt (a second
cardinal point of the sentence) is like the straits a channel joining
remote regions. When she thinks of the fabled cave from Gibraltar
to Morocco through which the 'monkeys go . . . when they die'
and then a few lines later of the banana taken 'out of a woman . . .
covered with limesalts', there is clearly a parallel at work: Bloom
and Gerty MacDowell have already compared newborn children to
monkeys, bananas are traditional monkey property, and
'limesalts' recalls the cave's stalactites and stalagmites, which are
made of limestone. The mating urge is really a desire to re-connect,
like the monkeys: 'theyre all mad to get in there where they come
out of' (*U* 760). Earlier, 'in a mist' she felt 'so old'; now, imaginatively taken 'near out of [her] skin' and clothes, she rejoins
her Gibraltar self and can say, 'Lord its just like yesterday to me'.
Having met Mulvey in May, she feels that she would like a 'new
fellow' every May (*U* 760). She did in fact meet Boylan then, and
the contrast between her two spring lovers recalls to what extent
things have in fact dwindled since Gibraltar. Her last memory of
Mulvey is of two people drifting apart and losing sight of one
another, looking at each other (a reprise of the contracting rondels
of 'Ithaca') through spyglasses. So back to Dublin, on the same
train that took her away:

> Frseeeeeeeeeeeeeeeeeeeefrong that train again weeping tone
> once in the dear deaead days beyond recall close my eyes breath
> my lips forward kiss sad look eyes open piano ere oer the world
> the mists began . . . (*U* 762).

Back in the old post-lapsarian haberdashery, she resolves to buy
some new clothes and work on her pronunciation, but her last

thoughts are of the loss of what she once had with Mulvey. 'I could have been a prima donna only I married him' (*U* 763). 'Prima donna' (she knows enough Italian to know this) means simply 'first woman', and Mulvey did make her feel like the first woman in the world, as she made him her first man. The Gibraltar journey which began with a baptism of sea and sun now ends next to a man with 'cold feet' in a flat without 'even a bath'.

Sentence 6 (763-70): Like the parallel sentence 2, sentence 6 returns to an unbearably claustrophobic Dublin. It seems that her first Byron, Mulvey, in effect set her up for her second, Bloom, who came along at just the right time to capitalise on what Mulvey had started, promising her another 'new world' of faraway places: 'telling me all the lovely places we could go for the honeymoon Venice by moonlight with the gondolas and the lake of Como he had a picture cut out of some paper . . .' (*U* 765). In fact, their one disastrous sea trip, which just for a moment reminded her of 'Catalan bay round the back of the rock' before they almost drowned, was enough to keep her planted where she is. By contrast with that memory of sea air, Dublin is full of the odours of things gone bad from being sealed up. The sentence begins with a fart which was probably caused by an overripe pork chop and ends with a discharge of stale blood. Arse and cunt, the cardinal points, are sealed-up chambers, microcosms of Dublin's locked cells, and pretty much indistinguishable in this most profane of Molly's sentences. Reminded of the reality of her home life and thus of her family, she concentrates her frustrated Gibraltar fantasies on the figure of Milly, always seen as a reincarnation of the youth she yearns to recapture: 'I'll cut all this hair off me . . . I might look like a young girl' (*U* 769). (An extreme reaction against fetishes, and of course another indication of the cardinal point.) As a mother, alas, she finds that she has to become an unwilling accomplice of the jailers; doubtless she represents to Milly what the old Gibraltar bishop 'that spoke off the altar his long preach about womans higher functions' represented to the young Molly. (Both object to girls on bicycles.) Milly's recent departure has been the latest in a series of sunderings, predicted by the plumpudding 'split in 2 halves' and other symbols of 'parting'. It signals Molly's apogee in her orbit away from Gibraltar.

Sentence 7 (770-76): 'Who knows', Molly begins, and the words set the tone for the sentence. She feels bewildered, lost in a prison of ridiculous old-man words like Dr Collins's 'omission'. Bloom is typical, for instance with his suggestion that she sing in French 'to be more classy' (*U* 771). It becomes clear now why the flowers he gave her for her birthday were poppies, and why she would not trust Dr Collins to give her chloroform (*U* 770). Trying to make some sense of this world, Molly begins by sweeping away all the man-made lies she knows, especially those of conventional religion—Buddhism, Judaism, Christianity, and Bloom's lottery scheme 'that was to be all our salvations' (*U* 772)—and turns to a private creed of superstition and nature worship. She interprets signs such as Milly's discharge, Bloom's pockets, cards and dreams. Her favourite word at this point is 'nature', as distinguished from male 'art'. She likes singing, for instance, with 'no art in it' (*U* 774). Men are artificers who refuse to make 'chambers a natural size so a woman could sit on it' (*U* 771). Their art may be defined as that which spoils nature, and the pinnacle of their achievement is a collection of abortions called 'Aristocrats Masterpiece'. In contrast is the natural creation of childbirth. Men become infants once again in this sentence (it is full of images of children), the cardinal points of which are, naturally, breasts and womb. Breasts also recall, as in sentence 3, woman-as-artist's-ideal. The two associations, motherhood and art, converge toward the end in the figure of Stephen, whom Molly's memory connects with Rudy, and whom she thinks of as a poet; he is also clearly a projected successor to the departed Milly. And there is one other office he can fill: when she says 'Im not too old for him' she is preparing for another return to Mulvey's Gibraltar. (If Mulvey is 'about 40' now, as she says, then during their courtship in 1886 he must have been 'about' Stephen's age of twenty-two.) Finally, he is yet another Byron. So the sentence which began with Dr Collins's big words about her insides ends with poetry, words with the regenerative powers which are otherwise the property of women: 'real beauty' (*U* 776) and rebirth:

> they all write about some woman in their poetry well I suppose he wont find many like me where softly sighs of love the light guitar where poetry is in the air the blue sea the moon shining so beautifully coming back on the nightboat from Tarifa the lighthouse at Europa point . . . (*U* 775).

Sentence 8 (776-83): Molly's last sentence is a wheel within a wheel, a circle which completes the larger circle of her monologue.

It begins with 'no' and ends with 'yes', moving from Dublin to Gibraltar to Dublin-Gibraltar and Bloom-Mulvey. Like love-letters and poetry it is mainly about connections, worked out with a fine sense of oxymoron ('so hard and at the same time so soft'), coinciding and interchanging contraries ('going to the other mad extreme'), paradoxical compounds ('a mixture of plum and apple'), and balance. The ideal is androgynous, both hard and soft. So Molly would like to be a man in order to appreciate a woman's body, and thinks approvingly that Bloom 'understood or felt what a woman is' (*U* 776, 782). The problem with most men is their provincialism: they 'dont know what it is to be a woman'. Sick of being 'always chained up', like Aristophanes in the *Symposium* she envisions a world coming back together: Bloom kissing her body and 'anything unnatural', including the halldoor, women needing to be 'embraced 20 times a day' (*U* 776). One reconciliation is between profane and sacred love, down and up. Even intercourse with Boylan is upward ('up to my neck nearly'), that is, toward the womb, which after all does have a neck. Profane love can serve the sacrament of rebirth: 'flowers all sorts of shapes and smells and colours springing up even out of the ditches' (*U* 782). All four cardinal points are in this final recapitulation, reconciled in the womb which generates new life, even from ditches. At first, in her enthusiasm for all connections and remembering the blissful wordlessness she enjoyed with Mulvey, Molly fantasises about the anonymous connection of prostitution, 'where nobodyd know me', but then bridles when that suggests the anonymous connection of murder, 'without a word'. In fact her final return to Gibraltar begins with a name: 'Dedalus I wonder its like those names in Gibraltar Delapaz Delagracia Santa Maria that gave me the rosary Rosales y OReilly' (*U* 779). 'Dedalus' is a compound, signalising, like 'Rosales y OReilly' and 'Valera', the fusion of Gibraltar and Dublin. With a name like that, Stephen the artist can join her in a ritual to re-evoke the peace and grace ('Delapaz Delagracia') of the past; together they will 'pretend we were in Spain'. (Stephen was searching for an epiphany this morning when he imagined the 'lost Armada' on the shores of Sandymount Strand; this is it.) Stephen is thought to be an expert in language, with the result that the 'preverbal' (*L* I, 170) Molly suddenly wants to be a student of (new) words. The enclosures of the earlier sentences are now, like the womb, homes, and she becomes, of all things, a conscientious homemaker who wants 'to do the place up' and get rid of the dust. Simply because he would make her home a worthwhile place to be, Stephen encompasses Byron and Rudy, the young Mulvey and the young Bloom, and turns Dublin into a picture of Gibraltar, bringing back the vision of her rose-youth ('I dont feel a day older'), and widening it to include Dublin. That is why she can decide to give Bloom 'one more chance'. She is a 'prima donna' once again, who like Eve would 'have to introduce myself not knowing me from Adam'. Adam's first job, to name the beasts and fowl, was both domestic and artistic; likewise Stephen and Molly would begin with the learning of words and names, moving from the unlettered universe discovered with Mulvey to the discrimination of particulars—not 'colours' but 'pink and blue and yellow', not 'plants' but 'jessamine and geraniums and cactuses'. As her ambition contracts to the realm of the domestic, her vision widens to the universal, the most important paradox in a concluding rhapsody that includes the traditional symbol for the fusion of water and fire in divine love, white rose married to red: 'shall I wear a white rose or shall I wear a red', 'the sea crimson sometimes like fire'.

'Penelope' is more than another chapter. It is a whole other story, for which *Ulysses* has prepared by blotting out and filing away the old one. The narrative remembers something almost completely new by first almost completely forgetting the old. It is as if the last rondel of 'Ithaca' had turned out to be a microscopic specimen which, when studied closely, reveals a 'new world'. If 'Penelope' bears certain anagogical resemblances to the old story—sailors, old men and young men, usurpers—it gives the effect not of filling it in or giving another angle on it, but rather of perhaps being the original from which it was derived, the book's closest approach to the untold story behind the whole endeavour, the confessional source promised in 'Scylla and Charybdis'. The next chapter examines in detail one dimension of that story.

7

In the Arms of Murphy

S. L. Goldberg notes the presence of what he calls 'a hidden character, the author himself' in the final chapters of *Ulysses,* although this character is 'not the real Joyce, of course'.[1] Actually, it is very close to the author's version of 'the real Joyce'. To Joyce, the one great event of his life was his meeting with Nora Barnacle. The story that unfolds during the last three chapters of *Ulysses* is hers, reshaped. In 'Eumaeus', the romantic attachments of Nora's Galway youth return to haunt Leopold Bloom. They are Michael Bodkin, whose death at the age of nineteen is memorialised in 'The Dead' and 'She Weeps Over Rahoon', and Willie Mulvey, the young Protestant left behind by Nora when she ran off to Dublin and her eventual meeting with Joyce. Of the two, the more important is Mulvey, who as the Mulvey of Molly's past has promised to reclaim his place:

> he said hed come back Lord its just like yesterday to me and if I was married hed do it to me and I promised him yes faithfully Id let him block me now flying perhaps hes dead or killed or a Captain or admiral its nearly 20 years if I said firtree cove he would if he came up behind me put his hands over my eyes to guess who I might recognize him (*U* 761).

Bearing some reminders of the dead Bodkin, Mulvey returns in *Ulysses* disguised as W. B. Murphy.

At first, Murphy seems to be nothing but a collage of clichés. In

135

an episode of murk and mystery, where 'sounds are impostures' and so are people, he is presented as the biggest imposture of all. His name signifies anonymity more than anything, being, as we learn in 'An Encounter' (*D* 28) the Irish equivalent of 'Smith', and his many tokens and tales seem to make him a kind of symbolic factotum. He claims, in Freudian fashion, to recall seeing someone named Simon Dedalus blast away a couple of eggs with a rifle; he recollects ports of call from all over the map; he carries around a symbolic knife, a revealing postcard and a provocative tattoo. Like Morpheus, with whom the narrator punningly identifies him (Joyce going so far as to supply his den with a hornhandled knife), he can evidently assume any form.

Most obviously, assuming the form of the returning sailor, he connects point by point with the Homeric story of the return to the swineherd's hut, but with one difference. The return told of in this episode is always an unhappy one: Enoch Arden, Rip Van Winkle, Alice Ben Bolt: 'And the coming back was the worst thing you ever did because it went without saying you would feel out of place' (*U* 651). And so the evidence suggests that Murphy will not get past the nearest prostitute or brothel. He deviates from his Homeric original as the homecoming theme deviates from the Homeric narrative.

In other words, Murphy is what Joyce calls him in the Linati outline—Ulysses Pseudoangelos. (He comes to us from the Black Sea, so he must have sailed past the site of Troy. His port in the Black Sea was 'Odessa'.) He is something of a Homer Pseudoangelos as well, having arrived this morning on a 'homing ship' (which makes him, of course, a 'homer')[2] with sails 'brailed' on the masts; he wears a blind man's glasses and spins a lot of fabulous stories. False Odysseus and false Homer, he may in some way be a symbol of aborted art. The 'meaning' assigned to the episode in the Linati outline is 'The Ambush at Home', and Richard Ellmann has argued that the ambusher is Murphy, intercepting the narrative of *Ulysses* with his own bogus version:

> With falsimilitude Murphy would ambush the verisimilitude that is claimed in *Ulysses,* and turn Aristotle's imitation of nature into mere fakery . . . If he could, he would deny the significance of this sixteenth episode . . . by exhibiting on his chest the tattooed number 16 in token of homosexuality. (This numerical sym-

bolism was, as Gilbert points out, well known on the Continent.)[3]

Ellmann is surely right that Murphy is the one who lies in ambush—there is no other candidate in sight—but his theory of what Murphy is ambushing and how he is doing it shows a good deal of straining. In what way does the introduction of a liar into a literary work ambush its verisimilitude? (Especially with Homer's heroic liar in the background.) As for the number 16, aside from Ellmann's source, Stuart Gilbert, there is no evidence to my knowledge that it represents homosexuality, and Gilbert's source is another author's reference to some traveller's recollection of a story told him by a Neapolitan prostitute.[4]

I do not think that Murphy, who after all seems at least interested in the whore of the lane, is homosexual or insinuating that anyone else is. He is, instead, an aging heterosexual whose presence constitutes a threat of ambush, not to literature or truth, but to Leopold Bloom. Odysseus returning to Penelope, Bloom is the one in danger of ambush, and Murphy is the one he should fear. As a compulsive liar who hates blacks and has a postcard from 'Santiago', Murphy fulfills in some ways Stephen's picture of the 'hornmad Iago', out to scuttle Bloom's Othello. As a sailor type he is an abandoner of women. The woman in this port is the Molly left on Gibraltar by Mulvey and, behind her, the Nora whose last vivid memory of home centered on Willie Mulvey, the successor to Michael Bodkin.

The first reason for suspecting Murphy's identity is his name, or rather his two names, since he also carries around a postcard addressed to 'A. Boudin'.

Mulvey-Bodkin/Murphy-Boudin is a double homonymity which seems too striking for coincidence, especially in an episode so concerned with name changes, for instance from 'Ledwidge' to 'Ludwig'. Aside from the postcard, Murphy also brandishes a knife—a bodkin, (see page 149 below). Joyce may have changed 'Bodkin' to 'Boudin' to suggest an exotic or desperate background, since the marching song of the French Foreign Legion is called 'Le Boudin', named for the 'boudin' or black pudding. The phonetic change from Mulvey to Murphy would have been sanctioned, and perhaps suggested, by two precedents which Joyce later exploited in *Finnegans Wake:* the L/R interchange, 'an extremely frequent form of alternation in Irish words', and the l—r exchanges characteristic of the 'little language' in Swift's *Journal to Stella*.[5] That change made, the replacement of 'v' with the phonetically related 'f' sound comes almost automatically. It is possible as well that the change was suggested by p. 321 of John O'Hart's *Irish Pedigrees* (1881 edition), where the stems of the two families are listed one after the other. There is no record that Joyce consulted O'Hart, but he was interested in pedigrees, and O'Hart would have been the source most readily available.

There are other puzzling things about Murphy. He claims that one of his two favorite books is Mrs Rhoda Broughton's *Red as a Rose is She* (*U* 659), a sappy piece of drawingroom fantasy which no ablebodied seaman would ordinarily be caught death with, but which, as a book about a rose-woman by a woman whose first name means 'rose', should remind us of Molly, Bloom's rose of Castille, whose skin became 'like a rose' under the Gibraltar sun, who wore a red rose for Mulvey, who later lay among the rhododendrons—'rose trees'—of Howth, thinking of roses, and who was born in 1870, the year the novel was published.[6] Its plot reflects poignantly on the Mulvey story: the heroine abandons her fiancé, a lieutenant in the navy, when she meets a better catch, and her old lover expires in foreign lands with her image still in his heart; the book concludes with a memory of his pathetic death. (In *Finnegans Wake*, this and another of Mrs Broughton's books, *Cometh Up as a Flower*, appear in the company of Issy and ALP, respectively.) Murphy's ship is the 'Rosevean'.

On two occasions in particular, Murphy—or his creator—seems determined to puzzle us, to let us know that something is there but not let us know what it is. In both instances, questions are raised and then dodged. The first is about Gibraltar:—'Have you seen the Rock of Gibraltar? Mr Bloom inquired. The sailor grimaced, chewing, in a way that might be read as yes, ay, or no' (*U* 629). The answer, Joyce's notes to the episode indicate,[7] should be yes; he was there 'nearly 20' years ago. Although Joyce doesn't allow Murphy to directly acknowledge any connection with Gibraltar, the episode does contain what seems like an indirect link—Murphy's fond memory of Captain Dalton, 'the best bloody man that ever scuttled a ship' (*U* 625). 'Captain Dalton' is the name invented by Arthur Conan Doyle for the captain of the *Dei Gratia*, the ship which in December 1872 discovered the famous derelict

Mary Celeste and brought it into Gibraltar. He was publicly accused by the Gibraltar attorney-general of having scuttled the crew.[8]

The second question is about the most challenging puzzle of the episode, Murphy's tattoo, 'an image tattooed in blue Chinese ink, intended to represent an anchor', above which is a 'full view of the figure 16 and a young man's sideface looking frowningly rather' (*U* 631). 'And what's the number for?' asks one of the resident loafers, to which the answer is only 'some sort of half smile, for a brief duration only, in the direction of the questioner about the number' (*U* 632). Most obviously, the tattoo is an emblem of *Ulysses,* the story of a mariner meeting a frowning young man sixteen years his junior.[9] But the number is singled out for special attention, and should be considered with special care. What is that 'sort of half smile' all about?

Like the grimace in response to the question about Gibraltar, the half smile in response to the question about '16' is dodging a connection with Molly and, behind her, Nora. Because '16' is a symbol of Nora. As everyone knows, 16 June is her day, the day, according to Joyce, that she began the arduous business of making him a man. Her number has been made an element of the architecture of *Ulysses*. Molly and Bloom have been together sixteen years, and Bloom is sixteen years older than Stephen—an arithmetical way of saying that Bloom's maturity exceeds Stephen's by the factor of his relationship with Molly, or, on another level, that the mature Joyce surpasses his younger self because of Nora. In *Ulysses,* the number is linked unobtrusively but repeatedly with Molly. In the cabman's shelter, for instance, Bloom enjoys showing around a picture of Molly 'when her years numbered barely sweet sixteen', her age when they met. In two cases, Joyce goes especially out of his way to associate her with the number. The blind which projects her 'luminous sign' in 'Ithaca' is said to originate from an establishment at '16 Aungier street' (*U* 702),[10] and the Claddagh ring (named after the old Spanish quarter of Galway) given her by Mulvey is remembered as being 'pure 16 carat gold' (*U* 762), even though there is no such weight for gold jewellery, and 'pure gold' is twenty-four karats. The Claddagh ring, as Joyce almost certainly knew, was according to legend originally devised by one of the Galway Joyces and inscribed with the mark of an anchor.[11]

So far I have been discussing the clues to Murphy's identity, as if Joyce had supplied nothing but. But of course Murphy has been disguised, in two ways in particular. First, his hair apparently is, or once was, the wrong colour. Though grey and balding, he is introduced as 'redbearded' (*U* 622) whereas Molly's Mulvey was blond. On the other hand, there is evidence that suggests that Nora's Mulvey, anyway, was red-haired, and at the least it seems clear that Joyce thought of the people of Nora's region as typically red-headed. His essay 'The City of the Tribes' reveals his impression that 'a Titian red predominates' among Galway's natives (*CW* 229). When, in a letter to Nora, he dismisses her former lovers as 'red-headed louts in the county Galway', he seems to have Willie Mulvey in mind.[12] Johnny MacDougal of *Finnegans Wake*, who represents the west and comes from the same Galway district as did both Bodkin and Mulvey,[13] is described as having 'ruddy' hair (*FW* 368.42). (In an early draft of *Finnegans Wake* MacDougal appears in one of his incarnations as 'MacMurphy'—*JJA* 6, 27.) Bloom himself has some generic notion of 'red-headed curates from the county Leitrim' (*U* 58), Leitrim being the county from which virtually all Mulveys come. So Murphy's red beard, which seems to distinguish him from Molly's Mulvey, may be Joyce's private signature of his connection with Nora's.

Second, the 'ancient mariner' Murphy seems too old to be lieutenant Mulvey, who was a young man eighteen years ago and is now, Molly guesses, 'about 40' (*U* 761). But we do not know how old Murphy actually is, and Frank Budgen, after whom Joyce modelled some of Murphy's features, was himself 'about forty' at the time. If Murphy seems to be an old man, so does everyone else in this 'antediluvian' episode of memories, fossils and fatigue. In fact his role as Ulysses Pseudoangelos requires him to look older then he is, since, as Stuart Gilbert explains, 'Ulysses Pseudoangelos' is Joyce's name for Odysseus after he has been disguised as an old beggar by Athena. Seeing the disguised Odysseus, Penelope comments, 'They [Odysseus and the beggar] are of an age, and now Odysseus' / feet and hands would be enseamed like his. / Men grow old soon in hardship.'

In fact, the number on Murphy's chest, along with its other significations, may also point to the change which has turned one kind of Odysseus into the other—romantic seaborn rover into false messenger and unwanted would-be usurper. Joyce was familiar with numerology, and all of the numerology texts which I have seen relate '16' to the sixteenth card of the Tarot's major arcana, a card which depicts two human figures falling from a lightning-struck tower. In general, it stands for the approach of some cataclysmic event—divorce, separation, ruin. If Murphy is an ambusher, bringing displacement or death, the number is right for him. In any case, I find it interesting that the day before Mulvey left Gilbraltar Molly pointed out to him 'OHaras tower I told him it was struck by lightning' (*U* 760). She fancies herself a prophet, and here she is, the tower an omen of departure (Mulvey left) and ruin (Murphy is a wreck), the '16' on Murphy's chest a token of both what he left and what he became.

Because in effect there are two Mulveys, as there are two Odysseuses—the Mulvey who returns in Molly's final rhapsody and who will always be associated with romance, roses, and youth, and the Murphy of the cabman's shelter, a sorry old sot for whom Gibraltar is a place he would prefer to forget. As Bloom under-stands, the first will always be before him in Molly's heart. But the second has been displaced: Bloom is going home to Molly, and he isn't. The usurpation or ambush taking place is in fact, like Murphy himself, 'equivocal' (*U* 658). Who is ambushing whom? Words like 'usurp' and 'ambush' are relative. Men in relation to women are, like Mulvey, lieutenants—place-fillers (Gardner, Molly's other previous lover, was also a lieutenant)—succeeding one another in the set role. When Bloom and Murphy stare at one another, either in a way would be justified in viewing the other as an ambusher, and the conflict cannot be resolved until Molly fuses them together on the last page. They meet in 'Eumaeus' as replicas of one another in a 'double image' 'two impostors' (*BM* 407,396) with equally dubious claims to sole possession. Joyce records in his notes: 'there are two sinbads (UL-Psagg-LB-WBM): wandering jew, he returns after each voyage, always recovers 7th goods lost in 6th'— *S* 153 (so Murphy's other favorite book, *The Arabian Nights Entertainment*). We can view these successive Sinbads as usurpers knocking one another off, or just as one another's lieutenant, each ambush a simple changing of the guard; in which case the mariner Murphy stands in relation to the symbolic mariner Bloom not as usurper to usurped, but as forerunner to follower, pilot to homing ship.

As in others of Joyce's writings, the first reading tends to recede into the second. Joyce's notes indicate with precision the nature of the 'equivocal' relationship between the usurpers. A passage in one of the *Ulysses* notesheets reads: 'Pilot boats, anchor painted on sail (white . . . P. Blue flag up on white').[14] The anchor and the blue-and-white colours are, of course, represented in the tattoo; so perhaps is 'P', an international signal of pilot boats, since it is the sixteenth letter of the alphabet. It seems that on some level Murphy functions as a pilot, and my own belief is that the level is a very literal one—that he leads Bloom, or would if Bloom would just follow him, directly to Molly as soon as he spots her. He spots her as the whore of the lane who makes her first appearance at the end of 'Sirens':

> A frowsy whore with black straw sailor hat askew came glazily in the day along the quay towards Mr Bloom. When first he saw that form endearing. Yes, it is. I feel so lonely. Wet night in the lane. Horn. Who had the? Heehaw. Shesaw. Off her beat here. What is she? Hope she. Psst! Any chance of your wash. Knew Molly. Had me decked. Stout lady does be with you in the brown costume. Put you off your stroke. That appointment we made. Knowing that we'd never, well hardly ever. Too dear too near to home sweet home. Sees me, does she? Looks a fright in the day. Face like dip. Damn her! O, well, she has to live like all the rest. Look in here (*U* 290).

The black straw hat, which in 'Ithaca' is sitting on the commode next to Molly's bed (*U* 730)—where Bloom did not notice it this morning, perhaps because it wasn't there then—repeats with a depressing difference the new 'white ricestraw hat' (*U* 760) that Molly bought to wear for her sailor boyfriend on their last day together. 'When first he saw that form endearing' is a motif connected, for Bloom, with his first vision of Molly and, from its place in *Martha,* with a vision of a lover disguised below her station. 'Horn' evokes his cuckolding by Blazes. That Bloom does not recognise the whore as Molly simply exemplifies a common feature of the technique of 'Sirens': people's appearances can be changed radically by influences such as sun and shadow. The whore's speech features the provincial 'does be' construction which, there is reason to believe, Joyce identified with the provincial Nora (see, for example, *FW* 620.12). She appears here as a whore because she has just recently given her self to Blazes Boylan and thus, according to the relentless relativism governing 'Sirens', has lost her value to him and to men in general. (Even Bloom, according to Molly, was 'trying to make a whore of me'—*U* 740.) 'Course everything is dear if you don't want it,' thinks Bloom as she passes by, and he pretends to concentrate on the blowsy melodeon which is yet another (cf. her melody, her melons) emblem of Molly. Molly is walking 'glazily in the day along the quay' because she is sleepwalking, like Amina in Bellini's *La Sonnambula*. If one follows carefully the sequence of *double entendres* from p. 282 to 289 ordered to correspond to Blazes' arrival at 7 Eccles Street and his lovemaking with Molly, it becomes apparent that just before the whore's appearance Molly has dropped off to sleep: 'Sleep! All is lost now.' Bloom has shortly before compared the innocent Amina, falsely accused by her fiancé when she sleepwalks into another man's bedroom, to the genuinely adulterous Molly—a poignant case of wishful thinking. Molly has been enabled, like Gerty later, to leave her body by sexual *ek-stasis,* and she has been transported telekinetically from 7 Eccles Street by virtue of the same authorial dispensation that has peopled *Ulysses* with ambulatory apparitions. 'Too dear too near to home sweet home': Bloom doesn't know the half of it.

When the whore returns in 'Eumaeus', wearing the old straw hat, she takes a look at the tattoo and vanishes:

Round the side of the *Evening Telegraph* he just caught a fleeting glimpse of her face round the side of the door with a kind of demented glassy grin showing that she was not exactly all there, viewing with evident amusement the group of gazers round Skipper Murphy's nautical chest and then there was no more of her (*U* 632).

Consider the language: 'a fleeting glimpse'; 'not exactly all there'; a 'glassy grin'; 'and then there was no more of her'. This is an apparition being described, and in fact 'apparition' is what Joyce first called her.[15] When Murphy goes after her, she has 'disappeared to all intents and purposes' (*U* 638). The fact that she is glimpsed in juxtaposition with the *Evening Telegraph* is a clue of sorts (Joyce has a funny notion of clues) which becomes comprehensible if we follow Joyce's chain of associations down the following list:

> telegraph
> telephone
> wireless
> thought transference
> hypnotise
> somnolent
> safe in the arms of Murphy (*JJA* 2, 36).

Three kinds of telecommunication leading to a fourth, telepathy, supposed by psychics to occur during a trance ('hypnotise'); 'hypnotise' leads to 'somnolent' in a shift from the Greek for 'sleep' to the Latin, and to the Murphy-Morpheus pun because Hypnos, god of sleep, is the father of Morpheus (see *U* 692 for Bloom's association of somnambulism with hypnotism, *U* 284 for his association of hypnotism with Molly). The glassy-eyed whore of the lane is the somnolent, somnambulent, telepathic, telegraphic projection of Molly's reverie: 'I was thinking would I go around by the quays there some dark evening where nobodyd know me and pick up a sailor off the sea' (*U* 777). She was not so much 'thinking' as day-dreaming, and when she dozed off her daydreams turned to dreams which transported her, through the dreamscape of the 'Nostos', in the arms of Morpheus towards the arms of Murphy. She is in the tradition of the Joyce female characters whose fantasies are realised in somnambulism, telepathy, telekinesis, or a combination: Polly Mooney, who drifts into a trance-like reverie in 'The Boarding House' (*D* 68) and who in *Ulysses* is a 'little sleepwalking bitch' (*U* 303); Gerty MacDowell, whose fantasies are enacted telekinetically; Milly Bloom, the 'somnambulist' (*U* 695); and Issy, who 'will dream telepath posts dulcets . . . and 'twill carry on my hearz waves my still waters reflections in words . . . to thee, Jack, ahoy, beyond the boysforus' (*FW* 460.19-27; see also 527.4-8). (Issy is sending a message to her sailor-lover, like Murphy from beyond the Bosphorous, with 'thought transference' which is also 'wireless' communication.) Molly was dreaming of sailors, of course, because her first lover was a sailor. Wearing a reminder of her old Gibraltar hat, her image finds the image it seeks, there is a recognition scene centering, in traditional fashion, on a tattoo, and her old lover comes out to meet her. What she in fact encounters explains her about-face: 'I suppose the half of those sailors are rotten again with disease—' (*U* 778). She vanishes from the quays, Murphy takes a breath of air and drink of rum—and he may feel that he needs it, what with apparitions appearing and disappearing before his eyes—and Bloom, who has not followed the pilot to his goal, goes on to make the journey safely on his own. (In *Finnegans Wake,* HCE in his role of young lover, sends a raven 'as my sure piloter'—*FW* 539.35-6—to his beloved.) This and similar episodes in Joyce's work were no doubt suggested first by an early letter from Nora: 'It seems to me that I am always in your company under every possible variety of circumstances talking to you walking with you meeting you suddenly in different places until I am beginning to wonder if my spirit takes leave of my body in sleep and goes to seek you, and what is more find you or perhaps this is nothing but a fantasy' (*L* II, 47). In this particular scene, there is also a precedent in the corresponding episode of the *Odyssey* (see XX, 91-4).

The apparitional presences of the cabman's shelter have forecast the 'equivocal' nature of Bloom's return home, and the extent to which it will be qualified by another return. 'Returning not the same' (*U* 377), Bloom has earlier mused, his thoughts embracing both his youthful infatuation with Molly and Molly's with Mulvey, and one major reason for the rich, borderless ambiguity of the conclusion of *Ulysses* is that it brings this doubleness much closer to the surface. The Penelope of *Ulysses* has another Odysseus besides Bloom—the sailor who gave her the Galway equivalent of an engagement ring and, promising to return, sailed off 'nearly 20 years' ago. His twenty years—Odysseus' time of absence—is about up now, and true to promise and type he has arrived, on a 'homing' ship full of bricks, as Odysseus comes home on an unpiloted, self-steering ship that is later turned to stone, to intercept and be intercepted by the second Odysseus.

Throughout *Ulysses*—it is a major reason for his abnegation—Bloom knows that his real rival for Molly is not Boylan, but her 'first':

First kiss does the trick. The propitious moment. Something inside them goes pop. Mushy like, tell by their eye, on the sly.

First thoughts are best. Remember that till their dying day.
Molly, lieutenant Mulvey that kissed her under the Moorish wall
beside the gardens (*U* 371).

Later, Molly's words confirm his: 'its only the first time after that
its just the ordinary do it and think no more about it' (*U* 740).
Standing on the beach while his wife may still be in bed with
Boylan, Bloom thinks less about him than about Mulvey and his
possible return:

Then I did Rip van Winkle coming back. She leaned on the
sideboard watching. Moorish eyes. Twenty years asleep in
Sleepy Hollow. All changed. Forgotten. The young are old. His
gun rusty from the dew (*U* 377).

Rip van Winkle here is both Bloom himself, trying to recapture the
moment on Howth, and Mulvey ('Twenty years' and 'Moorish' are
Mulvey cues) imagined returning after 'nearly 20' years. In
'Eumaeus', looking at Murphy leads Bloom into sympathetically
imagining stories of long-gone sailors returned from the sea peering
through windows into homes where they no longer belong; here,
imagining the same thing, often in the same images, 'rusty' gun, for
instance anticipating 'rustbearded' Murphy, he is thinking of
Mulvey. His musings about the returns of migratory birds, bees,
bats, sailors and lovers all trace back to an imagined return of
Molly's long-lost lover-sailor, as shown most clearly in his last
reverie: '*senorita* young eyes Mulvey plump bubs me breadvan
Winkle red slippers she rusty sleep wander years dreams return tail
end . . .' (*U* 482).[16]
  The idea is present to him throughout his day. It asserts itself
boldly in Molly's literary query in 'Calypso': 'Is she in love with
the first fellow all the time?' (*U* 64). It is working on Bloom when,
subconsciously recalling that Mulvey's letter to Molly was signed
'an admirer' (*U* 759), he makes his embarrassing substitution of
'wife's admirers' for 'wife's advisers' (*U* 313). Likewise, it is
probably working on Molly when she throws a coin to the sailor
outside her window. Philip Herring cites evidence from Joyce's
notesheets that Joyce had originally intended to cast this sailor as a
type of Lord Nelson, Molly as Lady Hamilton, and Bloom as the
displaced Lord Hamilton.[17] Francis Bulhof thinks that 'the one-

legged sailor . . . is probably identical with the sailor named Murphy.'[18] The two are so alike that the hypothesis is attractive, and both do sing 'The Death of Nelson'. But of course Murphy has two legs and the other has only one, although Joyce's notes show that he was originally just 'lame'. Murphy may or may not be lame: when he finally gets up his 'dumpy sort of gait' is inconclusive. It seems most likely that Joyce originally meant to cast the sailor of 'Wandering Rocks' as the returning Mulvey, using the Nelson-Hamilton paradigm, but decided that he wanted a separate character in 'Eumaeus' and added the one-legged detail to distinguish them.

Probably most revealing is Bloom's image of Molly in bed: 'Blackened court cards laid along her thigh by sevens. Dark lady and fair man' (*U* 75). For years, like most readers, I assumed that this passage and the later 'M.B. loves a fair gentleman' (*U* 333) must refer to Molly's assignation with Boylan. But Molly does not love Boylan, and he is not 'fair'. He is remembered, in fact, as having 'Brown brilliantined hair' (*U* 68). The return of the blond Mulvey and not Boylan's petty triumph is what has been foretold. It was foretold as well eighteen years ago by the books Molly happened to read—*Henry Dunbar, Molly Bawn, Moll Flanders, East Lynne, The Shadow of Ashlydat, The Moonstone* and *Eugene Aram* (*U* 756)—all of them on the theme of lovers, returns, and the return of lovers. Of special interest is the novel *Henry Dunbar*, since Molly made a point of lending it to Bloom with Mulvey's picture inserted between the pages (*U* 756). The story is about a man who returns home after many years in India (Molly's Mulvey was heading for India) and is ambushed and murdered by a usurper who assumes his name. The story is evidently working on Bloom when he thinks of Molly's past and recognises the extent to which he is Mulvey's usurper, and when he looks at Murphy and thinks about the Tichbourne case, Enoch Arden and other analogous tales of usurpation, ambush, fraud, mistaken identity and aborted homecomings. Although 'Sceptre' Boylan is defeated easily enough in the contest for Molly's heart, as 'Throwaway' Bloom must share his victory with Mulvey, a castaway himself—history repeating itself—Milly's doll, 'a boy, a sailor she cast away' (*U* 693).

History is repeating itself yet again with Milly; she has put aside her sailor doll and, having reached the age at which Molly met

Mulvey, is beginning a romance with a young man, evidently soon to sail away from her 'for the wars' (*U* 401). So Milly, the 'Same thing watered down' (*U* 89), in some ways seems to re-enact Molly's story—and so, in other ways, does another important *Ulysses* woman, Gerty MacDowell. Gerty has a roving lover who has recently left her life; like Nora's Mulvey he is Protestant, and his name, Reginald Wylie, could without too much fiddling have been derived from 'Willie Mulvey'. The Mulveys come from exactly the same place as the Reynolds family and may be an offshoot, and Reginald, as Joyce seems to have known, is a variant of Reynolds.[19] Willie Mulvey—Willie Reynolds—Willie Reginald—Reginald Wylie: The connection, at least as tractable as Stephen's name games in 'Eumaeus', accounts for an otherwise inexplicable pairing in one of Joyce's notesheets: 'MB & RW no nerves bad' (*BM* 490). 'RW'—there is no other candidate—is Reginald Wylie, 'MB' is always Molly Bloom, and 'nerves' is a cue for Bloom's thoughts about the returns of sailors, who need nerve to make their voyages (*U* 378). Unrelated in the narrative, Molly Bloom and Reginald Wylie can come together if we trace them back to their origins—Molly as Nora, the Protestant Wylie as the Protestant Mulvey, united in the Spanish-Irish city of Galway (see *CW* 229 for Joyce's Spanish vision of Galway) as Molly and Mulvey, their love sealed with a Claddagh ring from Galway, are united in the Spanish-English city of Gibraltar.

So the pattern multiplies and divides throughout *Ulysses:* Gerty thinking of Reginald Wylie while looking at Bloom, Milly re-enacting her mother's story in Mullingar, Molly reconciling herself to Bloom by conflating him with the Mulvey whose later incarnation she would not recognise or desire, Bloom seeking reincarnations of the one time on Howth through projections on Gerty ('Made me feel so young'—*U* 382), Milly, and, of course, Martha Clifford.[20] For Bloom the lesson—the Murphy lesson—is always the same, of 'An unsatisfactory equation between an exodus and return in time through reversible space and an exodus and return in space through irreversible time' (*U* 728). The lesson, simply, is that we all become Murphys sooner or later, as when Bloom, becoming Rip van Winkle, is forced to see that his dreaming return to his courtship with Molly is actually a peek at Milly and her boy friend, and that his memory has become a ghost of events: 'O Papli, how old you've grown!' (*U* 542). Like Adam in a sadder garden, he wakes from his nightmare to find it true—he really *is* Rip van Winkle—and feels the way that Murphy would if he knew the facts. He discovers the inevitability of displacement, the way that time can make people unwanted usurpers on their own past selves, and turn their loves and loyalties into weapons against them. Starting from an awareness that, all signs indicate, came to him most forcibly through his experience with Nora and knowledge of his supposed rivals, Joyce explores again and again, through *Ulysses,* the evidently inevitable connection between place and displacement, doubling lovers and interchanging usurpers as he almost obsessively reverts to the Murphy story and its attendant images.

The Murphy story first seems to have taken command of Joyce's imagination, as he approached and entered his twenty-fifth year, during his brief stay in Rome. There he conceived *Ulysses* and most likely 'The Dead'. Two years later he made his pilgrimage to the Galway scenes of Nora's youth that he had memorialised at the end of 'The Dead' and wrote her the famous letters which can still startle by the intensity of their desire and jealousy: 'I am tortured by memories'; 'I am so jealous of the past' (*L* II, 232, 281). The catalyst for this extraordinary correspondence was Vincent Cosgrave's false boast that he had been Joyce's secret rival with Nora during the weeks following Bloomsday. The lie was exposed, but not before it upset Joyce profoundly. Over ten years later, while composing the penultimate episode of *Ulysses,* he was to remember the incident and its effects in a typical fashion: the time from the Blooms's marriage until their last act of 'complete carnal intercourse', as tabulated in 'Ithaca', is just one day less than the time from 16 June 1904 until the incident with Cosgrave.[21]

Whatever else this may mean, it certainly suggests that the Cosgrave incident remained for Joyce a turning-point in his life with Nora, a wound (to use the language of Richard Rowan) of his romantic notions of sacramental exclusiveness which was never to heal, and to which, like Stephen's version of Shakespeare, he was constantly returning. Four years later, about to begin serious work on *Ulysses,* he wrote down a series of associations centred on Nora which, while evidently trying to almost telepathically evoke her early life, unite the themes of 'The Dead' and *Ulysses.* For instance: 'Dagger: heart, death, soldier, war, band, judgment, king' (*E* 118). The words connect with Michael Bodkin, translated into 'dagger', with his fictional counterpart Michael Furey who died, perhaps of a broken heart, and who returns like the soldier-saint Michael to pass judgment on a man part of whose name means 'king', and with Molly's boyfriend Lieutenant Gardner, who met death in the Boer war while fighting as a soldier for his king, carrying Molly's Claddagh band, with its figures of a heart and a king's crown. Like much of *Ulysses*, 'The Dead' is about a long-lost lover, and behind both is the same essential story, Nora's. Predictably, the two have much, both great and small, in common. Lieutenant Mulvey's home town of Cappoquin (*U* 759), for instance, is in one version of the song the site of the fatal events of 'The Lass of Aughrim', which reminds Gretta Conroy of Michael Furey and reminded Joyce of Nora in Galway.[22] (In 'The Dead', the song's theme is adumbrated by the table talk of Mt Melleray monastery, which is located just outside Cappoquin.) The two works seem to share a common attitude toward their subject. When Bloom, standing on the beach, tells himself that Mulvey will always be the 'first' in Molly's affections, he is simply revealing the knowledge that comes to Gabriel in the Gresham Hotel. (Like Gabriel, he learned of it in the small hours following a memorable party, the Glencree dinner.) And the two have similar visions. Gabriel, re-enacting the moment in 'The Lass of Aughrim' when Lord Gregory dreams that his dying lover has come to his door,[23] senses the ghost of Michael Furey; Bloom, remembering a Gaiety performance of the past, senses the 'phantom ship' (*U* 376) of the Flying Dutchman Vanderdecken (projected by rays of waning sunlight on a cloud, in an effect which probably recalls the magic lantern illusion typically used in stage productions of the story), returning like the Flying Dutchman Murphy (see *U* 636 for the equation) to usurp the place of the faithful landlubber Eric. (Like the returning Vanderdecken, Murphy has been gone from home for seven years.) Bloom's equation of Mulvey with Vanderdecken and of himself with the displaced Eric explains the otherwise unaccountable hostility he reveals in 'Circe' toward 'These flying Dutchmen or lying Dutchmen' (*U* 479). It also helps explain Molly's peculiar recollection of Mulvey 'now flying' (*U* 761). (Note, incidentally, that the Freudian slip of 'rover' for 'over', which Bloom makes at the end of his tirade on p. 429, applies to Murphy, previously a sailor on the *Rover* and 'himself a rover' (*U* 630)—and see also p. 153 below. It is clear that Bloom's 'Flying Dutchman' speech is mainly concerned with sexual usurpation.) In 'Exiles', the theme recurs with a twist: Bertha returns from over the sea in the company of Richard, and Robert Hand, the would-be usurper, must convince her to stay put. The irony of his position is underscored when, like Nora's young lover and Gretta's, he waits secretly in a dark garden in the rain, but has nothing more romantic to show for it than wet clothes. The opposite irony of Richard's position, that he must be both husband and free spirit, Eric and Flying Dutchman, is brought home in Bertha's closing words to him: 'O, my strange wild lover, come back to me again!'

In all these works, Nora's two Galway lovers have been fused into one character. Murphy is both Murphy and Boudin, Mulvey and Bodkin; Michael Furey stands under the apple tree like Mulvey and dies like Bodkin;[24] Robert Hand like Bodkin embalms a dead love and, like Mulvey, continues to stand at the window. In a way familiar to all readers of Joyce, a collection of private associations has been made into an archetype which seems at different times to have its source in either autobiography or myth.

In *Ulysses* the myth most in control, behind even the *Odyssey* and *The Flying Dutchman,* seems to be Ibsen's *The Lady from the Sea,* which Joyce certainly knew well, and which tells the story of a red-bearded former sailor arriving on an English boat to reclaim his love pact, sealed with a ring, to a woman now married. As in *Ulysses* the returning lover is disguised by his new-grown beard and greater age, but bears a token of recognition on his chest, a breast-pin with a bluish-white pearl. Like Mulvey he was considered possibly drowned; like Murphy he is suspected of having done in one of his mates, and is finally rejected.[25] In *Finnegans Wake* the myth most in control is certainly *Tristan and Isolde,* which in the Joseph Bédier version Joyce used is full of stories of Tristan, disguised as leper or beggar, returning to lure his first love from the side of her legal husband. One of these 'rearrivals' is the subject of the first complete sentence's first clause—in which Joyce takes pains to sound the Murphyean 'rover' (*FW* 3.4)—and remains at the heart of the book thereafter. Again, the female's former lovers are frequently Murphys, particularly in the famous 'Anna Livia Plurabelle' chapter. There, though the two gossiping washerwomen disagree over the identity of ALP's first lover, a Murphy is behind both main candidates. The first, 'a dynast of Leinster, a wolf of the sea' (*FW* 202.24), has been traced by Brendan O Hehir to the historical figure Diarmaid MacMurchadha, whose last name is the Gaelic original of Murphy.[26] (A toothless wolf of the sea,

W. B. Murphy is called an 'old seadog'.) MacMurchadha is still remembered in Ireland as an odious invader and wife-stealer, as we find in *Ulysses* (*U* 324) when Bloom is implicitly compared to the man whose wife he stole. The second candidate for ALP's first lover, the reverend Michael Arklow (*FW* 203.19), has been identified by Edward Kopper, Jr as 'undoubtedly Father Michael Murphy, the Irish patriot', called 'Arklow' because of his role in the 1798 siege of Arklow and because of the monument to him there.[27] (Joyce's 'Eumaeus' notes indicate that he originally intended to have Murphy hail from the same town—*BM* 412.) As a lecherous priest he is in the tradition of Stephen's fancied rival Father Moran.[28] Joyce seems to have been genuinely jealous of priests, a feeling probably exacerbated by Nora's fond memory of Michael Bodkin, who died in the church, and in general the strong piety of her 'roomyo connelic relation' (*FW* 326.3)—particularly Mrs Barnacle, who forced the break-up of Nora's courtship with the Protestant Mulvey.[29] All this perhaps explains why Gretta's lover in 'The Dead' should verge on apotheosis as St Michael, avenger of the Church Militant. From *FW* 444.6 to 446.26, Shaun, lecturing Issy on her immodesty, becomes, certainly, Nora's sadistic uncle Tom Healy, beating Nora for deceitfully 'Cutting chapel' to go walking with Willie Mulvey,[30] probably as well Mrs Barnacle laying down the law against Protestants, and I think as well the dead Michael Bodkin, accepted by the family because of his faith, promising to return as a papal 'nuncio' and displace his replacement, sending messages from heaven via a 'pretty arched godkin of beddingknight'. The rival, again, is a sea wolf, leaving 'corsehairs' on Issy's frock.

As in *Ulysses*, in *Finnegans Wake* the story of the mother's courtship is repeated in the next generation, divided between Mulvey-type and Bodkin-type, wild excommunicant rover and angelic wraith. When Shem and Shaun compete for Issy, they divide into the roles established in the previous chapter by the two Murphys, wolf and monk. (That they are both Murphys explains why they reduce into a 'mariamyriameliamurphies' (*FW* 293.10-11) while shifting sides in the book's formal centre.) Shem is the exiled 'Warewolff' (*FW* 225.8) to whom the mother, a 'mate of the Sheawolfing class' (*FW* 49.33) is most attracted; Shaun is the repressed Father Michael. In the children's games chapter, the earlier conflict between sea-wolf Murphy and Arklow Murphy is re-enacted as the two fight over Issy: 'If Arck could no more salve his agnols from the wiles of willy wooly woolf!' (*FW* 223.2-3). (Issy is the lamb.) Shaun-Michael is the one on the side of the agnols, like his father trying to keep ALP home and off the sea, when aroused ready to become authoritarian, as in his later sermon: 'You'll ging nae*maer* wi' *Wolf* the Ganger' (*FW* 444.31; my italics). Shem is 'Rovy the Roder' (*FW* 228.24), Murphean Red Rover, wolf of the sea, wolf, wolfdog, and dog, in one of his thwarted approaches running off as a dog, returning to receive a warning from Issy that he should stop ('Please stoop') because 'she's marrid', and approaching her anyway disguised as a sailor (*FW* 227.19-233.14).[31] Issy's words to him are Nora talking to her reappearing lover and telling him about Joyce: 'Is you zealous of mes, brother? Did you boo moiety lowd? You suppoted to be the on conditiously rejected? Satanly, lade! Can that sobstuff, whingeywilly! Stop up, mavrone . . .' (*FW* 232.21-4).

When we consider that Shem and Shaun represent respectively their father's wild youth and domestic middle age, it becomes clear that as wolf-Murphy and monk-Murphy they reveal a polarisation in their mother's attitude toward their father between the same two male types that divided Molly's monologue, between romantic rover (Vanderdecken, Mulvey) and faithful hubby (Eric, Bloom). As Michael H. Begnal has suggested, another instance of the same division occurs in the 'Norwegian Captain' episode of the third chapter of the second book.[32] The wild captain who gets roped into marrying the daughter of the ship's husband is another wolf of the sea, a 'marelupe' (*FW* 325.30) who swears the 'kersse of Wolafs' on his rival (*FW* 319.27). He originates in the young HCE who first courted ALP, and his manner has reminded Edward A. Kopper of W. B. Murphy.[33] Displaced, the tame and homebound Kersse echoes Bloom's attack on the romantic Mulvey as one of the 'buccaneering Vanderdeckens' when he calls him a 'bugganeering wanderducken' (*FW* 323.1), and in fact the daughter like her mother before her has been dreaming of just such a lover, 'titting out through her droemer window for the *flyend* of a *touchman* over the wishtas of English Strand' (my italics), who like Mulvey will come as a 'phantom shape' and like Murphy will also be a 'Sinbads' and a 'rover' (*FW* 327.22-7). The returning Flying Dutchman here is the 'round the worlder wandelingswight' who was buried at 76.10-78.6, a passage richer than any other in Dutch words, in an underwater coffin which was also a submarine and is now a ship, bringing him back, his pockets full of Dutch coins,[34] 'hiberniating after seven oak ages' (*FW* 316.15-16) to reclaim his lover, only like Murphy to face ambushers 'laying low for his home gang in that eeriebleak mead . . . to fitten (him) for the Big Water', again (*FW* 313.8-317.20). Throughout most of *Finnegans Wake* the young Vanderdecken-Sinbad-Norwegian captain figure has aged into the unromantic Eric-Ship's husband who stays on land with a 'poached fowl' (*FW* 380.24), the Barnacle goose handed him by 'Meister Capteen Gaascooker'—goosecooker (*FW* 323.14)—after he has finished making free with her for a time, but in her concluding reverie ALP, like Molly and Bertha, is able to recall his days of glory: 'And stand up tall! Straight. I want to see you looking fine for me . . . You make me think of a wonder-decker I once. Or somebalt thet sailder, the man me gallant, with the bangled ears' (*FW* 620.6-8). In intermittently reconciling to her husband, ALP in effect condemns the Flying Dutchman to drowning, which happens to be the typical fate of the Man Servant, who is often cast as a spurned Dutchman, 'an exsearfaceman' (*FW* 429.20) speaking in 'Dutchener's native' (*FW* 430.14), 'Secke sign van der Deckel' (*FW* 530.20) bringing 'gingin! gingin!' (*FW* 116.19), a proverbially Dutch liquor, frequently pickled in it or some other drink.[35] As such he is paired with Kate the Slop, who as Adaline Glasheen has suggested is probably a portrait of 'what Nora would have been had she not eloped',[36] her name perhaps deriving from Nora's memorable performance as Katherine in *Riders to the Sea*.[37]

Like the return of Gretta's lover in 'The Dead', which Joyce's brother Stanislaus once called a 'story of ghosts',[38] the Norwegian captain's return is 'ghustorily spoeking', 'like the dud spuk of his first foetotype' (*FW* 323.36-324.01). The two types of return went together in Joyce's work from the start. When, as 'Postumus', the sacrificed hero is told that 'Nobody will know or heed you . . . if you . . . come . . . to beg in one of the shavers' sailorsuits' (*FW* 377.9-11), there is surely a reminder of the disguised Odysseus begging in the swineherd's hut, and so the Ulysses Pseudoangelos of *Ulysses*, W. B. Murphy, a beggar where once he was lord. Michael Furey, Murphy, to an extent Robert Hand, and the many haunters of *Finnegans Wake* have according to Stephen's definition of a 'ghost' all 'faded into impalpability through death, through absence, through change of manners', to become blurry, penumbral figures produced through the unavoidable double vision of a lover trying to see through the present into the past. Their lives mingle with ghostly doubles, and the older they get, the more of them they meet: the Earwicker household is nothing but. The ending of *Ulysses* and all of *Finnegans Wake* suggest that the ghosts that haunted Joyce most came increasingly from the life of the woman he loved and lived with. The characteristic swooning ecstasy of the Joycean ending—Gabriel drifting off into the shadow-land of Michael Furey, Bloom composing himself with a hypnagogic chant about his rival, Sinbad the Sailor, the rhapsodic yieldings of Molly and ALP—was evidently forged to a great extent in the days when Joyce was reconciling himself to the power his lover's past had over him, and was evidently annealed on the day when it seemed to have overcome him. From that experience one essential story moved to the centre of his art, the story of the returning lover whose abortive usurpation reveals the transience of his replacement. It is present in 'The Dead', 'Exiles' and above all in the two major works written completely, first draft to last, in the presence of the woman from whom it was learned, and whose autobiography is as much a part of the work of James Joyce as is his own.

8

Proteus and Antaeus

Having completed one book set on the date of his first assignation with Nora and centred in the house where he regained his faith in her, Joyce then wrote another book named in part for her residence at the time, Finn's Hotel,[1] and set on her birthday, 21 March. When it was finished he commemorated it with a 'ring which was James Joyce's most precious present to his wife, and which Nora always wears: a big, magnificently set aquamarine—the stone symbolic of the River Liffey—the present commemorating the day he wrote *finis* to *Finnegans Wake*'.[2] The aquamarine is one of the two birthstones for March. The other, the bloodstone or heliotrope, is of course the answer to Issy's riddles to Shem, in the first chapter of Book II. In that chapter Issy is in effect acting out her mother's hints that she wants her birthstone for a birthday present—a characteristic action of the two principal female characters (e.g. 201.5, 276 No. 3, 280.24ff).

Unless one counts her husband's 'paying me his duty on my annaversary' (*FW* 493.45)—the marital copulation recorded in the penultimate chapter—it seems clear that ALP never does get her present. Instead, as 'Santa Claus' (*FW* 209.22) (the role probably has to do with Nora's Galway residence in the shadow of St Nicholas's Church), she reverses things and gives to her children 'the birthday gifts they dreamt they gabe her' (*FW* 209.27-8). There follows a long list of these gifts, concluding with a shorter list of women, many of them recognisably versions of Nora (for instance 'Grettna Greaney and Penelope Inglesante'), the total number of whose names problematically makes fifty-four, ALP's number,[3] receiving 'a moonflower and a bloodveine' (*FW* 212.1-16). In earlier drafts (*FDV* 127), 'bloodveine' was 'bloodstone'.

Nora's birthday, 21 March, was an ideal date for a universal book. It is the usual date of the vernal equinox,[4] and so New Year's Day according to the Hindu, Egyptian, early Roman and Zodiacal calendars, the day after the anniversaries of the births of Ovid and Ibsen and the beginning of Napoleon's one hundred days, four days after St Patrick's day, and likely to be in the middle of Lent. It is what Joyce calls it at one point, the Plotinian fountainhead, the origin of Anna Livia's Plurability, on which all things converge: '. . : looking wantingly around our undistributed middle between males we feel we must waistfully woent a female to focus and on this stage there pleasantly appears the cowrymaid M. whom we shall often meet below who introduces herself upon us at some precise hour when we shall again agree to call absolute zero or the babbling pumpt of platinism' (*FW* 164.5-11). This moment is to time what Molly's Gibraltar was to space.

Nathan Halper has already argued that the date of *Finnegans Wake* is in March sometime near the equinox, pointing out that since dusk falls as the bells are ringing six the day and night must be about evenly divided, that everything about the book suggests spring rather than autumn, and that in the first complete sentence Joyce distorts 'Tristan' to 'Tristram', thus smuggling in Aries, the Zodiacal sign commencing 21 March. But he misses the date by two days, I think, because of his belief that the year should be 1922 (when Joyce began thinking of the book) and that the sleeper's night dawns on a Sunday, specifically the Third Sunday in Lent.[5] Without lingering to dispute the particulars of Mr Halper's pioneering article, I think that with a little arithmetic a much better case can be made for another date.

We know, with a reasonable amount of precision and certainty, the ages of three of the family members, on one level at least. ALP is fifty-four: 'a more than quinquegintarian' (*FW* 111.06), 'if you can spot fifty I spy four more' (*FW* 10.31). (Her age, it has been noted, spells LIV in Roman numerals.) Her daughter Issy, having been born on a Leap Year's 29 February,[6] is seven birthdays old, thereby refracting into the seven rainbow girls, and so somewhere between twenty-eight and thirty-one. HCE, like his wife, is in his mid-fifties. Given the fact that three of his most important avatars,

Wellington, Swift and Mohammed, all had trouble with younger women when they were fifty-five, and that Joyce began writing *Finnegans Wake* with a description of the male principal as 'between fifty-four and fifty-five', fifty-five would seem to be a likely figure. But Joyce later revised this passage to 'between fiftyodd and fiftyeven years of age', and there are several suggestions that the correct number is fifty-six: at 443.22 HCE is described as 'well over or about fiftysix or so', at 495.30 his coat of arms is registered V.I.C. 5.6, on 497 there is recalled the celebration of his recent 'five hundredth and sixtysixth borthday', and in the concluding summary of his career, on the last two pages before the *Ricorso,* we are given a series of numbers which total fifty-six.[7] One of Joyce's notes reads 'biography begin in middle at 28' (*JJA* 3, 31); it seems most likely that the biography is that of HCE.

Finally, Shem and Shaun. Because they are always 'multiplicating' (*FW* 281.18), 'doublin their mumper all the time' (*FW* 3.8), their age is the hardest to fix. On the other hand, if they're doubling their number all the time, it ought to be one of the powers of two. At times they are four, eight, and so forth, but the point of departure seems to be thirty-two: they are variously described as 'Two overthirties' (*FW* 494.32), 'totalling . . . two and thirty' (*FW* 497.9), and 'too the trivials' (*FW* 581.22), and they are persistently connected with the numbers two and three together, in either order.

So: the husband is fifty-six, the wife fifty-four, the sons thirty-two, and the daughter between twenty-eight and thirty-one. As it happens, there was one period during which all the ages of the family of James Joyce met these specifications: between Nora's fifty-fourth birthday on 21 March and Giorgio's thirty-third birthday on 26 July 1938.

The date of *Finnegans Wake* is 21 March 1938. This date accounts for many of the book's strongest echoes. It was a Monday, the traditional wash-day (the two washerwomen are at their work), usually the first day of the week in Joyce's sequence (for instance at *FW* 301.20-2) and, as 'moon-day' the most appropriate day for a night book. (That it is also the wife's birthday explains why she should be 'menday's daughter'—*FW* 117.5.) When, late at night, the television in the pub advertises the week's programmes, it begins with Tuesday, tomorrow (*FW* 325.6-11).[8] When, on the next morning, ALP announces McGrath's funeral, it is on 'by creeps o'clock toosday' (*FW* 617.20-1), Tuesday, today. When HCE recalls the encounter in the park on the previous Thursday, he is remembering a meeting with a lowdown sort who addressed him in Gaelic on 17 March, St Patrick's Day— understandably unsettling for an insecure Anglican in the newly established Republic of Ireland. When the Gospel reading for the third Sunday in Lent echoes in his mind, it is not, as Nathan Halper suggests, an anticipation of tomorrow's service—HCE is not all that religious, and would hardly know it in advance—but a memory of yesterday's.[9] He is in the thoroughly wiped-out state revealed throughout *Finnegans Wake* because as a suburban publican depending heavily on the bona fide trade (his regular customers are described as 'statutory persons' (*FW* 220.36), 'a bundle of a dozen of representative locomotive civics, each inn quest of outings'— *FW* 221.3-4), he is recovering from his busiest, wettest day and night of the week; he is 'Sunday King' (*FW* 276.27-277.1), 'the sabbatarian' (*FW* 229.19), and Monday is his day of rest. Finally, the single most distinct indicator of the date is the sound of bells from the annual Sechseläuten festival of Zurich, and although in Joyce's time the festival was celebrated in April, throughout most of its history it occurred on the first Monday of the vernal equinox —which means that in 1938 the bells, according to the old schedule, would have rung exactly when we hear them (*FW* 213.15-16), at six p.m. on Monday, 21 March.[10]

In writing *Ulysses,* a book set in the past, Joyce could have Myles Crawford predict the First World War; in writing *Finnegans Wake,* set in the future, he played the same sort of tricks in reverse. At *FW* 609.25-610.13, as dawn breaks, the morning star is what it in fact was on the morning of 22 March 1938, Jupiter, a 'Diminussed aster' fading out but also a crowned king of gods announced by 'Juva' to the sound of 'tonobrass' and revealing (a joke of which Joyce was uncommonly fond)[11] a prominent red spot—his 'rugular lips'. Joyce could have determined the morning star for a future date by going to any competent astrologer, but since the Jupiter details were evidently not added until some time in 1938[12] it seems probable that instead he simply made use of an almanac or newspaper when 1938 rolled around. (Like *Ulysses, Finnegans Wake* took him much longer than planned, and so outran its future.) We know that while writing the book Joyce filled it with the latest news and the kind of science-fiction technology either just developed or expected in the reasonably near future: television and atom-splitting, not space ships and time machines. And he dragged in, with more than the ususal degree of strain, Sheridan Le Fanu's *The House by the Churchyard,* a novel set in Chapelizod about a Phoenix Park murder written sixteen years before the Phoenix Park Murders, and so an ideal analogue for this other Chapelizod book set sixteen years later than when Joyce began planning it.

The sixteen-year figure was of course an obvious choice for the author who in 1922 had just finished a book about two Ur-Joyces sixteen years apart in age. *Ulysses* had been a day book, set at a precise time in the past, to a great extent about the reconciliation or lack of reconciliation across that talismanic space of time: *Finnegans Wake* would be a night book, a prophetic 'somnione sci-upones' (*FW* 293.7-8) envisioning a precise time in the future, developing the problematic connection between the author at forty and a portrait of the artist as an almost old man, sixteen years later. Having reached at forty what *Finnegans Wake* calls the middle of life's journey, the zenith of the arc (*FW* 129.32-3) which ends at eighty, Joyce turned from a book in which he had projected his future by studying the past to a book evoking his past and what can only be called future past by studying the future. In letters and conversation he repeatedly compared himself writing *Finnegans Wake* to a man boring into a mountain from two sides, and superstitiously remarked that something seemed to happen to people when he put them in the book; the two sides of the mountain were 1922 and 1938, and the root superstition was that what he was writing was literally prophetic.

In a way, then, *Finnegans Wake* is a crystal ball.[13] There is a crystal set in the Earwicker house, bringing news from faraway, and the comparison of radio waves to messages from the beyond, whether past or future, was a commonplace among spiritualists in the twenties and thirties. At other times, as in *Ulysses,* the crystal ball doubles as a magic mirror, like the one that transports Bloom at the end of 'Nausicaa', carrying us into a future which of course reflects the past. At the very end, before returning to the beginning, 'We pass through grass behush the bush to', and 'grass' is also 'glass', by virtue of Gaelic's L/R. interchange[14] and the fact that the Alice Liddell who went through Lewis Carroll's looking glass had for her middle name 'Pleasance', whence her persistent connection in *Finnegans Wake* with grass and 'wonderlawn'. So we pass through glass back to the first page where, as Adaline Glasheen has remarked, everything is backwards,[15] and where we are immediately told of a number of events which have not yet occurred but will soon.

These events are the story of Joyce's personal and public career, from youth to late middle age—the main co-ordinates of the life lived from Stephen Dedalus's twenty-two to the fifty-odd years of the Rory O'Connor figure, blind drunk and superannuated, with whose portrait Joyce began the writing of 'Work in Progress'. Reading over his letters and biography from this period, one can easily see why, looking ahead, Joyce should have cast himself as 'that joky old man, poor he . . . the king of them all overwhelmed with ruin smiling through his old tears' (*FDV* 204). He had recently suffered a severe eye attack and, like Earwicker (*FW* 129.32-3), had had his teeth removed (*L* III, 71). After the immense labor of *Ulysses* he found himself exhausted, two years older than the Bloom who had felt himself getting old, with two children who had reached adolescence. The story told by the first complete sentence of *Finnegans Wake* (which, as Bernard Benstock has shown, names all members of the Joyce family)[16] repeated at the very end of the third book and run through at least twice in between, is a seven-stage story of the life of James Joyce, father and author.

For the reader's convenience, the following summary of each of these seven stages is preceded by the first, second, third, etc. clauses from each of the four sequences. They come from 3.4-14, 104.10-14, 126.16-24 and 589.20-590.3.

I. 'Sir Tristram, violer d'amores, fr'over the short sea, had passencore rearrived from North Armorica on this side the scraggy isthmus of Europe Minor to wielderfight his penisolate war;'

'Amoury Treestam and Icy Siseule,'

'thought he weighed a new ton when there felled his first lapapple;'

'First for a change of seven days license he wandered out of his farmer's health and so lost his early parishlife.'

Stage 1: the meeting with Nora, the young ALP (a 'lap-apple' because Alice Pleasance Liddel becomes APL becomes apple—a very common equation in the book), as momentous as Newton's with his apple. The liaison was consummated after a passage across the North Sea to Armorica (Newhaven-Dieppe) and thence to Zurich's Gasthaus Hoffnung,[17] in German 'hope', for which concept the universal symbol is the anchor—'pas-*encore*'. It signals Joyce's final departure from his father's house and the loss of his early life. The year is 1904.

II. 'nor had topsawyer's rocks by the stream Oconee exaggerated themselse to Laurens County's gorgios while they went doublin their mumper all the time;'

'saith a Sawyer til a Strame,'

'gave the heinousness of choice to everyknight betwixt yesterdicks and twomaries;'

'Then ('twas in fenland) occidentally of a sudden, six junelooking flamefaces straggled wild out of their turns through his parsonfired wicket, showing all shapes of striplings in sleepless tights.'

Stage 2: the birth of Giorgio, conceived, Joyce believed (*L* II, 232), in the Gasthaus Hoffnung, born after repeated doubling of the egg fertilised in female Oconee by male rocks. He is born accidentally of a sudden—a month earlier than the father calculated[18]—flamefaced and wild, and given the heinous name of Joyce. The year is 1905.

III. 'nor avoice from afire bellowsed mishe mishe to tauftauf thuartpeatrick:'

'Ik dik dopedope et tu mihimihi,'

'had sevenal successivecoloured serebanmaids on the same big white drawringroam horthrug;'

'Promptly womafter in undated times, very properly a dozen generations anterior to themselves, a main chanced to burst and misflooded his fortunes, wrothing foulplay over his fives' court and his fine poultryyard wherein were spared a just two of a feather in wading room only.'

Stage 3: the birth of Lucia, looking ahead to all the tragic 'misflooded . . . fortunes' that are to follow in consequence. She cries 'mishe mishe'—'I I'—because she is named for the patron saint of eyes: hence 'IssY'. (And because her mother's letters, ALP, add up to 111 according to the Kabbalic practice of gematria, and so Issy's two vertical lines make her a chip off the block, or leaf off the tree, or as here two feathers from a Barnacle goose.)[19] She is greeted and baptised by the boy baby—'tauftauf'—who will grow up to be a type of Patrick and Peter. As Lucia she is the guardian of Joyce's eyes and the seven colours which enter through them, so she refracts into seven 'successivecoloured serebanmaids'. The sight left to the father is like two of the seven ducklings in the Anderson fairy tale, saved from the flood. There seems to be an allusion to the father pacing the rug of the maternity ward's waiting room, but the biographical sources are no help in pinning it down. The time is 1907-8.

IV. 'not yet, though venissoon after, had a kidscad buttended a bland old isaac:'

'Buy Birthplate for a Bite,'

'is a Willbeforce to this hour at house as he was in heather;'

'Next, upon due reflotation, up started four hurrigan gales to smithereen his plateglass housewalls and the slate for accounts his keeper was cooking.'

Stage 4: a half-blind old eye-sick, shut in a glass house which is also the House of Commons of Butt and Wilberforce, a fragile and vulnerable centre of paternal authority, he has to contend with the challenges and demands of his growing Gaelic son. The time is around 1915, with the First World War in the background.

V. 'not yet, though all's fair in vanessy, were sosie sesthers wroth with twone nathanjoe.'

'Which of your Hesterdays Mean Ye to Morra?'

'pumped the catholick wartrey and shocked the prodestung boyne;'

'Then came three boy buglehorners who counterbezzled and crossbugled him.'

Stage 5: general warfare among the siblings, against one another, against themselves, and all against father. The girl has split into two sisters and fights with the boy, who is now Nat and Joe—two people, and an upside-down version of the split-in-half father as Jonathan Swift. Both offspring of the House of Commons—a public house—the boys go at it like Catholics and Protestants at the Boyne. It is no accident that the father is in the crossfire, since all attacks are really at him. With the Irish Civil War in the background, the year is 1922.

VI. 'Rot a peck of pa's malt had Jhem or Shen brewed by arclight'

'Hoebegunne the Hebrewer Hit Waterman the Brayned,'

'killed his own hungery self in anger as a young man'

'later on in the same evening two hussites absconded through a breach in his bylaws and left him, the infidels, to pay himself off in kind remembrances.'

Stage Six: takes us into the post-*Ulysses* era. Having finally finished the job he began in *Portrait* by killing off his young self in *Ulysses*, [20] he suffers a more severe attack of glaucoma which robs him of the remaining two parts of his vision left over from the attack recorded in Stage 3. As 'hussites', the hussies are rebels, 'infidels'—note the two 'i's—against the paternal Noah-Bloom-Mohammed, and the consequence of their desertion is that, like Joyce during many of the days following 1922, the father can only sit alone in the darkness, with the 'remembrances' that are becoming *Finnegans Wake*. The blindness is a revenge of the son(s), brewing the liquor—'wood alcohol' (*FW* 70.27)—that Joyce suspected, perhaps correctly, aggravated his eye condition. [21] It is brewed by 'arclight' because the arc is the rainbow seen from Noah's ark and so a sign of the glaucoma which first manifested itself in the 'spinning rainbows' radiating from the 'arc lights' of Zurich. [22] (So HCE wears seven colours, as Joyce wore the three colours corresponding to the three major phases of glaucoma as a charm against the disease.) The time is the mid to late 1920s.

VII. 'and rory end to the regginbrow was to be seen ringsome on the aquaface.'

'Arcs in his Ceiling Flee Chinx on the Flur,'

'found fodder for five when allmarken rose goflooded;'

'Till, ultimatehim, fell the crowning barleystraw, when an explosium of his distilleries deafadumped all his dry goods to his most favoured sinflute and dropped him, what remains of a heptark, leareyed and letterish, weeping worrybound on his bank-rump.'

Stage 7: glaucoma is caused by excessive pressure of fluid against the iris, and so is always associated for Joyce with water, weeping, and floods: 'My left eye is awash and his neighbour full of water, man / I cannot see the lass I limned for Ireland's gamest daughter man . . .' [23] Here, bankrupt, his fortunes ruined by the flood, with not even the one end of the spectrum registering on his eyes, he wonders, quite naturally, how he can feed his family. The time is the 1930s, after the Wall Street crash.

As always with Joyce, this sequence can accommodate other chronologies, including one, I think, beginning with Joyce's own birth, followed next by the arrivals of Stanislaus and various sisters, and concluding with the author wearing out his one pair of trousers at his short-lived bank job in Rome, [24] where he conceived

Ulysses. But the main dimension is the arc of the Joyce family's history from 1904 to February 1922 to 1938, and the age permutations of the family members occur as factors of the 1938 numbers, reckoned backwards. Issy, I suspect, divides into Snow White and Rose Red because in early 1922—the period of Stage 5, when all the divisions begin—Lucia was fourteen, the age at which Milly Bloom has her first menstrual period (*U* 736), and just forty years younger than the age at which ALP has her last menstrual period:[25] her forty years' flood will be governed, like her mother's, by bloodstone and moonstone. Giorgio, his alliterative name midway between James-Joyce and Shem-Shaun, from early 1922—again, the same schismatic year—to early 1938 has doubled his number from sixteen to thirty-two, and so twinned himself.

The main point is that behind the temporal and seasonal fractionings into the two, the four, the seven, the twenty-eight, and so on, into the infants, children, adolescents and youths of earlier years whose memory makes up most of the book, is discernible what we begin to see as the sun comes up: a family of four, with one brother and sister—'brightner and sweetster' (*FW* 598.12-13), father and mother, each the product and sum of certain established multiplicands and addenda. The book is the dream of a fifty-six year old Irish publican, recalling his past, who is in turn the dream of James Joyce, forecasting his future. Like Gabriel and Bloom, HCE is Joyce's imaginary portrait of himself, had he not made his decisive departure from Ireland. That is why the book so often resolves, often very movingly, into direct confession or appeal, as when ALP's valedictory turns out to be the coaxings of a wife dressing her blind husband and guiding him over the landscape, describing the sights and trying to cheer him up: 'Come! Give me your great bearspaw, padder avilky . . . Not such big strides . . . huddy fuddy! . . . You know where I am bringing you? . . . And I'll be your aural eyeness . . . You'll know our way from there surely.'

So, for instance, it makes most sense to think of the *tertium quid* into which Shem and Shaun are forever coalescing or threatening to coalesce as not so much a Brunonian coincidence of contraries as the shadowed origin of which the twins are a later bifurcation. They are, that is, one person, as such a reincarnation of their sleeping father, and their polarisation into two is on the primary level a partition of his body, squeezed in half by the tight belt (he is trying to look slimmer) which has left a black and blue ring around his middle (*FW* 564.24-5). They are the two ends of the earwig which will supposedly fight one another if it is cut in half,[26] 'you all over' (*FW* 620.17) as ALP tells her husband. This becomes clearest at the end when we get a glimpse of the male offspring in bed, 'tightly tattached as two maggots to touch other', Kevin the 'farhead bode', Jerry with his 'bespilled . . . foundingpen' (*FW* 562.21-563.6). They are top half and bottom half, the father's shirt and pants, brain and genitals, and thence, in a progression which suggests that Joyce may have agreed with Pound that the deepest mental activity involves a co-ordination of those two bundled concentrations of nerve endings, they become northern hemisphere vs southern hemisphere (the belt is the equator)[27] 'hairytop on heeltipper' (*FW* 483.18), '*dio in cap* vs *diavolo in coda*' (*FW* 466.18), god vs dog, pipe and cad (from HCE 'cap-a-pipe', *FW* 220.26), white chessmen vs black chessmen, firefly vs beetle, tennis champion son vs mongrel, Mookse vs Gripes, dove vs raven, up vs down, Patrick vs snake, monk vs wolf, wheat vs rye.

And since the dreamer is fifty-six, when the heyday in the blood is proverbially tame, they fall naturally into one other fundamental opposition—past vs future. The young Joyce remarked on the male's 'extraordinary cerebral sexualism' (*L* II, 192) and in 'The Holy Office' bragged that he had been saved from the dreamy dreaminess of the Æ circle by dint of vigorous exercise both above the neck and below the belt, but for the dreamer of *Finnegans Wake* the wisdom of the blood has receded into memories of his flaming Shemian Norwegian Captain, Tristan,[28] corsair, seawolf youth, and perhaps in compensation he envisions the future as a Shaunian accumulation of denatured wisdom in his 'vaultybrain' (*FW* 159.25), which keeps getting mixed up with the accumulation of food in his belly. So he has become—it is his most remarked feature—very fat: 'One sees how he is lot stoutlier than of formerly' (*FW* 570.16-17). Most simply, the passage from Book I to Book III, from Shem to Shaun, past to future,[28] raven to dove originates in the dreamer's remembered passage from thin to fat and from dark hair to grey: he 'passed for baabaa blacksheep till he grew white woo woo wooly' (*FW* 133.24).

Joyce symbolises the common origin of Shem and Shaun with the Claddagh ring, that Galway artifact which, as I have suggested, he almost certainly associated with his ancestral history. The twins are the two hands, coming together to frame one heart supporting one crown. (See, for example, *FW* 27.4, 174.9-10, 188.3, 189.21-4, 191.23-4, 224.33, 252.15, 384.26ff, 464.23-4, 610.11-12.) In the act of reuniting, they refigure their paternal original: the Claddagh ring becomes the belt around HCE's middle and, somewhat earlier, the hoop around the Shaun-barrel, containing and restraining the Shem-brew inside. Most likely, the Claddagh ring has come to have these associations because it was the engagement or wedding band that the sleeper put on at the major division of his life. It is certainly true, in any case, that he habitually wears two constricting bands, a tight belt and a wedding ring, and that they have worn lines in his flesh which have become, over the years, emblematic of the major dividing line of his life—the day that he got married, started getting fat, and changed from Norwegian captain to Ship's husband, from Shem to Shaun. The division is compounded in his mind by the presence of a thirty-two year old son, representing in one way his past, in one way his future, sleeping in a nearby room which is reached by way of stairsteps inlaid in a checkerboard pattern (*FW* 560.9). 'Thirty-two' and 'checkerboard' suggest division into black and white forces on a chessboard and the doublings and divisions of squares and square roots—so he envisions his wife running to the room 'in eight and eight sixtyfour', in 'a nanny's gambit', with a 'knightlamp' (*FW* 559.35-6). The eschatological cast of the struggle comes from the picture over the mantle in the sleeper's room: 'Michael, lance, slaying Satan, dragon' (*FW* 559.10-11).[30] The demarcations worn into his flesh by belt and ring suggest to the sleeper that the struggle re-enacts his own divisions, and the ring by itself has become the symbol for reconciliation and inner peace.

Similarly, the other main characters originate in a richly detailed here-and-now underlying the dream's metamorphoses. HCE becomes mountain and house because he is so fat, 'big as a house'. (Contrary to wide belief he is not literally a hunchback, although remembering his slim original he does think of the growth around his middle as a deformity—'the large fungopark he has grown'—*FW* 51.20.) ALP's flowing hair, trinkets, and gauzy underwear becomes the Liffey, its pebbles and its salmon weir. Issy is leap year, looking glass and rainbow girl because of her date of birth, her girlish vanity, her mirror and the tints of the cosmetics on her dressing table; the immediate cue for her appearances in the dreamer's dream is the multicoloured patchwork quilt on his bed.

Her pale double is her earlier self before she reached, at fourteen, the age of puberty and make-up. She becomes Issy—Is-sY, eye-eye, I-I, IsIs, IrIs—because as the rainbow, Iris, she is a charm against the dreamer's glaucoma, a Saint Lucia to gather up and restore the shattered rainbow of his vision, as Isis gathered up and restored the dismembered Osiris. As I-I she metamorphoses into the two Isoldes, thence into the 'ii' chirped by the birds in the zoo (*FW* 244.30) and the birds themselves (the dots are the heads)[31] thence into the two candles (the dots are the flames) lit by her father while courting her mother (*FW* 626.14), the two dots of 'i' in Morse code, the two peas in a pod of the Pranquean's riddle and, finally, I think, into the '11' which combines with her brother's number to form the '1132' floating mysteriously around in the dreamer's mind.[32]

Contrary to a number of modern critics, then, there is a carefully planned literal level underlying the metamorphoses of *Finnegans Wake* which the reader is allowed to discern. If he were meant to be adrift in words and images, he would not be shown a fully-furnished household and given the means of seeing how the language of the book has metamorphosed from those fixtures; he would not be shown the checkered staircase, for instance. Books meant to cast the reader adrift have indeed been written, mainly by imitators of Joyce convinced that *Finnegans Wake* is a gorgeous swamp of glittering phonemes, an Irish Albert Memorial of blarney and bric-a-brac, or *A Vision* set to music, but they are imitating a book which does not exist. In *Finnegans Wake* Joyce continued to explore the same subject that had fascinated the young Stephen Dedalus who read Skeat by the hour: not words by themselves but where they came from and how they were made. He constructed *Finnegans Wake* so that the reader would wonder and by degrees discover where its visions come from and how they are made. It is, I am convinced, a law of *Finnegans Wake* that the clues necessary to find the phenomenal determinants of any sequence are always given somewhere, and I do not think it too large a statement that the essential activity of the book is the transformation of those determinants into the poetry on the page. Joyce regularly presents both pumpkin and gold carriage because he continues to be as interested as ever in the way the mind and senses working together turn one into the other.

What readers of *Finnegans Wake* probably need most is a

catalogue of the pumpkins. They need a thoroughly reductive account of what really happens—and there really is a reality here—in order to experience the book's incandescent arcs between ground and sky, the alchemy which enlarges, embroiders, couples, uncouples, multiplies, weaves, gilds, blurs, occults, refracts, illuminates and transforms its givens, never quite past the point of recognisability. The usual dangers of reductive analysis, of fixing on the idea that Stella *is* Penelope Devereux or Lilliput the Walpole court, do not apply to this book which no one is in any danger of finding too easy. As of now, reading *Finnegans Wake* is too often like reading about the 'testoon of costliest bronze' in 'Cyclops' without understanding that it is really a penny: we miss the point, which is neither the penny nor the 'testoon' but the way one becomes the other.

That is of course a prescription for another book. As a small sample of what needs to be done, I will now go over the book's shortest chapter, called 'Mamalujo' by Joyce, which most critics have seen as mainly an account of Tristan and Iseult sailing away in the ship which holds their bridal chamber. That story is certainly there, but in order to see how it arises we need first to see its origins, the pumpkins and pennies. Thus the following will be mainly an account of the pumpkins and pennies.

The active participants are the dreamer—I will call him HCE because I have to call him something—and the household cat. Next in importance are the wife, who is lying next to HCE, the daughter whose bedroom is the cat's dormitory (*FW* 461.19), and the four bedposts above the sleeper's bed. The chapter covers pp. 383-99.

383.1-384.5: The 'ark' sounds are the cat's squawking, waking up HCE by degrees. The factitious 'bark'-'mark'-'lark' rhymes illustrate a dreamer's tendency to assimilate stimuli into set associative patterns, to turn 'any sound that comes to our ears during sleep . . . into a dream'.[33] The second rhyme 'bark', for instance, is produced by the associative chain Meow—cat—dog—bark. The sound comes from 'Overhoved' because the cat is at the bed's head; hence it reminds the dreamer of the cries of birds, of sea-birds because he is very drunk from his recent indulgence—the bedposts keep turning around—and consequently feels seasick. The chapter's sea sounds, its 'oceans of kissening' (*FW* 384.19), come from the drink-induced rushing in the sleeper's ears and the storm outside, the thunder from which (*FW* 353) probably woke up the cat in the first place. The vertiginous, bottomless, undulant rhythm of the sentences is another instance of imitative form by an author who knew what it was like to occasionally look at the world through an alcoholic haze. When HCE opens his eyes (*FW* 383.17) he sights the cat, 'the wildcaps', in the doorway, spinning around, then 'kemin in so hattajocky' to his 'solans'. The 'sighing and sobbing' (*FW* 384.4-5) is the sound of the storm outside. 'Moykle ahoykling!' is another meow for attention.

384.6-386.11: Eyes open, HCE looks at the four posts, the four masts of the ship imagined to go with the sea, here the 'four master waves' because he is still feeling very much overwhelmed with what he has done to himself. Trying to get his bearings and stop the spinning, he focuses on the posts as points of the compass. To focus on something is to project: the posts become old men because he is feeling very old himself, for obvious reasons—as old as King Mark, the name he first heard in the cat's squawk. So the four men become, like Mark, voyeurs, observing from above the bed a coupling of young lovers, derived from HCE's memories of youth, which is also, because of the cat's presence (the four are introduced eating fish) a cat playing with and eventually eating a goldfish, 'in her ensemble of maidenna blue, with an overdress of net, tickled with goldies, Isolamisola . . . '. Isolde is of course Issy, recalled here because the cat is her pet. The goldfish episode is undoubtedly an actual occurrence in the family annals, as the entire chapter is a pastiche of distant memories evoked by events. In projecting these memories onto the bedposts, HCE is evidently able to imagine himself as freed from his burden of years: as the bedposts become the old voyeurs, coveting his daughter, he returns to her lover, his early Tristan self, with the blue eyes, proper shape and undivided sense of self—both right hand and left hand of the Claddagh ring—of the time before his affliction with bad eyes, obesity and age: 'her bleaueyedeal of a girl's friend, neither biguly nor smallnice . . . with his sinister dexterity . . . '. Since Issy sleeps with the cat, he becomes, in reliving his youth, the cat.

The next page (385) is a capsule history of cat memories: their cult in Egypt (thinking of the past and looking at the cat, HCE sees a sphinx), their unlovely habit of leaving 'tribluts' of prey on doorsteps, a delightful picture of kittens (thinking of his own youth and seeing the cat, HCE sees a kitten) watching the 'mad dane'—

the household dog—like Elizabethans at a bearpit, and a final recollection of the victimised goldfish, her mouth to the water surface, which like Issy's mirror reflects her image: 'reflecting on the situation, drinking in draughts of purest air serene and revelling in the great outdoors . . . '.

386.12-388.9: Having circled around to the foot of the bed, the cat leaps '(up)' onto the bedspread (the '(up)'s are also the rising gorge of HCE) and shows its green eyes through the murk: 'so nice and bespectable and after that they had their fathomglasses to find out all the fathoms . . . '. One of the main contrasts of the episode is between the purblind human and the cat, with its proverbial ability to 'remembore . . . throw darker hour sorrows': to remember the past but also to bore through the dark with its green eyes. Pp. 386-7 describe an encounter between semiconscious human and importunate cat: it approaches HCE and wife, 'the auctioneer there dormont . . . at the darkumound number wan' (he is indeed a dark mound beneath the covers) 'beside that ancient Dame street, where the statue of Mrs Dana O'Connel', and, first negotiating the bed's lumps and folds and then prancing impudently up and down HCE's mountainous middle with its tail erect, reminds HCE of a *dressage* demonstration from his college days:

> . . . going to the tailturn horseshow . . . and the shoeblacks and the redshanks and plebeians and the barrancos and the cappunchers childerun [a cat's progress up the length of HCE's body] . . . highstepping the fissure and fracture lines, seven five threes up, three five sevens down, to get out of his way . . . like hopolopocattls, [note the buried 'cat'] erumping around their Judgity Yaman [not having been shooed away, the cat gets rambunctious] and all the tercentenary horses [three hundred years old: roughly the horse's life expectancy of thirty or so years times the cat's nine lives] and priesthunters from the Curragh, and the confusionaries and the authorities, Noord Amrikaans and Suid African cattleraiders [we are off on another tour of HCE's body, here seen as northern and southern hemispheres] . . . all over like a tiara dullfuoco [here we go, beginning atop the head like a furry tiara] in his grey half a tall hat and his amber necklace and his crimson harness and his leathern jib [this is the farthest reach of the cat's progress; now it starts doubling back toward the face] and his cheapskin hairshirt and

his scotobrish and his parapilagian gallowglasses [we are now ready to look the aroused HCE, earlier dubbed the 'jaypee', in the eyes]: (how do you do, jaypee, Elevato! . . .)

For the remainder of p. 387 HCE brushes the visitor away temporarily ('Get out of my way!') and, awakened, gazes at the 'whate shape' of his sleeping wife and recalls, in another reprise of the family history, the main events of his life with her, concluding with a memory of his eye attack, transformed by the sound of the rain outside, the sight of his form under the covers and thoughts of the drowned Martin Cunningham into a vision of himself beneath the waves: 'the arzurian deeps o'er his humbodumbones sweeps'. Which brings things back (388.1-9) to the King Mark and Tristan story.

388.10-389.39: The cat keeps up a chorus of background cater- waulings from the floor ('Mat speaking!') but HCE's main thoughts continue to circle around his wife and his past with her. He hugs and kisses her, 'poghuing her scandalous', and imagines himself seen from the bedposts as 'the gouty old galahat'. So centred on her are his thoughts that when his nausea catches up with him and he throws up and spits into a bedside bowl he still imagines himself as gazing into her eyes: ' . . . while his deepseepeepers gazed and sazed and dazecrazemazed into her dullakbloon rodolling olo- sheen eyenbowls by the Cornelius Nepos, Mnepos. Anumque, umque, Napoo'.

389.30-392.12: This hilariously recounts HCE's attempt to uri- nate and then dress himself while the room is spinning around him. Having 'shoved the wretch in churneroil' and checked the 'croniony' at his bedside, he sits up on the edge of the bed, aims at the fireplace, and, when he misses ('all nangles, sangles, angles and wangles') starts laughing uncontrollably, which of course only makes things worse: ' . . . raining water laughing, per Nupiter Privius, only terpary . . . '. One reason he laughs at making the floor a temporary privy is that he hits the cat, who becomes 'Dion Cassius Poosycomb, all drowned too'. The passage contains many references to divorce and parting because HCE has left his wife's side. Despite the 'misoccurs' he decides to forge ahead, downstairs, where he will feed the cat and himself. He pads across the 'stamped bronnanoleum', which because of the 'Neptune's mess' he has made has become like the Giant's Causeway, a meeting of land and water. 'Sculling over the giamond's course-way', intending to 'hersute' himself, he arrives 'at the rim of the rom' and sits 'on his two bare marrowbones' on the room's one chair. Since the chair is draped with his wife's clothes, 'hersute' (*FW* 559.8), he apologised for his 'hunnish familiarities' with her. This incident and the 'divorce' overtones are enough to turn him, I think, into Nora's disreputable and wayward father, trying to excuse his abandonment of Mrs Barnacle: 'there were faults on both sides.' Having particular difficulty with the buttons, HCE slowly and clumsily gets dressed.

392.14-396.3: Like HCE, ALP wears a Claddagh ring, probably as an engagement band. On her hand, it is his last sight before setting out, and calls up memories of their courtship, the mother-in-law recalled on p. 391, and, since his wife has like himself grown too fat for it, of age and approaching death: 'They were all so sorgy for poorboir Matt in his saltwater hat, with the Aran *crown* [my italics] [Joyce associated the ring with the Aran Islands] or she grew out of, too big for him, of or Mnepos and his overalls, all falling over her in folds [HCE in the final stages of getting dressed]—sure he hadn't the *heart* [my italics] to pull them up—poor Matt, the old perigrime matriarch, and a queenly man, (the porple blussing upon them!) [Mrs Barnacle's militant Catholicism] . . .with her face to the wall [a literal fact and an intimation of death: ALP has just reminded HCE of her aged mother] . . . amid the rattle of hailstones, kalospintheochromato-kreening, with her ivyclad hood . . .' [wife's snoring; the sound suggests hailstones because of the rain outside]. Incredibly enough—perhaps his vomiting cured the nausea—HCE is hungry, so with thoughts of meatloaf ('Matt. And loaf') and other foods dancing in his head he pulls himself up (the '(up)'s start coming back), with the immediate result that his brain starts buzzing ('he poled him up his boccat of vuotar and got big buzz for his name .'.'.'), and heads for the downstairs kitchen, still thinking of 'the lovely mother of periwinkle'. (The word he is searching for, and which will come to him[34] on the last page, is 'Barnacle'.) I suspect that at the bottom of p. 392 and top of 393 he inserts his dentures. Meanwhile the cat, sensing human movement and hence the possibility of food, becomes active again. Like HCE it has been reliving its past 'in dreams of yore' (compare the 'hearthdreaming cat' of *Ulysses*), particularly the memories of kittenhood's terrors just revived by its master's strange and inconsistent behaviour: he acts nicely and then goes and does *that*. 'So frightened', it recalls HCE as an inscrutable two-handed engine at the door, calling it and the other kittens of the litter in one minute ('come in, come on, you lazy loafs!') and then putting them out the next ('come out to hell, you lousy louts!') with no apparent reasons, and in general the 'puddled and mythified' state of growing up in a house full of humans: 'when nobody wouldn't even let them rusten, from playing their gatspiels [cat gospels] crossing their sleep by the shocking silence, when they were in dreams of yore, standing behind the door, or leaning out of the chair, . . .' and so on, including memories of running from a turkeycock ('dadging the talkeycook that chased them') and licking up table scraps and crumbs, 'to collect all the bits of brown'. Well, at least HCE fed them: following him with 'their night tentacles', the eyes reaching out like tentacles through the darkness, 'dooing a dunloop' around him as he heads for the kitchen, correctly reading his signals that 'left no doubt in his minder' that he is going to come across with 'their passion grand, that one fresh from the cow'—that is, milk—jumping up his leg in anticipation as he pours it into a bowl, the cat becomes an ecstatic worshipper, awaiting and then receiving a communion of the Milky Way in theological language recalling (*FW* 245.11-3) the earlier discussion between the fish about their fish-gods: '[the milk] exteriorises on this ourherenow plane in disunited solod, likeward and gushious bodies [is put on the floor] with (science, say!) perilwhitened passionpanting pugnoplangent intuitions of reunited selfdome (murky whey, abstrew adim!) [it is lapped up] in the higherdimissional selfless Allself [and swallowed] . . .'. The cat's frenzied behaviour, open mouth and Issy associations produce the obvious sexual dimension of both this scene and the chapter's climax (*FW* 395.25-396.3), which is literally a description of HCE tossing a sausage (*FDV:* 'I won't dream of a sausage of his not even for catsmeat') to the waiting cat: 'with ripy lepes to ropy lopes . . . when, as quick, is greased pigskin, Amoricus Champius, with one aragan throust, druve the massive of virilvigtoury flshpst the both lines of forwards (Eburnea's down, boys!) rightjingbangshot into the goal of her gullet.' The soccer associations arise because sex and athletics are two things that HCE thinks he left behind him at forty, when 'his stumps were pulled' (*FW* 129.33).

396.4-399.36: Page 396 mainly describes the cat's worrying ('doing a lally a lolly a dither a duther') and then swallowing ('Plop') the meat, after which it purrs its 'mummurrlubejubes'. HCE's Mark-ish reflections about his desertion by his young lover arise because the cat, true to its kind, has ungratefully run off with its prey into a corner. The 'throust' into the gullet is 'aragan' because as HCE feeds the cat, his wife, having been wakened by all the commotion, is simultaneously lighting their bedside Argand lamp (200 pages later it will still be lit): 'she renulited their disunited.' Its glow from the bedroom upstairs is what reminds HCE of her 'firstclass pair of bedroom eyes' and 'beaufu mouldern maiden name', and what draws him back to her. He ascends the stairs (the '(up)'s return one last time) as the cat, 'after doing the mousework', returns to his usual spot in Issy's room in 'the top loft'. As at the end of 'Penelope', the two scenes, of youth and age fuse, HCE removing his teeth (*FW* 397.21) and glasses (*FW* 397.35) and settling in next to his wife with a final concatenation of sevens, the cat 'going to dodo sleep atrance, with their catkin coifs', next to Issy's two I's: 'churles and vassals, in same, sept and severalty and one by one and sing a majalujo'—a chorus. There follows a prayer before going to sleep, introduced as an 'oremus prayer and homeysweet homely' for the whole household, which turns out to be compounded of the events just experienced: the 'Nine' lives of the cat, the 'blueblack' night, the mother of pearl (changed into 'daughter of pearl') buttons of the shirt, the 'glut of cold meat', the wife's 'snore', the 'highsteppers' of the horseshow, the toss ('I tossed that one') to the cat, the 'wet' on the floor, the 'goosegreasing' of the feeding, the 'eiderdown bed'. Like HCE himself, it all comes back round to the woman, the 'Barnacle' goose (even her eiderdown quilt is a cue) from 'the barony of Bohermore', a district of Galway. Printed as a poem, it is obviously not: instead it is HCE's subsidence into sleep, as he tries to convince himself with the forced imposition of stanzaic structure that his thoughts have form and thus meaning, assimilating the events of the last fifteen minutes or so into what matters most, his wife. As such, it is an epitome of the whole book.

It is possible that none of this happens. It may be that the events are a dream of a man who stays in a four-poster bed and envisions himself awakened by his daughter's cat, that only his spirit leaves the bed, as Molly Bloom's does when she dreams of picking up sailors, and so sleepwalks down to the cabman's shelter. Indeed, on one level it undoubtedly all is a dream, the dream of James Joyce about the dream of a Chapelizod publican. The fact remains that its logic, like the logic of the hallucinations in 'Circe', is anchored in events and things and the reverberations from them: a mewling cat, a lit lamp. Like Antaeus, it keeps returning to a hard and solid ground floor of irreducible facts from which its protean visions renew their strength before progressing through allotropic metamorphoses whose apprehension is the main business of reading the book. Well before he spends his time studying the libretto of Wagner's *Tristan,* for instance, the serious reader of 'Mamalujo' would do much better to get quite drunk in the company of a cat. It is still the story of Stephen on the beach with Tatters: a mind crammed with memories looking at a moving object, formulating intermediary emblems which are recorded on the page. Those emblems reveal an author at least as sensitive to the nuances of everyday experience as he was when describing another cat-and-man encounter in *Ulysses,* registering the 'avid shameclosing eyes' and 'dark eyeslits narrowing with greed'. The obscurity of the book comes mainly from its author's way of 'leaving out, of course, foreconsciously the simple worf' (*FW* 174.1). In 'The Sisters' he never says, 'I groped my way to my chair because my pupils were dilated from the stay in the brightly-lit room'; here he never says, 'Entering the room, the cat reminded him of his daughter Issy, in whose chamber it customarily slept.'

All the same, such intersections of subject with object are at the heart of everything that happens. Far from being a 'decentred' universe, *Finnegans Wake* is the most centred universe imaginable. One of its most remarkable features, considering when it was written (I speak as an American), is that there is no Babe Ruth in it. Nor, so far as I can see, is there any mention of the single most publicised event of the mid-thirties, the abdication of Edward VIII to marry Mrs Wallis Simpson. Instead we get Napoleon— Josephine, Daddy Browning and Peaches, and a host of other analogues to one of the few major stories—an older man lured from his wife by younger women. If 'universal' means encyclopaedic, then this is not a universal book. Everything is included and weighted insofar as it relates to the essential concerns of a certain man, HCE, in a certain place, Chapelizod, at a certain time, 21 March 1938, and these co-ordinates are in turn important insofar as they reflect James Joyce remembering the Sechseläuten bells of the city in which he consummated his love for the true centre of the book, the Nora Barnacle whose birthday it commemorates. Using one of the images that recurs throughout his books, we may picture the relationship between vision, symbol, hallucination, and so on and their sources as a series of concentric circles, a calibrated permutation of encounters between noumenal self and phenomenal world, determined according to set laws worked out early in life by an author whose weak and failing sight gave him a special interest in the mechanics of vision. In *Finnegans Wake* he gathers up and enormously expands the experiments with perception recorded in his earlier works. As in *Chamber Music*, a willow drooping into a river is anthropomorphically transformed; as in *Dubliners*, a lit lamp becomes a moon; as in *A Portrait of the Artist as a Young Man*, a structure becomes a ship; as in *Ulysses*, concentrating on a red triangle induces a vision, and one kind of jogging quadruped mutates easily into a picture of another. 'Why all this fuss and bother about the mystery of the unconscious? What about the mystery of the conscious? What do they know about that?' Joyce asked Frank Budgen,[35] while in the middle of writing a book one of whose points is that *Othello* is at least as interesting a story as *Oedipus Rex*. Working at a time when the new art of cinema was realising on the screen the metamorphoses which had previously been mechanically produced by diorama, panorama, magic lantern, dissolving view, and the scrim-and-spotlight epiphanies of the Transformation Scene, when animated cartoons as a matter of course depicted fish in a 'school', with professor and blackboard, and tables and chairs prancing around on their 'legs', and a book entitled *The Long Arm of the Law* shooting out a long arm to grab a prisoner escaping from between the covers of a book entitled *Prison Escape* and flinging him into flames spouting from Dante's *Inferno*, James Joyce gathered all he had learned with his previous works and spent his last years writing, in *Finnegans Wake*, the epic of his great theme: the way the mind, in concert with the body and its senses, works.

Abbreviations

B: Herring, Philip F., ed., *Joyce's Notes and Early Drafts for Ulysses: Selections from the Buffalo Collection,* Charlottesville 1977.

BM: Herring, Philip F., ed., *Joyce's Ulysses Notesheets in the British Museum,* Charlottesville 1972.

CP: Joyce, James, *Collected Poems,* New York 1957.

CW: Joyce, James, *The Critical Writings of James Joyce,* eds Ellsworth Mason and Richard Ellmann, New York 1959.

D: Joyce, James, *Dubliners,* eds Robert Scholes in consultation with Richard Ellmann, New York 1967.

E: Joyce, James, *Exiles,* New York 1951.

FDV: Hayman, David, *A First-Draft Version of Finnegans Wake,* Austin 1963.

FW: Joyce, James, *Finnegans Wake,* London 1939.

JJA 1: *James Joyce Archive,* Michael Groden, gen. ed., 'Ulysses: "Circe" and "Eumaeus": A Facsimile of Manuscripts and Typescripts for Episodes 15 (Part II) and 16', prefaced and arranged by Michael Groden, New York and London 1977.

JJA 2: 'A Facsimile of Buffalo Notebooks VI.B.5—VI.B.8', prefaced and arranged by David Hayman, New York and London 1978.

JJA 3: 'A Facsimile of Buffalo Notebooks VI.B.9—VI.B.12', prefaced and arranged by David Hayman, New York and London 1978.

JJA 4: 'A Facsimile of Buffalo Notebooks VI.B.13—VI.B.16', prefaced and arranged by David Hayman, New York and London 1978.

JJA 5: 'Finnegans Wake, Book II, chapter II: A Facsimile of Buffalo Notebooks VI.C. 1, 2, 3, 4, 5, 6, 7', prefaced and arranged by Danis Rose, New York and London 1978.

JJA 6: 'Finnegans Wake: A Facsimile of Drafts, Typescripts, and Proofs', vol. I, prefaced by David Hayman, arranged by Danis Rose with the Assistance of John O'Hanlon, New York and London 1978.

JJA 7: 'Finnegans Wake, Book IV: A Facsimile of Drafts, Typescripts, and Proofs', prefaced by David Hayman, arranged by Danis Rose with the assistance of John O'Hanlon, New York and London 1977.

L I: Joyce, James, *Letters of James Joyce,* vol. I, ed. Stuart Gilbert, New York 1965.

L II, L III: Joyce, James, *Letters of James Joyce,* vols II and III, ed. Richard Ellmann, New York 1966.

P: Joyce, James, *A Portrait of the Artist as a Young Man,* ed. Chester G. Anderson, New York 1968.

S: Connolly, Thomas E., ed. *Scribbledehobble: The Ur-Workbook for Finnegans Wake,* Evanston 1961.

SH: Joyce, James, *Stephen Hero,* eds John J. Slocum and Herbert Cahoon, New York 1963.

SL: Joyce, James, *Selected Letters of James Joyce,* ed. Richard Ellmann, New York 1975.

U: Joyce, James, *Ulysses,* New York 1961.

Note: References to Joyce's 'schema' are to the table of *Ulysses* correspondences included in Stuart Gilbert's *James Joyce's Ulysses,* New York 1958, p. 30. References to the 'Linati schema' are to the altered and expanded outline included in the back of Richard Ellmann's *Ulysses on the Liffey,* New York and London 1972.

Notes

Chapter 1
PROTEUS AND NARCISSUS
(pp. 1-12)
1. Power (1974), 75.
2. McHugh (1977), 76.
3. Gordon, 229-31.
4. Atherton (1955), 20.
5. Vico, 232-3; see also Seidel, 44-5.
6. Hart (1962a), 9.
7. Budgen (1955), 12; Vico 280.
8. Scholes and Kain, 167.
9. Hayman (1956), 160-1. For more on Jousse and Joyce, see also David Hayman in Bonnerot, 209-21; Louis Bonnerot in Bonnerot, 223-42; Weir, 313-25; and Eugene Jolas in Beckett, 3-25.
10. Lefèvre, 70.
11. Singer, 84.
12. Campbell and Robinson, 298.
13. Norris, 44-7.
14. Cf. Kenner (1978), 12; Gross, 32.

Chapter 2
THE DIALOGUE OF *DUBLINERS*
(pp. 13-27)
1. Stanislaus's Italian account of Joyce's first plan for *Ulysses* reads: 'Aveva pensato ad una vignetta da inserire nel volume, un quadro tolto dalla prima novella, 'Le Sorelle', del vecchio prete colpito da emiplagi e sprofondato nella poltrona, accanto al fuoco. Lo voleva simbolo della vita irlandese, dominata dia preti e semi-paralizzata,' Stanislaus Joyce (1941), 26. Ellsworth Mason's widely consulted translation (Joyce, 1950) renders the beginning of the last sentence as 'Joyce meant it as a symbol of Irish life', with 'it' seemingly referring to Flynn's portrait in 'The Sisters'. But the translation supervised by

181

the author himself (Stanislaus Joyce [1949], 502) reads: 'This was to have been a symbol of Irish life.' The tense here indicates that the 'This' refers to the never-written scene for *Ulysses* rather than 'The Sisters'.

2. Walzl (1962), 183-7 and Stein both see Joyce's change in revision of Father Flynn's death date from 2 July to 1 July as symbolically significant (see also Reynolds, 336). 2 July is the Feast of the Precious Blood of Our Lord Jesus Christ—thus, the argument goes, an ironic comment on Flynn's failed priesthood. But it would have been impossible for Flynn not to die on some feast day on the calendar of Joyce's day, and most of them could be seen as applicable to 'The Sisters' in some way. The original date, 2 July, happens to be the Joyful Feast of the Visitation of the Virgin to Elizabeth, and although Walzl says that this particular feast would be symbolically irrelevant to 'The Sisters' (Walzl [1973], 405), nothing could be easier than to demonstrate its ironic reflection on a story named for two childless women, one of whom is named Elizabeth.

3. Eileen Kennedy, 336. See also Goldman (1966), 13-14 and Walzl (1973), 408.

4. Goldman thinks the resentment may be mutual (Goldman [1966], 14).

5. Reprinted in Scholes and Litz, 247.

6. Brooks and Warren, 422.

7. Brandabur, 26.

8. Fritz Senn in Hart (1969), 37.

9. Fritz Senn in Hart (1969), 28.

10. Brandabur, 47-8. See also Degnan, 152-6.

11. Wachtel, 80.

12. San Juan, 97, 100.

13. Boyle (1963), 3-6.

14. Hagopian, 272-6.

15. Carpenter & Leary, 3-7.

16. M.J.C. Hodgart in Hart (1969), 119.

17. David Hayman in Hart (1969), 127.

18. Kenner (1978), 12.

19. Richard M. Kain in Hart (1969), 137.

20. Foster, 102.

21. Brendan P. O Hehir, in Moynihan, 120; Knox, 221.

22. Knox, 221-2; Florence Walzl in Scholes and Litz, 438-43.

23. Kenner (1978), 40.

24. O'Connor (1956), 299; see also Collins (1967), 82 and (1970) 48; Tindall, 37; and Kelleher, 473.

25. Blum, 49.

26. Hart (1962b), 14.

Chapter 3
THE DIALOGUE OF *ULYSSES*
(pp. 29-45)

1. Kenner (1956), 124.
2. Cf. Warner, 22-3.
3. Budgen (1955), 12. See also Hart (1962 b), 93; Carver, 201-14; West, 60.
4. Schutte, 32.
5. Gwynn, 63-4, quoted in Schutte, 32.
6. Dowden, 60.
7. Adams (1962), 129.
8. Campbell, 3-18. Cope's early discussion of this word (Cope [1954], 228-9) is of questionable value because of its author's belief that the word is in *Finnegans Wake,* not *Ulysses*. Ellmann (1972), 28, and Boyle (1978), 18 have useful discussions.
9. See Robert Kellogg, in Hart and Hayman, 168.
10. Budgen (1967), 119.
11. *Pace* Sultan, 153.
12. Cf. Origen's Sabellian mockery of the Trinity: 'I, the Lord, founded myself as the beginning of my own ways for the sake of my works,' Pelikan, 192.
13. *Pace* Kellogg in Hart and Hayman, 151 and Noon, 117, who deprecate Eglinton. See Lennam, 386-97 for evidence that Eglinton plays Laertes to Stephen's Hamlet in a duel of wits; Laertes, after all, kills Hamlet.
14. Kain, 351.
15. Quoted in McIntyre, 173.
16. E.g. see Goldberg, 291; Goldman (1966), 89; Hardy, 197.
17. Adams (1962), 186-7.
18. Kellogg, in Hart and Hayman, 178-9.

Chapter 4
THE IDEA OF ORDER IN DUBLIN
(pp. 47-64)

1. French, 3-4.
2. Henke, 23.
3. Bernard Benstock in Hart and Hayman, 12.
4. Levenston, 265.
5. I must here take issue with Hugh Kenner's argument that Stephen has recently broken his glasses and so cannot see distant objects clearly even though his vision of his coat sleeve remains sharp. First, Stephen isn't specifically myopic—his vision, like Joyce's, is bad at any range, as we find in *Portrait* when he can't do his homework without his

glasses. If he can see his coat sleeve clearly, as Kenner grants, he can see clearly. Second, he does see distant objects sharply—the mailboat clearing the harbor mouth to Kingston, about a mile away (*U* 5), the faint whitening of the water, 'inshore and further out' (*U* 9), the distant chalkscrawled backdoors (*U* 41). When in 'Circe' he says that he broke his glasses 'yesterday' (*U* 560) he is simply too drunk to see straight—he cannot manage to bring a cigarette in contact with a match. See Hugh Kenner in Hart and Hayman, 353-4; see also Wasson, 195, 207; Killham, 274; Hayman, 19; Bernard Benstock in Hart and Hayman, 4. Finally, see Budgen (1967), 56 for an exchange with Joyce which indicates that Stephen is sharp-eyed enough to discern the masts and yards of a ship off in the distance.

6. McCarthy, 193-205.
7. Peake, 180-1.
8. French, 84.
9. Tindall, 156.
10. Scholes and Kain, 31.
11. Maddox, 52.
12. Ellmann (1959), 14.
13. Gilbert, 187.
14. Gilbert, 187, 186.
15. Maddox, 99; Hart and Knuth, 16.
16. Ellmann (1972), 72.
17. Gorman, 168.
18. Hayman, 78.
19. McLuhan, 19.
20. Adams (1967), 143.
21. French, 8-9; Shloss, 336-7.
22. Swanson, 390-1; Herring (1974), 374-5.
23. Anderson, 30-1.
24. Adams (1962), 94.
25. E.g. Melvin J. Friedman in Hart and Hayman, 132.
26. Maddox, 66; cf. *U* 151.
27. Kenner (1978), 55-6.
28. Miller, 7.
29. Clive Hart in Hart and Hayman, 181-216.
30. Clive Hart in Hart and Hayman, 181-216; see also Hart in Hart and Knuth, 38-9.
31. Budgen (1967), 122.
32. Budgen (1967), 124.

Chapter 5
THE ROMANTIC TEMPER
(pp. 65-110)
1. Power (1974), 45.

2. Power (1974), 46.
3. Power (1974), 74.
4. See Ellmann (1972), 104 and Peake, 150.
5. Scholes and Kain, 96.
6. One critic, Jackson I. Cope, has bizarrely taken Joyce's selection of 'souse' as a sign of creative interplay that forecasts the triumph and love and art etc., but of course the overtones of 'souse', in a barroom full of souses, are considerably less heartening. The OED Supplement's first listed instance of 'souse' as a synonym for 'drunk' is from 1915, before the composition of 'Sirens'. See Cope in Hart and Hayman, 238ff.
7. See Bowen, 249-52 and Solomon (1976), 93.
8. Budgen (1967), 139; see also Fritz Senn in Bonnerot, 40.
9. Maddox, 74.
10. Budgen, (1967), 163-4; see also David Hayman in Hart and Hayman, 251, 263.
11. For the journalistic origin of much of the chapter's parody, see French, 148, Groden, 133, Herring (1977), 146, and Schneidau, 93.
12. Budgen (1967), 165.
13. Colum, 328.
14. Suggested by David Hayman in Hart and Hayman, 245, 257.
15. As Hugh Kenner has pointed out about the negotiations in which Bloom is participating, 'we can hardly deny that someone named Bridgeman lent money in good faith, and that what is proposed is to defraud him on a technicality,' (Kenner [1977], 389). And 'Bridgeman' is a Jewish-sounding name, and Joe Hynes' comment on the manoeuvers is 'that's a good one if old Shylock is landed.'
16. French, 156.
17. Pointed out by Darcy O'Brien, 159, and demonstrated at length by Fritz Senn in Hart and Hayman, 277-312.
18. Summer, 73-4.
19. Kenner (1956), 258.
20. Dumoutet, 30-32.
21. Dumoutet, 16; Jeremy, 234-5.
22. Henke, 156.
23. Glasheen (1963), 20. My thanks to Professor John V. Kelleher for first pointing this out to me.
24. Raleigh, 154-67, shows that Bloom's shameful 'secret life' is mainly from the Holles Street period.
25. Fritz Senn in Hart and Hayman, 299.
26. Goldman (1966), 95; French, 171; Hayman (1970), 84-5.
27. J. S. Atherton in Hart and Hayman, 326.
28. Fritz Senn in Hart and Hayman, 300.

29. Gordon (1979), 158-72.
30. Sultan, 248ff.
31. Kenner (1956), 259.
32. Maddox, 181.
33. The following calculations assume that the standard edition represents the fullest development of Joyce's plan for the episode, and that the paragraphing is as he wished it. See Litz, 106 and Gabler, 177-82.
34. Weiss, 11.
35. Abrams, 35, 167.
36. Ellmann (1972), 136.
37. Herring (1972), 323; see also the entry under 'Joachim' in the *New Catholic Encyclopedia* and Blamires, 163-4.
38. Weiss, 2; French, 174.
39. Gordon (1979), 171. 'Try it on' can also accommodate Triton, the sea-god who is swamping Odysseus' crew.
40. Joyce's two known sources for this chapter's literary history, George Saintsbury's *A History of English Prose Rhythm* and William Peacock's *English Prose from Mandeville to Dickens,* both place Carlyle ahead of the position to which Joyce assigns him (see J. S. Atherton in Hart and Hayman, 313-39).
41. Marilyn French, 169 suggests that the episode is presided over by Postverta, goddess of prophecy. Also see Herring (1972), 172.
42. Partridge, 41. My thanks to Professor John V. Kelleher for confirming that such substances could well have been around in a red light district of the period, and for pointing out that Yeats experimented with hashish while in Dublin. I also call attention to the 'drugged' smell coming from the folds of Zoe's clothes (*U* 501), the general stoned-out demeanour of the whores, and the Gautier-ish ambience of Mrs Cohen's drawing room.
43. Norman Silverstein in Harmon, 30.
44. Hugh Kenner in Hart and Hayman, 346; Herring (1977), 211.
45. Blodgett, 28.
46. Tindall, 159.
47. Blodgett, 28.
48. Maddox, 128.
49. '. . . the crystal which has ever found most favour for the purposes of "crystallomancy" . . . is the *Beryl* . . . ' Melville, 7.
50. Hugh Kenner in Hart and Hayman, 348.
51. I must here once again take issue with Hugh Kenner, this time with his suggestion (Hart and Hayman, 353) that Stephen hurt his hand while slugging Mulligan during a scuffle at the Westland Row Station. If it happened Bloom witnessed it, but in 'Eumaeus' he goes out of his way (*U* 620) to warn Stephen not to trust Mulligan, and one does not bother to warn one person against another if they have just been in a fist-fight.

Further, Stephen is playing the pianola at Mrs Cohen's, and it seems unlikely that he would be doing that if his knuckles were bruised, or in any event that he could have done that without noticing the state of his hand. What does make him notice it is that Zoe 'traces lines on his hand' (*U* 562) and that he has just been reminded of the pandying of sixteen years ago. Since both sensations would be localised in the palm, it seems logical to assume that the palm, not the back of the hand, is what is tingling, probably from the moment about twenty minutes ago when Stephen impetuously whacked a cast-iron lamp post with enough force to make the gaslight flicker.

52. From a 1965 RCA recording.
53. McCarthy, 202.
54. Cf. Hart and Knuth, 24.
55. Schneider, 308.
56. Goldman (1966), 98.
57. Ellmann (1959), 156-7. Note the metrical signature: 'Blazes Boylan' and 'Vincent Cosgrave' are both double trochees; 'Malachi Mulligan' and 'Oliver Gogarty' are both double dactyls.
58. See especially Groden, 133-4 and Herring (1977), 146.
59. Respectively, 'The Hostile Environment' and 'The Manhating Orc'. As Ellmann makes clear (Ellmann [1972], 141), the Orc of 'Circe' is the environment, which is certainly hostile. See also Pearce, 378-84.

Chapter 6
UNDER THE MICROSCOPE
(pp. 111-133)

1. Segal, 44.
2. Maddox, 160.
3. Gerald L. Bruns in Hart and Hayman, 369.
4. See Byrd, 9-21.
5. Clarke, 74-5.
6. Cf. French, 221.
7. Atanasijevic, 30; see also Michel, 102.
8. Hugh Kenner has been suggesting controversial answers to some of these questions in a series of articles beginning with 'Molly's Masterstroke' (1972).
9. French, 227.
10. See Blake, 239, Hardiman, 17, and O Flaherty, 40-41. Special thanks to Dr Paul Walsh of the Department of Archeology, University College, Galway. Mr T. H. Joyce of Dublin reports hearing that the artifact dropped in Margaret Joyce's lap was 'the origin of the popular Claddagh ring' (letter to the author dated 5 October 1979.) Other tales about the Claddagh ring link it to the Joyce family (see note 11 in chapter 7). Molly Bloom received one from her first lover, and James

Joyce mentioned it in his travel notice about Aranmor for *Il Piccolo della Sera* (*CW* 234).

11. Not quite to everybody: Stanley Sultan finds a tendency for the monologue to move from acceptance of Bloom to rejection and back to acceptance (Sultan, 415-50), Robert Boyle (in Hart and Hayman, 414), suggests that the first four sentences parallel the second four, Diane Tolomeo (439-54) argues the contrary, that the second four are a mirror image of the first four and C. H. Peake (298-321) traces a four-part circular progress from Bloom to Boylan to Mulvey to Stephen, then back to Bloom. I agree with Peake's outline, although I am less concerned with the males themselves than with what 'Penelope' makes them represent. Despite these contributions, Edwin R. Steinberg was unquestionably speaking for the great majority in 1973 when he noted the absence of any apparent 'organizing principle' to the chapter's eight sentences (Steinberg, 222), as was Hugh Kenner in 1978, referring to its 'liquid formlessness' (Kenner [1978], 98).

12. Hart (1962 b), 94-5.

13. Frank O'Connor in Garrett, 26 points out Boylan's correspondence to the sun, which is always blazing and boiling. Boylan flashes a white disc, his hat, wherever he goes; his gaze makes the shopgirl in Thornton's turn red; Molly compares him to a lion, the animal of the sun.

Chapter 7
IN THE ARMS OF MURPHY
(pp. 135-155)

1. Goldberg, 35. See also Robert Kellogg in Hart and Hayman, 178-9, and Maurice Beebe in Bates and Pollock, 22.
2. Atherton (1974), 73.
3. Ellmann (1972), 155.
4. Gilbert, 364.
5. O Hehir, 393 and Solomon (1969), 31, 137-8.
6. For Molly's year of birth, see Niemayer, 172-3 and Raleigh (1977), 396-7.
7. The 'Eumaeus' notes record what seems to be an earlier version of Bloom's question about Gibraltar and Murphy's answer: 'Seen Gibraltar? LB to seaman. Altro!'—*BM* 412.
8. See 'J. Habakuk Jephson's Statement', included in *The Captain of the Polestar and Other Tales*, London 1890. The story was presented as fact, and reportedly convinced a number of readers. Probably the most influential account of the Mary Celeste mystery (Fay, 141), it has misled many, Joyce included, into misspelling the vessel's first name as 'Marie'. This is how the name appears in a passage of Molly's

monologue left out of all published versions of *Ulysses,* in which memories of the 'Marie watchyoucallit' lead immediately into thoughts of Mulvey. (The Rosenbach manuscript shows the note added in Joyce's hand.)

9. Tindall, 218.

10. The actual address was 17 Aungier Street, not 16. Hart and Knuth (63-4) trace the discrepancy to a misprint in *Thom's Directory* for 1904. Two of the three *Thom's* entries, however, are correct.

11. 'There are several popular versions of the origin of the Claddagh Ring, the two best-known of which attribute it to the Joyce family, one of the so-called "Tribes of Galway" . . .'. According to one of the stories, Richard Ioyes (Joyce), after being freed from slavery by a moorish goldsmith, 'brought with him the idea of the "Claddagh Ring"—some of the rings stamped R.I. and bearing the mark of an anchor (thought to signify hope) are believed to be his work'. Quotations are from a brochure entitled 'The Claddagh Ring', obtained at the Galway City Museum; n.d., n.a., 4. As I mentioned in chapter 6, the other well-known story is that it was dropped by an eagle into the lap of Margaret Joyce. For evidence of Joyce's continuing identification with the Galway Joyces, see Bruni, 153. For evidence of his continuing fascination with '16', see Dalton (1964), 5-6. I do not believe it has been noted that Joyce's abbreviation for Nora, 'N. B.', cross-sums to sixteen.

12. See James Joyce, *Selected Letters of James Joyce,* ed. Richard Ellmann, New York, 1975, 183. Earlier in the letter Joyce has been quizzing Nora about her involvement with 'that boy you were fond of', and his later dismissal of the 'red-headed louts' seems to be an unconvincing repudiation of any jealousy toward the 'boy'. Since Michael Bodkin was dark (*E* 118), her other Galway lover, Mulvey, must have been the red-head if anyone was. In *Finnegans Wake,* when an aged version of ALP recalls the wild lover of her youth, a footnote comments, 'Frech devil in red hairing!' (*FW* 268.35).

13. See Glasheen (1963), 159. Garvin, 108, establishes Mulvey's home in Prospect Hill, in the Bohermore district of Galway—Johnny Mac-Dougal's district. The death certificate of Michael Bodkin, on file at the Public Records Office, Dublin, lists his residence as Prospect Hill.

14. Herring (1969), 301.

15. In the first draft of 'Eumaeus', Bloom thinks about Murphy chasing after the whore of the lane: 'Bloom who had a shrewd suspicion he went out as a maneuver after a female ~~apparition~~ attraction . . .' (*JJA* 7, 341).

16. The passage from 'plump' to 'wander' has been erroneously left out of all published editions of *Ulysses.* Quotation is from Groden (1975), 50. Note, especially, 'sleep wander'.

17. Herring (1977), 44-5.
18. Bulhoff, 331.
19. He makes the following notation in one of his notebooks: 'Ragnal- = Reginald' (*JJA* 7, 34). Edward MacLysaght equates 'Reynolds' with 'Mac Rannell', or '*Mac Raghnaill*' in Gaelic, which as 'Raghnall' 'is equated with Reginald' (MacLysaght, 254, 257). For the connection between the Reynolds family and the Mulveys or (another branch) Mulvys of Leitrim, see O'Hart, 151-2, 168, 172, 321.
20. Raleigh (1978), 220.
21. See *U* 736. For Joyce: From 16 June 1904 to 6 August 1909 equals five years and fifty-one days. For Bloom: from 8 October 1888 until 27 November 1893 equals five years and fifty days. (The Blooms' wedding day, 8 October, no doubt celebrates 8 October 1904, when Joyce and Nora left Ireland together.) I cannot account for the one-day discrepancy, but 'Ithaca' is full of small slips of the sort: there is another one-day error, for instance, in figuring Rudy's age at death. J. F. Byrne, 157, recalls that the Cosgrave incident prompted Joyce to tally and memorialize the time passed since his meeting with Nora, and much later Louis Gillet, 93, noticed Joyce's attachment to a 'secret calendar'.
22. See Kennedy and Lomax (IV) for a recording of the song in which the lovers meet 'that night in Cappoquin'.
23. Like the lass of Aughrim, Willie Mulvey was evidently kept from the door of his lover by her mother. According to the memory of my Galway informant, Mrs Barnacle took Mulvey aside and convinced him to break off the romance, thus bringing about the poignant farewell in Nora's garden.
24. Recent research by John Garvin (Garvin, 110) and Nathan Halper (Halper [1975], 273-80) confirms that Michael Bodkin is buried in Rahoon Cemetery on the outskirts of Galway, rather than, as stated by Richard Ellmann and before him Herbert Gorman, the town of Oughterard. This site was first identified by Susan and Thomas Cahill (133-4). Since the Michael Bodkin buried in Rahoon died in 1900, four years before Nora left for Dublin, the young man standing in her garden was most likely his successor Willie Mulvey. In conflating the two Galway stories, one of a lover standing in the wet and the other of a lover who dies, Joyce may have been affected by his memories of Parnell, whose death resulted from his having stood in the rain in Galway.
25. Tysdahl, 176-8, demonstrates how the story of *The Lady From the Sea* functions in *Finnegans Wake* as a variant of the *Exiles* story.
26. O Hehir, 107. Professor O Hehir has very kindly explained the derivation for me in a letter dated 9 September 1977, from which I quote:

. . . which dynast of Leinster could be called a wolf of the sea? None was known for seafaring or piracy. "Wolf of the sea" in Irish is cu mara—no help there. But "sea-wolf" is muirchu. Now cu literally means "dog" (Old Irish) or "hound" (Modern Irish). The animal called "wolf" in English is called in Irish faolchu, literally "wild-dog" or "wild-hound." Strictly, therefore, there is no word precisely meaning "wolf" in Irish, but the lexical element cu in all contexts of wildness signifies a wolf rather than a dog. And the word faolchu in military contexts means, by metaphor, a warrior. The language has very many words meaning "warrior," and among them, in the archaic language, was cad (later cath). Murchadh or Muirchad therefore appears to mean "Sea-warrior," but Muirchu (lit. "Sea-hound" or "Sea-wolf"; but cu = "wolf" = "warrior") also means "Sea-warrior." In Modern Irish pronunciation Murchadh and Muirchu are pronounced so much alike as to make little difference (in this context -adh is pronounced -u, and the genitive -adha is pronounced -u (i.e., -oo). In fact the third element in Diarmaid Mac Murchadha (murukhu) is pronounced identically to Murchu. (*Mac Muirchu is however grammatically impossible, Mac Muirchon being required.)

27. Kopper, 12; see also Pakenham, 212-14.
28. *P* 221, and see Glasheen (1977), 192, 200 for the suggestion that Father Michael is Michael Bodkin crossed with the Father Moran who sexually molested Nora when she was a girl. Interestingly, the Morans come from the exact same region as do the Mulveys; see McGivney, 14-19.
29. My source is a Galway native and former neighbor of the Barnacles who wishes to remain anonymous.
30. Ellmann (1959), 164-5.
31. See Carlson, 138 and Tysdahl, 176-8 for the *Lady From the Sea* dimension of this passage.
32. Michael H. Begnal in Begnal and Eckley, 99-100.
33. Edward A. Kopper in Begnal and Senn, 121.
34. Campbell and Robinson, 201.
35. Hart (1962b), 125.
36. Glasheen (1977), 94.
37. Gorman, 257.
38. Stanislaus Joyce (1950), 20.

Chapter 8
PROTEUS AND ANTAEUS
(pp. 157-178)

1. A connection confirmed at *FW* 514.18: '.i..' .o..1', which seems to call for 'Finn MacCool' but in fact fits 'Finn's Hotel' Glasheen (1977), 94.

2. Van Hoek (1950), 25.
3. If you count the first and last names of each recipient, count 'Fox-Goodman' and 'Frances de Sales' as single names, and count 'Una Bina Laterza' and 'Trina La Mesme' as two names each. This last step may be justified if we note that 'Una Bina' seems to be a splitting-up of Italian 'Unanima' into the Italian for 'one' or 'twinned' (or Latin for 'a pair'); together, 'Una Bina Laterza' and 'Trina La Mesme' are both representatives of the twins. For the connection between 'Grettna Greaney' and Nora, see Glasheen (1977), 110. 'Penelope', of course, is a version of Molly Bloom, in turn a version of Nora.
4. Hart (1962 b), 73-4, argues that (1) the intersection of Book I and Book II takes place on the vernal equinox, and (2) that Book II is the book devoted to the present. So it follows that the 'present' of *Finnegans Wake* is 21 March.
5. Nathan Halper in Dalton and Hart, 72-90.
6. Budgen (1967), 294; see also Halper (1976), 100.
7. From *FW* 589.19 to 590.3: 'upper ten and lower five', 'seven days license', 'six junelooking flamefaces', 'a dozen generations', 'fives' court', 'two of a feather', 'four hurrigan gales', 'three boy bugle-horners', 'two hussites'. As usual, there are borderline possibilities: 'As one generation tells another', which could be one, two, thirty, thirty-one, thirty-two, etc., and 'heptark', seven. But the above numbers seem clearly to be meant to stand out as a sequence, especially since in a passage reviewing the Joyce career (see pp. 162-5 below), they add up to the talismanic ages twenty-two (ten plus five plus seven) and then (plus six plus twelve) forty. 'Seven days license', which corresponds to the ages sixteen to twenty-two, probably refers to Joyce's wild bachelor life before Nora.
8. See Christiani, 166 for a translation.
9. Nathan Halper in Dalton and Hart, 84. As Halper points out, this is known as 'Oculi Sunday'. In 1938 it fell on 20 March.
10. Senn (1960), 1-23. Senn leaves some question as to whether, in the event that Monday falls on the twenty-first, the festival would be celebrated then or a week later, but see Trümpy, 77 for an account of a Sechseläuten on 21 March 1831.
11. In 'Oxen of the Sun', the narrative enacts a cometary journey from the sun outward past each planet in order, and Jupiter's presence is announced by, among other things, the bright red triangle on a bottle of Bass, followed by Saturn's rings as 'a veil of what do you call it gossamer' (see Gordon, 166-8). On at least two other occasions in *Finnegans Wake*, Jupiter appears along with its 'redhot turnspite' (231.32-3), 'Redspot his browband' (582.31).

12. See the chronology supplied by editor Danis Rose to *Finnegans Wake* Notebook IV, 155-7, *JJA* 7, 145.
13. ' . . . the favorite shade of this crystal utilized by ancient seers was the pale winter-green beryl or 'aquamarine' . . . '—again, Joyce's *Finnegans Wake* gift to Nora (Melville, 13).
14. O Hehir, 393.
15. Glasheen (1965), 18.
16. Benstock (1966), 61.
17. Ellmann (1959), 190.
18. Ellmann (1959), 211.
19. Joyce makes the kabbalic derivation of '111' from 'ALP' in *JJA* 4, 253.
20. *L* I, 168: 'Bloom and all the Blooms will soon be dead, thank God.'
21. Ellmann (1959), 227.
22. Gorman, 259.
23. Ellmann (1959), 561.
24. Ellmann (1959), 234.
25. Hart (1962a), 60.
26. Kenner (1956), 284.
27. Hart (1962a), 117 points out Shem's identification with the antipodes.
28. 'T when I was young'—Joyce's note (*JJA* 4, 75). 'T' is Joyce's sign for Tristan.
29. See Hart (1962b), 19.
30. Kenner (1956), 298.
31. Mercanton (1938), 44, and see Mercanton (1967), 95 for testimony that this interpretation was 'faite avec la collaboration de Joyce'.
32. See McHugh (1976) 47 for a second probable dimension of '1132'.
33. Ellmann (1959), 560.
34. Cowan (1971), 21.
35. Ellmann (1959), 450.

Bibliography

Abrams, M. H., *Natural Supernaturalism; Tradition and Revolution in Romantic Literature*, New York 1971.

Adams, Robert M., *Surface and Symbol: The Consistency of James Joyce's Ulysses*, New York and London 1962

Adams, Robert M., *James Joyce: Common Sense and Beyond*, New York 1967.

Anderson, Chester, 'Leopold Bloom as Dr. Sigmund Freud', *Mosaic* VI (Fall 1972), 23-44.

Atanasijevíc, Ksenija, *The Metaphysical and Geometrical Doctrine of Giordano Bruno*, trans. George Vid Tomashevik, St Louis, n.d.

Atherton, J. S., 'The Gist of the Pantomime', *Accent* XV/1 (Winter 1955), 14-26.

Atherton, J. S., *The Books at the Wake*, New York 1974.

Baron, Gabrielle, *Marcel Jousse, introduction à sa vie et à son oeuvre*, Belgium 1967.

Bates, Ronald and Henry J. Pollock, ed., *Litters from Aloft: Papers Delivered at the Second Canadian James Joyce Seminar*, Tulsa 1971.

Beckett, Samuel, *et al*, ed., *Our Exagmination Round his Factification for Incamination of Work in Progress*, London: New York 1972.

Begnal, Michael H. and Grace Eckley, *Narrator and Character in Finnegans Wake*, Lewisburgh, 1975.

Begnal, Michael H. and Senn, Fritz, ed., *A Conceptual Guide to Finnegans Wake*, USA 1974.

Benstock, Bernard, 'Lucia', *A Wake Newslitter* III/3 (1966), 61.

Blodgett, Harriet, 'Joyce's Time Mind in *Ulysses:* A New Emphasis', *James Joyce Quarterly* V/1 (Fall 1967), 22-9.

Blum, Morgan, 'The Shifting Point of View: Joyce's "The Dead" and Gordon's "Old Red" ', *Critique* I (Winter 1956), 45-66.

Bonnerot, Louis, ed., *Ulysses: Cinquante Ans Après*, Paris 1974.

Bowen, Zack, 'The Bronzegold Sirensong: A Musical Analysis of the Sirens Episode in James Joyce's *Ulysses*', in Eric Rothstein and Thomas K. Dunseath, *Literary Monographs* I, Madison 1967, 255-98.

Boyle, Robert, S. J., ' "Two Gallants" and "Ivy Day in the Committee Room" ', *James Joyce Quarterly* I/1 (1963), 3-9.

Boyle, Robert, S. J. *James Joyce's Pauline Vision: A Catholic Exposition*, USA 1978.

Brandabur, Edward, *A Scrupulous Meanness: A Study of Joyce's Early Works*, Urbana 1971.

Brooks, Cleanth and Robert Penn Warren, 'An Intepretation of "Araby" ', in *Understanding Fiction*, New York 1944, 420-23.

Budgen, Frank, *Further Recollections of James Joyce*, London 1955.

Budgen, Frank, *James Joyce and the Making of Ulysses*, Bloomington and London 1967.

Bulhof, Francis, 'Agendath Again', *James Joyce Quarterly* VII (Summer 1970), 237-41.

Byrd, Don, 'Joyce's Method of Philosophic Fiction', *James Joyce Quarterly* V/1 (Fall 1967), 9-21.

Byrne, J. F., *The Silent Years*, New York 1953.

Cahill, Susan and Thomas, *A Literary Guide to Ireland*, New York 1973.

Campbell, Joseph, 'Contransmagnificanjewbangtantiality', *Studies in the Literary Imagination* III/2 (October 1970), 3-18.

Campbell, Joseph and Robinson, Henry Morton, *A Skeleton Key to Finnegans Wake*, New York 1964.

Carlson, Marvin, 'Henrik Ibsen and *Finnegans Wake*', *Comparative Literature* XII/2 (1960), 133-41.

Carpenter, Richard and Leary, Daniel, 'The Witch Maria', *James Joyce Review* (1959), 3-7.

Carver, Craig, 'James Joyce and the Theory of Magic', *James Joyce Quarterly* XV/3 (Spring 1978, 201-14.

Christiani, Dounia Bunis, *Scandinavian Elements of Finnegans Wake*, Evanston 1965.

Clarke, Howard W., *The Art of the Odyssey*, Englewood Cliffs, New Jersey 1967.

Collins, Ben L., 'Joyce's "Araby" and the Extended Simile', *James Joyce Quarterly* IV/2 (Winter 1967), 84-90.

Collins, Ben L., 'Joyce's Use of Yeats and of Irish History: A Reading of "A Mother" ', *Eire* V/1 (Spring 1970), 45-66.

Colum, Padraic, *The Road Round Ireland*, New York 1926.

Cope, Jackson I., 'Test Case for a Theory of Style', *ELH* XXI/3 (September 1954), 221-36.

Cowan, Thomas A., 'What Shall I Call a Research Project on the Four Evangelists', *A Wake Newslitter* VIII/2 (1971), 19-24.

Dalton, Jack, 'More Numbers', *A Wake Newslitter* I (February 1964), 5-7 and addendum (June 1964), 10.

Dalton, Jack P. and Clive Hart, eds, *Twelve and a Tilly: Essays on the*

Occasion of the 25th Anniversary of Finnegans Wake, Evanston and London, 1966.

Degnan, James P., 'The Reluctant Indian in Joyce's "An Encounter" ', *Studies in Short Fiction*, VI/2 (Winter 1969), 152-6.

Deneau, Daniel P., 'Joyce's "Minute" Maria', *The Journal of Narrative Technique* II/1 (January 1972), 26-45.

Dowden, Edward, *Shakespeare, A Study of His Mind and Art*, London 1975.

Dumoutet, E., *Le Désir de Voir L'Hostie*, Paris 1926.

Ellmann, Richard, *James Joyce*, London 1959.

Ellmann, Richard, *Ulysses on the Liffey*, London and New York 1972.

Fay, Charles Eden, *Mary Celeste, the Odyssey of an Abandoned Ship*, Salem 1942.

Foster, John Wilson, 'Passage Through "The Dead" ', *Criticism* XV/2 (Spring 1973), 91-108.

French, Marilyn, *The Book as World*, Cambridge 1976.

Gabler, Hans, review at Rosenbach manuscript, *Library* V/32 (June 1977), 177-82.

Garrett, Peter K., ed., *Twentieth Century Interpretations of Dubliners*, Englewood Cliffs, N.J. 1968.

Garvin, John, *James Joyce's Disunited Kingdom*, Dublin: New York 1976.

Gilbert, Stuart, *James Joyce's Ulysses*, New York 1958.

Gillet, Louis, *Claybook for James Joyce*, trans. Georges Markow-Totevy, London and New York 1958.

Glasheen, Adaline, 'The Opening Paragraphs', *A Wake Newslitter* II/6 (1965), 1-22.

Glasheen, Adaline, *A Second Census of Finnegans Wake*, Evanston 1963.

Glasheen, Adaline, *A Third Census of Finnegans Wake*, Berkeley 1977.

Goldberg, S, L., *The Classical Temper*, New York and London 1961.

Goldman, Arnold, 'The Journeywork of the Magus' (review of *The Classical Temper* by S. L. Goldberg), *Essays in Criticism* XII/2 (April 1962), 198-203.

Goldman, Arnold, *The Joyce Paradox*, London 1966.

Gordon, John, 'Notes in Response to Michael Seidel's "Black Panther Vampire" ', *James Joyce Quarterly* XV/3 (Spring 1978), 229-35.

Gordon, John, 'The Multiple Journeys of "Oxen of the Sun" ', *ELH* XLVI/1 (Spring 1979), 158-72.

Gorman, Herbert S., *James Joyce*, New York 1939.

Groden, Michael, 'Toward a Corrected Text of *Ulysses*', *James Joyce Quarterly* XIII/1 (1975), 49-52.

Groden, Michael, *Ulysses in Progress*, Princeton 1977.

Gross, John, *James Joyce*, New York and London, 1970.

Gwynn, Stephen, *Experiences of a Literary Man,* London 1926.

Hagopian, John V., 'The Epiphany in Joyce's "Counterparts" ', *Studies in Short Fiction* 1/ (Summer 1964), 272-6.

Halper, Nathan, 'The Grave of Michael Bodkin', *James Joyce Quarterly* XII/3 (1975), 273-80.

Halper, Nathan, 'Leap Year', *A Wake Newslitter* XII/3 (1975), 273-80.

Hardiman, James, *History of the Town and County of Galway,* Galway 1928.

Hardy, Barbara, 'Form as End and Means in Ulysses', *Orbis Litterarum* XIX/4 (1964), 194-200.

Hart, Clive, 'Explications—for the greeter glossary of code', *A Wake Newslitter* I/1 February 1962), 3-10.

Hart, Clive, *James Joyce's Dubliners: Critical Essays,* New York and London 1969.

Hart, Clive, *Structure and Motif in Finnegans Wake,* London 1962.

Hart, Clive and Hayman, David, eds, *James Joyce's Ulysses,* Berkeley and London 1974.

Hart, Clive and Leo Knuth, *A topographical guide to James Joyce's Ulysses,* Colchester 1976.

Hayman, David, *Joyce et Mallarmé,* Paris 1956.

Hayman, David, *Ulysses: The Mechanics of Meaning,* Englewood Cliffs, N.J. 1970.

Henke, Susan, *Joyce's Moraculous Sindbook,* Columbus 1978.

Herring, Philip, 'Experimentation with a Landscape: Pornotopography in *Ulysses*—The Phallocy of Imitative Form', *Modern Fiction Studies* XX/3 (Autumn 1974), 371-8.

Herring, Philip, '*Ulysses* Notebook VIII.A.5 at Buffalo', *Studies in Bibliography* XXII (1969), 287-310.

Jeremy, Sister Mary, *Scholars and Mystics,* New York 1962.

Joyce, Stanislaus, 'James Joyce: A Memoir', *The Hudson Review* II/1 (Spring 1949), 487-514.

Joyce, Stanislaus, *My Brother's Keeper,* London 1958.

Joyce, Stanislaus, *Recollections of James Joyce,* trans. Ellsworth Mason, USA 1950.

Joyce, Stanislaus, 'Ricordi di James Joyce', *Letteratura* V/4 (1941), 23-35.

Kain, Richard M., 'James Joyce's Shakespeare Chronology', *Massachusetts Review* V (Winter 1964), 342-55.

Kelleher, John V., 'Irish History and Mythology in James Joyce's "The Dead" ', *The Review of Politics* XXVII/3 (1965), 414-33.

Kennedy, Eileen, 'Another Look at "The Sisters" ', *James Joyce Quarterly* XII/4 (Summer 1973), 362-70.

Kennedy, Peter and Alan Lomax, *The Folk Songs of Britain* (disc), New York 1961.

Kenner, Hugh, *Dublin's Joyce,* Boston 1956.

Kenner, Hugh, *Joyce's Voices,* Berkeley 1978.

Kenner, Hugh, 'Molly's Masterstroke', *James Joyce Quarterly* X/1 (Fall 1972), 19-28.

Kenner, Hugh, 'The Rhetoric of Silence', *James Joyce Quarterly* XIV/4 (Summer 1977), 382-94.

Killham, John, ' "Ineluctable Modality" in Joyce's *Ulysses', University of Toronto Quarterly* XXXIV (April 1965), 269-89.

Knox, George, 'Michael Furey: Symbol-Name in Joyce's "The Dead" ', *Western Humanities Review* XIII (1959), 221-2.

Kopper, Edward A., 'Some Additional Christian Allusions in the *Wake'*, *The Analyst* XXIV (March 1965), 5-22.

Lefèvre, Frédéric, 'Marcel Jousse: Une Nouvelle Psychologie du Langage', *Les Cahiers d'Occident* I/10 (August 1927), 9-190.

Lennam, Trevor, 'The Happy Hunting Ground', *University of Toronto Quarterly* XXIX/3 (April 1960), 386-97.

Levenston, E.A., 'Narrative Technique in *Ulysses*: A Stylistic Comparison of "Telemachus" and "Eumaeus" ', *Language and Style* V (Fall 1972), 260-75.

Levin, Harry, *James Joyce,* Norfolk 1960.

Litz, A. Walton, review of Rosenbach Manuscript, *James Joyce Quarterly* XIV/1 (Fall 1976), 101-11.

MacLysaght, Edward, *The Surnames of Ireland,* Dublin 1973.

Maddox, James H., *Joyce's Ulysses and the Assault Upon Character,* New Brunswick 1978.

Mercanton, Jacques, *Les Heures de James Joyce,* Lausanne 1967.

Michel, Paul Henri, *The Cosmology of Giordano Bruno,* New York 1973.

Miller, J. Hillis, The *Disappearance of God,* Cambridge 1963.

Moynihan, William P. ed., *Joyce's The Dead,* Boston 1965.

Nebeker, H. E., 'James Joyce's "Clay": The Well-Wrought Urn', *Renascence* XXVII/3 (Spring 1967), 123-38.

Niemayer, Carl, 'A "Ulysses" Calendar'; *James Joyce Quarterly* XIII/2 (1976), 163-93.

Noon, William T., S. J., 'Joyce's "Clay": An Interpretation', *College English* XVII/2 (November 1955), 93-5.

Noon, William T., S. J., *Joyce and Aquinas,* New York 1957.

Norris, Margot, *The Decentered Universe of Finnegans Wake,* London and Baltimore 1974.

O'Brien, Darcy, *The Conscience of James Joyce,* Princeton 1968.

Mathews, F. X., 'Punchestime: A New Look at "Clay" ', *James Joyce Quarterly* IV/2 (Winter 1967), 102-6.

McCarthy, Patrick A., 'The Riddle in Joyce's *Ulysses', Texas Studies in Literature and Language* XVII/1 (Spring 1975), 193-205.

McGivney, Jr., 'The Morans and the Mulveys of South Leitrim', *Ardagh and Clonmacnoise Antiquarian Society Journal*, I/3 (1932), 14-19.

McHugh, Roland, *The Sigla of Finnegans Wake*, Austin 1976.

McHugh, Roland, 'Night Mail to Cork', *A Wake Newslitter* XIV/5 (October 1977), 76.

McIntyre, J. Lewis, *Giordano Bruno*, London 1903.

McLuhan, Herbert M., 'Joyce, Mallarmé, and the Press', *The Interior Landscape*, ed. Eugene McNamara, New York and Toronto 1969, 5-21.

Melville, John, *Crystal Gazing and Clairvoyance*, New York 1974.

Mercanton, Jacques, 'L'esthétique de Joyce', *Études de Lettres* XXXVI (October 1938), 20-46.

O'Connor, Frank, *The Mirror in the Roadway*, New York 1956.

O'Flaherty, Roderick, *Iar Connacht*, ed. James Hardiman, Galway 1946.

O'Hart, John, *Irish Pedigrees*, Dublin 1881.

O Hehir, Brendan, *A Gaelic Lexicon of Finnegans Wake*, Berkeley 1967.

Pakenham, Thomas, *The Year of Liberty*, London 1969.

Partridge, Eric, *A Dictionary of the Underworld*, London 1949.

Pearce, Richard, 'Experimentation with the Grotesque: Comic Collisions in the Grotesque World of *Ulysses*', *Modern Fiction Studies* XX/3 (Autumn 1974), 378-84.

Peake, C. H., *James Joyce: The Citizen and the Artist*, Stanford 1977.

Pelikan, Jaroslav, *The Emergence of the Catholic Tradition (100-600)*, Chicago 1971.

Power, Arthur, *Conversations with James Joyce*, Dublin: New York 1974.

Power, Arthur, *From the Old Waterford House*, London n.d.

Raleigh, John Henry, 'On the Chronology of the Blooms in *Ulysses*', *James Joyce Quarterly* XIV/4 (1977), 395-407.

Raleigh, John Henry, *The Chronology of Leopold and Molly Bloom*, Berkeley and London 1977.

Reynolds, Michael, 'Feast of the Precious Blood and Joyce's "The Sisters" ', *Studies in Short Fiction* VI (1969), 336.

San Juan, Epifiano, *James Joyce and the Craft of Fiction*, Cranbury, N.J., 1972.

Schneidau, 'One Eye and Two Levels: On Joyce's "Cyclops" ', *James Joyce Quarterly* XVI/1&2 (Fall 1978 & Winter 1979), 95-104.

Schneider, Ulrich, 'Freemasonic Signs and Passwords in the "Circe" Episode', *James Joyce Quarterly* V/4 (Summer 1968), 303-11.

Scholes, Robert and Kain, Richard M., *The Workshop of Daedalus*, Evanston 1965.

Scholes, Robert and A. Walton Litz, eds, Viking Critical Edition of *Dubliners*, New York 1971.

Schutte, William, *Joyce and Shakespeare*, New Haven 1957.

Segal, Charles Paul, 'The Phaecians and Odysseus' Return', *Arion* I/4 (1962), 17-64.

Seidel, Michael, *Epic Geography: James Joyce's Ulysses*, Guildford and Princeton 1976.

Senn, Fritz, 'Some Zurich Allusions in *Finnegans Wake*', *Analyst* XIX (1960), 1-23.

Shloss, Carol, 'Choice Newseryreels: James Joyce and the Irish Times', *James Joyce Quarterly* XV/4 (Summer 1978), 325-38.

Silverstein, Norman, 'Evolution of the Nighttown Setting', in Maurice Harmon, ed., *The Celtic Master*, Chester Springs 1969.

Singer, Dorothy Waley, *Giordano Bruno, His Life and Thought*, New York 1950.

Solomon, Margaret C., *Eternal Geomater: The Sexual Universe of Finnegans Wake*, Carbondale 1969.

Solomon, Margaret Co., 'Striking the Lost Chord: The Motif of "Waiting" in the Sirens Episode of *Ulysses*', in Kathleen McGrory and John Unterecker, eds, *Yeats, Joyce, and Beckett: New Light on Three Modern Irish Writers*, Lewisburg 1976, 74-108.

Stein, William Bysshe, 'Joyce's "The Sisters" ', *Explicator* XXI (1962), Item 2.

Steinberg, Edwin R., *The Stream of Consciousness and Beyond in Ulysses*, USA 1973.

Sultan, Stanley, *The Argument of Ulysses*, Columbus 1964.

Summer, Joseph H., *George Herbert*, Cambridge 1968.

Swanson, Roy Arthur, 'The Pun or Allegory in Joyce's "Lestrygonians" ', *Genre* V (December 1972), 385-403.

Thomas, Brook, 'Not a Reading *of*, but the Act of Reading *Ulysses*', *James Joyce Quarterly* XVI/1&2 (Fall 1978 & Winter 1979), 81-94.

Tindall, William York, *A Reader's Guide to James Joyce*, New York 1959.

Tolomeo, Diane, 'The Final Octagon of *Ulysses*', *James Joyce Quarterly* X/4 (1973), 439-54.

Trümpy, Hans, 'Press und Volskunde', *Schweizer Volksunde* LI/6 (1961), 73-8.

Tysdahl, B. J., *Joyce and Ibsen*, Olso and New York 1968.

Vico, Giambattista, *The New Science*, trans. Thomas Goddard Bergin and Max Harold Fisch, Ithaca 1948.

Van Hoek, Kees, 'I Met James Joyce's Wife', *Irish Digest* XXXV (1950), 23-5.

Wachtel, Albert, 'The Genesis of Constructive Self-Destruction in Joyce's *Dubliners*', *Spectrum* XVI/1-2, 75-84.

Walzl, Florence L., 'A Date in Joyce's "The Sisters" ', *Texas Studies in Literature and Language* IV (1962), 183-7.

Walzl, Florence L., 'Gabriel and Michael: The Conclusion of 'The Dead', in Scholes & Litz, Viking Critical Edition, 438-43.

Walzl, Florence L., 'Joyce's "The Sisters": A Development', *James Joyce Quarterly* X/4 (1973), 375-421.

Warner, William B., 'The Play of Fictions and Successions of Styles in *Ulysses'*, *James Joyce Quarterly* XV/1 (Fall 1977), 18-35.

Wasson, Richard, 'Simon Dedalus and the Imagery of Sight: A Psychological Approach', *Literature and Psychology* XV (Fall 1965), 195-209.

Weir, Lorraine, 'The Choreography of Gesture: Marcel Jousse and *Finnegans Wake'*, *James Joyce Quarterly* XIV/3 (Spring 1977), 313-25.

Weiss, Deaniel, 'The End of "Oxen of the Sun" ', *The Analyst* IX (March 1956), 1-16.

West, Philip J., 'Classical Memory Culture in Joyce', *Modern Language Studies* III/1 & 2 (Spring & Fall 1973), 60.

Index